FAMILY
LIFE, DEATH AND
FOOTBALL

MICHAEL CALVIN

FAMILY
LIFE, DEATH AND
FOOTBALL
A YEAR ON THE FRONTLINE
WITH A PROPER CLUB

ICON BOOKS

This edition published in the UK in 2012 by
Icon Books Ltd, Omnibus Business Centre,
39–41 North Road, London N7 9DP
email: info@iconbooks.co.uk
www.iconbooks.co.uk

Previously published in 2010 by Integr8 Books

Sold in the UK, Europe, South Africa and Asia
by Faber & Faber Ltd, Bloomsbury House,
74–77 Great Russell Street, London WC1B 3DA or their agents

Distributed in the UK, Europe, South Africa and Asia
by TBS Ltd, TBS Distribution Centre, Colchester Road
Frating Green, Colchester CO7 7DW

Published in Australia in 2012
by Allen & Unwin Pty Ltd,
PO Box 8500, 83 Alexander Street,
Crows Nest, NSW 2065

Distributed in Canada by
Penguin Books Canada,
90 Eglinton Avenue East, Suite 700,
Toronto, Ontario M4P 2YE

ISBN: 978-190685-026-5

Typeset in New Baskerville by Marie Doherty

Printed and bound by
CPI Group (UK) Ltd, Croydon, CR0 4YY

For: My Family.
Thanks for yesterday, today and tomorrow.

About the author

Michael Calvin is one of the UK's most versatile sports-writers, having feigned expertise in everything from frog jumping to Aussie Rules football. He has worked in more than 80 countries, covering six summer Olympics and six World Cup finals. He was named Sportswriter of the Year for his despatches as a crew member in a round-the-world yacht race. He has twice been named Sports Reporter of the Year, has featured in the British Press Awards on four occasions, and has won awards for his coverage of sports for the disabled. He established a global reputation during a decade as chief sports writer with the *Daily Telegraph,* and has held similar positions at *The Times, Mail on Sunday* and *Sunday Mirror.* He took a five-year sabbatical from journalism to help set up and run the English Institute of Sport, which offers strategic support to 35 Olympic sports. When asked by Kenny Jackett what possessed him to choose Millwall as the subject for this book, he admitted: 'I thought it was worth a punt.' Jackett laughed and said: 'Some punt. Some season …'

www.michaelcalvin.com

Contents

Chapter 1
Family Ties

The knife penetrated Alan Baker's ribcage, in the fourth intercostal space, just beneath the right nipple. It sliced through veins, nerves, and arteries, puncturing a lung. His breath came in short, searing bursts, and he suffered severe blood loss, but he was lucky. Had the blade been wrenched to the left, instead of the right, it would have hit his heart. The officer from the Police Support Unit, who helped save his life after he had stumbled through an alleyway before collapsing outside a bus garage 300 yards from Upton Park, would have been a coroner's witness. His assailant, hidden in a melee of at least eleven attackers, estimated by police to be aged between their early twenties and mid-forties, would have been the central character in a murder inquiry.

The hunt was conducted, with feral efficiency, just after 8.00pm on what the headline writers designated, with a tiresome lack of originality, as football's night of shame. Only the dates – in this case Tuesday 25 August 2009 – change. The themes of social dysfunction, institutional arrogance and ritual criticism are constant. Baker was a Millwall season ticket holder, a former fireman of impeccable character who was systematically separated from nine members of his family as they attempted to reach the second round Carling Cup tie at West Ham. The rumour that he had died, given credibility by the sinister atmosphere of choreographed violence, swept through the ground. The following day, Neil Harris, his idol, was at his hospital bedside.

Harris, scorer of Millwall's goal in a 3–1 extra-time defeat, was shocked to discover the victim's identity. He had met Baker during a holiday in Portugal that summer. They had shared ice cream, discussed football folklore and the common challenges of family life. As the team's spiritual leader, Harris led them off during the second of three pitch invasions, when a youth ran across his path and drew his hand across his throat in an unmistakable mime of malevolence. He was as scared as he had been during an exemplary career, which had entered its thirteenth season. 'It's the only time I have ever felt threatened on the pitch', he admitted. 'Anyone could have walked past, slashed the back of your leg with a knife, or worse. You are basically putting your fate in the hands of idiots. You're hoping they are not mad enough to do you harm.' During the initial invasion, when he was abused as 'a fucking wanker' and 'Millwall scum', he had been able to smell the alcohol on fans' breath. Local pubs, and bars serving home fans at the ground, had remained open, despite warnings.

In the circumstances, no one gave a thought to Kenny Jackett, the Millwall manager, who considered the scenes the worst he had witnessed in 32 years in football. He had only three outfield players as substitutes, and compiled his game plan from a borrowed DVD and a single scout's report compiled by Steve Jones. It was a masterpiece of economy and tactical insight, almost too good for the common good. Jackett had spotted West Ham's limitations out of possession, their reluctance to track laterally, as Gianfranco Zola's system required. He had recognised the potential of exploiting one-on-one situations in wide areas. His preparatory work, on the training ground, took Millwall to within three minutes of a victory that would have caused even more bloodshed.

Ken Chapman, Millwall's security and operations advisor, believed the match finished only because of West Ham's 87th-minute equaliser, a Julien Faubert cross swept in by Junior Stanislas. The goal prompted the first incursions, and quelled, temporarily, the pitched battle between home fans, stewards and police, which was building to a crescendo in the north-west corner of the ground. Chapman, who spent 33 years in the Metropolitan Police, the last five as borough commander in Lewisham, was monitoring events at home with an air of foreboding, sadness, and exasperation. His sense of duty was offended.

He shared intelligence, but had been excluded from the planning process by West Ham's Safety Advisory Group, which comprises club officials, police representatives, and assorted bureaucrats. Chief Superintendent Steve Wisbey had been involved in policing football matches for 29 years, but was in his first season as match commander at Upton Park. He was dismissive of Millwall's protests about being limited to 2,300 tickets, less than half of what they were entitled to under competition rules. He gave more weight to the advice of Louisa Elliston, a functionary from the Football Licensing Authority. Chapman's fears of problems created by ticketless Millwall fans were realised when between 200 and 300 gained entry to the away end, little more than three minutes after kick-off. Initial reports that they had stormed an exit gate were clarified by CCTV footage, which revealed a white-coated steward opening the door, outwardly. It took precisely 80 seconds to herd them into the lower tier of the Sir Trevor Brooking Stand.

The resultant surge was apparent in the directors' box, where the Millwall delegation was aghast at the antics of Gianluca Nani, West Ham's technical director. He was urging those around him to get to their feet in response to chants of 'Stand up if you hate Millwall'. Visiting chairman

John Berylson chastised himself for lacking the presence of mind to capture Nani's crass behaviour on his mobile phone. The American businessman was eventually smuggled out of Upton Park in the back of a taxi, ordered by the driver to avoid eye contact with fans spilling into the road. He felt outraged, but finally understood the psyche of the club that had become an unlikely passion. He, too, felt a primal sense of belonging.

Andy Ambler, his chief executive, was in damage limitation mode. The Football Association, fearful of the global impact of the images of civil unrest, had England's 2018 World Cup bid to protect. Gerry Sutcliffe, a notably ineffective successor to Richard Caborn as sports minister, duly condemned events as 'a disgrace to football'. Moral anger was stoked by accusations of racist conduct on both sides. Millwall were tethered to their reputation, which encouraged assumptions of culpability. The club's Community work, in an area squeezed between the twin extremes of deprivation and gentrification, would be an important mitigating factor, but a draconian response was apparently inevitable. The FA charged West Ham on four counts of failing to control their fans, Millwall three. Accusations of racist abuse directed at West Ham striker Carlton Cole and Millwall substitute Jason Price were toxic.

Millwall's defence would be led by Jim Sturman QC, a Ramones fan who combined the intensity of a two-minute garage band thrash with the arcane courtesies of the courtroom. He had reason to identify with the underdog. In a profession shaped by the conventions of an Oxbridge education, he had become one of Britain's best barristers despite emerging from Reading University with a 2:2 in law. He was irritated by the fleeting indignity of being exposed, in a government report, as the first lawyer to earn more than £1 million in a year from legal aid.

He had spent a decade in football's disciplinary process, as both prosecutor and defender, and intuitively understood the parameters of Millwall's problem. It chimed with his experience of defending Colin Stagg, acquitted of murdering Rachel Nickell in 1994. Three words, ingrained on the brain of the most humble junior solicitor, summarised Millwall's plight: hue and cry. 'When there is a pressure to get a result, conscious or subconscious, injustice often happens', Sturman explained. 'If there is a desire to do something, or a perception someone's got to pay, hue and cry occurs. Colin Stagg is a classic example. It took us eleven years to show they always had the wrong man.'

'No One Likes Us. We Don't Care.' Not so much an anthem as a way of life. Millwall's notoriety is their birthright. I was an outsider who orbited another world in which players were desensitised to reality, clubs were quietly stolen by asset strippers, and supporters were disenfranchised. As a journalist I was deemed to occupy a place on the evolutionary scale somewhere between a sloth and a sewer rat. 'It's a calculated risk', said Jackett, when he announced to his staff that the board had agreed to give me unrestricted access to the club's activities over the 2009–10 season. The odds on that being a bad idea shifted at West Ham, on a night on which it was safer to leap to conclusions and exhume half-forgotten outrages, instead of interrogating the truth. It was an open goal for anyone inclined to do a hatchet job.

Matt Le Tissier unleashed the hounds of hell when he sent Millwall to Upton Park in a draw conducted in the Sky Sports studio. Most players banned their families from attending. The volatility of the fixture reflected a warped social history. The rivalry had soured, mutated. It defied rational analysis of the fault lines in the relationship between dockers and shipbuilders, founding fathers of each club. The heresy of scab labour, early in the last century, was

given a murderous dimension in a subsequent generation by gangland wars involving the Krays and Richardsons. The game was a tribal ritual, an end in itself.

The tone was set by the charmer who posted on a Millwall message board, minutes after the draw had been made: 'I'm so excited I don't know whether to polish my knuckleduster or have a wank.' The talk was of 'old faces, out in force'. This was to be football's equivalent of a Sex Pistols reunion gig, an invitation for middle-aged men to recreate the havoc of their youth. Throw in the Socialist Workers' Party, the British National Party and their fellow travellers in the English Defence League, and you had an anarchist's wet dream.

Chapman, who gathered his security team at 6.00am the day after the draw, listened to the usual intelligence chatter. He looked beyond the bravado of supposed emissaries from Rangers and Celtic pledging to fight for Millwall and West Ham respectively. He was concerned by the brevity of a thirteen-day planning cycle, and the fact that the game would end in the dark. The inevitability of a result meant that one tribe would be seething with resentment. His team identified three pubs as principal meeting points for hooligan factions. One was in the City, the second in Bermondsey, and the third was fluid, but in the Woolwich area. Suggestions that a series of organised clashes would begin at the Bluewater Shopping Centre in the early afternoon were discounted, because it would be too easy for security staff to control access and egress. The trouble would flare along tube and overground railway lines, where policing was sporadic.

The mood on Millwall's team bus was subdued as it arrived two hours before kick-off. While it waited at the traffic lights, before turning right into Green Street, some players stood in the aisle to get a better look at Bobby Moore's

statue, swathed in green plastic sheeting as a protection against desecration. Jack, the driver, wryly revealed that the tinted bus windows were 'brick-proof, but not bullet-proof'. Small knots of West Ham fans extended middle fingers in salute, but the gesture was just a surly form of foreplay. They were more interested in fuelling their prejudices behind the boarded-up windows of the Boleyn pub.

I disembarked in a quiet corner of the club car park, with a ticket for the away end in my back pocket. As a precaution, I picked up a pre-arranged media pass, and wandered past the black-suited Boleyn bouncers, filtering fans into a bar that radiated heat, the scent of stale beer, and the hum of humanity. Queues formed outside the pie'n'mash shops in Barking Road, where police patrolled two by two. Convoys of vans containing colleagues in full riot gear sped past, sirens blaring. Millwall fans, arriving at East Ham station on a southbound tube, had emerged to smash the windscreen of a passing car. They dragged the occupants, an Asian couple, out on to the road, and were ready to fight their way westwards.

I doubled back towards the epicentre of the trouble in Green Street, south of Upton Park tube station. At around 6.30pm, 75 minutes before kick-off, a chant of 'Let's go fucking mental', from drinkers corralled behind a wire-mesh fence adjoining the Queens pub, was the signal for a barrage of bricks, bottles, and beer cans. An older group of West Ham fans, clustered outside a chicken shop on the opposite side of the road, caught the police in a pincer movement. One officer, detached from the group when he attempted to retrieve acrylic glass riot shields from an adjoining street, was hit by a vodka bottle, thrown at point-blank range.

An Asian man, filming the scene from his flat overlooking the square, which normally housed a street market, was

providing the narrative for the night's rolling news. He made the mistake of glorifying his impact in a Sky TV interview. Two days later, as he attempted to enter his home at 11.30pm, he was assaulted by four well-dressed white men who, according to police, were aged between 35 and 45. It was deemed petty revenge, rather than a racially-motivated attack. No one was brought to trial, despite thorough examination of CCTV footage. No one was surprised.

Millwall fans arriving at Upton Park tube, before its closure, were told by police that their safety could not be guaranteed. Some turned back. Those determined to attend were largely unprotected as they walked down side streets and through an alleyway that led to the ground. Ominously, mounted officers chased a gang of West Ham fans out of Tudor Road, one of the principal access routes to the away end. I retraced my steps towards the ground and walked through a maze of garages behind the Bobby Moore stand towards the visitors' entrance in Priory Road.

It quickly became clear that the police were undermanned. More than 900 officers were allocated to the previous game between the clubs at Upton Park, a 1–1 draw in April 2005. Chief Superintendent Wisbey, conscious of draining resources across London, made do with 500, with the promise of another 200 being available from the Commissioner's reserve. Gangs, armed with bottles, walked with impunity from a nearby estate towards the visitors' gates, which were guarded by stewards. It was not until fifteen minutes before kick-off that police in Level One public order equipment, fireproof overalls, a visored NATO helmet, and shin and elbow guards, took over.

The policing strategy unravelled quickly. A second group of ticketless Millwall fans were herded into the away end. Wisbey and his deputies broke the chain of command by leaving the stadium control room at half time. Until they

returned, more than half an hour into the second half, Ron Pearce, West Ham's security officer, had no means of calling for reinforcements. His stewards struggled to maintain a semblance of control. This calamitous lack of communication, as the disorder in the north-west corner gained in intensity, was condemned by both clubs. It was, however, outside the FA's remit. The regulatory commission could make observations about the implications of the policing procedures but had no power to cross-examine senior officers. Chief Superintendent Wisbey declined to respond to my repeated requests for comment.

I retreated to the press box, having concluded it was unsafe even to approach the visitors' turnstiles. I sat behind a reporter, under unaccustomed pressure from his news desk. He stopped watching the game, typed the words 'Millwall', 'West Ham' and 'trouble' into Google, and began to copy and paste a familiar litany of mayhem. Two deaths in the eighties: one on a tube at Embankment in central London, the other at New Cross, when West Ham fans were intercepted after a game at Crystal Palace. The tired old legends of such hooligan firms as the Bushwackers and the Inter City Firm were resuscitated. Myths are woven on nights such as these. They become unchallenged history, holy writ in cyberspace. It is a sanitised process, a world away from pain and blood, bubbling at the back of a victim's throat.

The chaos on the tube meant the Baker family were late, and had to walk through unfamiliar territory. They wore no Millwall colours, but were directed to the wrong entrance. This made them conspicuous, and they were ambushed. The gang chased the family, which scattered, before Alan and his sons Harry and Charlie, aged seventeen and eighteen, were surrounded. At crisis point, deep-seated personal values dictated events: 'I'm very proud of my roots', Alan

explained, without any sense of bravado. 'I brought my boys up to be men, to face their fears. We stood together.'

They were kicked, punched, and bitten in what police described as a 'sustained and brutal attack', but fought back. Alan was isolated, and stabbed by one of eleven men whose descriptions were circulated by Newham's Violent Crime Unit. A twenty-year-old man was arrested in connection with the stabbing. He was bailed, never charged. For the victim, it was a surreal experience, relived through a series of stark, recurring images: 'I first noticed these bobbles of blood, dropping on to the pavement. I know this sounds crazy, but I was convinced it was tomato sauce. I was angry because I thought someone had smeared me with a hamburger.'

He was rejoined by his sons in the alleyway leading into Priory Road. Blood gushed from the wound when Alan lifted his blue and white striped sweater to investigate. Charlie's instinctive response, to jam his hands across his father's chest to stem the flow of blood, gave him precious time. Harry alerted the medically-trained PSU officer, who kept vigil as Alan was rushed to hospital, where he received seventeen units of blood and had twice to be resuscitated.

Alan Baker remains an unwilling symbol of a club burdened by its history. He refused all requests to come forward before, out of respect to Harris, he agreed to speak to me for this book. 'It's funny but, as a fireman, I was in many life-threatening situations', he said. 'It's not until it happens to you that you realise just how many people play a part in keeping you alive. I owe my life to about 50 people, who helped me from the time I was stabbed, to the time I was discharged. Incredible. I know I shouldn't be here.'

Alan has a special status in football's extended family. He proves it can be the people's game, in the most forbidding of circumstances. Harris often visited him at home during

his recuperation. He gave him the shirt he wore during the match. There was a simple motivation for his generosity: 'I'm a player, he's a fan. We represent the same thing. All of a sudden, because you've gone through his front door, you're family.'

Family.

It's a concept that covers a multitude of sins, enduring values like loyalty, trust and unconditional love. You're on the wrong shelf if you're looking for one of those factional romps involving lovely, lovely geezers dressed in Harrington jackets and surgical masks, tearing up town centres. This book has, as its central subject, a group of working men bound by the challenge of collective achievement. They've allowed me to study the nature of allegiance, the humanity that football is in danger of forfeiting. They represent an endangered species in an age of empty celebrity, a team greater than the sum of its parts. The pressures that assail them, an ordinary yet extraordinary group of sportsmen, will also shape the lives of strangers. Join me in a search for the game's soul, which can begin in only one place, the sunlit uplands of childhood.

Chapter 2
The Ghost of Billy Element

Billy Element was born to score goals: 112 in a single season for our boys' team. He had pinched features, a pudding bowl haircut, and a watchful, predatory nature. I remember him smiling only once, when he chipped a goalkeeper with a penalty kick. At the age of twelve he had the keys to the magic kingdom, far beyond a council estate built on a sewage farm in West Watford. Scouts flattered his family with the relentlessness of Tudor courtiers, and he signed for QPR, then an emerging force in the old First Division. We envied his ability, the breadth of his ambition. Football was his release, his salvation, our dream. We prayed his stardust would settle on us, like the white parachutes of dandelion seeds that carried on the wind when we blew them off their stalks. We were young, naive, and about to be ambushed by reality.

One summer's morning, an ambulance parked alongside the ash trees that doubled as our goalposts on the patch of grass outside Billy's house. He emerged in a makeshift shroud of blankets, and left a vacuum that took 35 years to fill. His memory was summoned when Kenny Jackett was driving me to a core stability class for his Millwall squad, run by an aerobics instructor with a stereotypical fondness for drum'n'bass remixes of Phil Collins' greatest hits. Kenny had grown up believing that Billy had swallowed his tongue. My theory that he had died of meningitis was confirmed in a mobile telephone call to Tony Wilson, a childhood friend.

Billy's death, once a blur of bewilderment, acquired sudden clarity. He symbolised the fragility of life, the privilege of talent, and the dark truth of the oldest football cliché in the book, about taking one match at a time.

Holywell Estate, where we grew up, was hardly Fort Apache. The newly-built houses quickly became homes. People took pride in making something of their flint-strewn gardens. The Highwayman, the solitary pub, had its fair share of cartoon brawls and comedy copping off, but lacked menace. Mediocrity, rather than the petty villainy that pre-occupied the local police, was its curse. Too many regulars accepted self-imposed limitations, and drifted on the ebb tides of everyday life. We vowed to be different.

I was among the bigger boys strutting their stuff on King George V Playing Fields, one of 471 in the UK named after the founding father of the House of Windsor. Kenny was one of the younger kids who played on Caractacus Green, a small patch of grass named after the tribal chieftain who led British resistance to the Romans. We each carried boy-hood traits into manhood. Kenny was dogged, quietly deter-mined, and easy to underestimate. I was uncoordinated, compulsively competitive, and had too much to say for myself. Sport offered us social mobility without compromis-ing the reference point of our background. We followed our parallel careers at a distance. Our fathers swapped sto-ries in the pension queue at the post office, and sustained our faith in the unfashionable fundamentals of family, hon-esty and hard work.

The highlight of my football career was selection as a ballboy for Watford in the 1969–70 season. Our washed-out bottle green tracksuits itched like a penitent's hair shirt. We changed next to the home dressing room, savouring the incense of liniment and the murmurs of the crowd that filtered through a frosted fanlight. I was thrilled by the

intimacy of the setting, the insights into human nature that even a Third Division club could provide. Vicarage Road was where I saw my first grown man cry, on 21 February 1970. He was a Liverpool fan, sagging against a wire-mesh fence beside the wooden hut that housed the Supporters' Club. He had mutton chop sideburns, and wore a long red and white scarf, studded with pin badges, over a donkey jacket. Bill Shankly's team had lost 1–0 in the FA Cup quarter final on a moonscape pitch, and I convinced myself I was centrally involved in the goal.

Through the modern miracle of a 52-second clip on YouTube, I can see myself, aged twelve, throwing the ball to Ray Lugg, a midfield player recruited from Middlesbrough earlier in the season. I hop from foot to foot, as he takes a short throw to Stewart Scullion, the obligatory Scottish wing wizard of the era. Lugg moves into space, receives the return pass, and nutmegs Peter Wall, the covering full back. The flight of his cross, a gentle out-swinger, is directly in my eyeline. It is met by a diving header from Barry Endean, which evades goalkeeper Tommy Lawrence, the fabled Flying Pig. Endean, a water buffalo of a centre forward, gave me a sudden affinity with girls of my age, drooling over soft-focus posters of Donny Osmond and David Cassidy. I was smitten.

Endean lasted another season with Watford, and became a builder in his home town, Chester-le-Street. Lugg emigrated to the United States. Their fifteen minutes of fame allowed me to understand what I wanted to do with my life. I observed a moment of sporting and social significance from a privileged vantage point. I felt the pulse of a community, sensed the spirit of that broken man on the wire. Shankly decided, there and then, that he had to break up his first great Liverpool side. Within a year he had ended the careers of Ron Yeats, Ian St John, Geoff Strong and Lawrence. Ray Clemence, Larry Lloyd, Steve Heighway,

John Toshack and Kevin Keegan developed the dynasty. I met Shankly shortly before his death, in 1981, and told him of the ballboy's role in his downfall. 'Aye, son', he said, in that Cagneyesque growl, 'a bitter day, son. Bitter.' I broke professional protocol and asked for his autograph on the double album of his reflections on football. That has happened only twice since – Pele signed a Manchester United programme, Nelson Mandela his autobiography.

Endean's goal was my passport, my tipping point. I appalled Trog Turner, my terminally uptight grammar school headmaster, by abandoning my A-levels for a job on the local newspaper. Since then, I've watched sport in more than 80 countries, seen its enduring glory and recurring tragedy in one man, Muhammad Ali. I've sailed the wrong way around the world, studied dinosaur fossils in the Gobi Desert, politely declined the offer to purchase a machine gun and a two-kilo block of cannabis resin in the lawless border between Pakistan and Afghanistan. I've raced around the Arctic Circle and Amazon Basin in politically incorrect car rallies, and even kept my Mum happy by getting my photo in the paper. Would I have swapped it all for a short career as a journeyman centre half?

Probably.

Kenny was no journeyman. He was a cultured left back, equally at home in central midfield. He played for Watford in the 1984 FA Cup final, winning 31 caps for Wales and making 428 appearances for his only club before he was forced to retire with a chronic knee injury at the age of 28. He forged a reputation as an outstanding youth coach and won promotion with QPR as assistant manager. He managed Watford and Swansea, working for Sven Goran Eriksson at Manchester City before taking over at Millwall in November 2007. Unusually, in an institutionally insecure profession, he has never been out of work. His understated personality

is responsible for a low media profile that fails to register the respect in which he is held in the game.

His story begins, like so many, in a study of a relationship between father and son.

Frank Jackett was a wing half, a defensive midfield player in modern parlance, who signed for Watford from Pontardawe Athletic in 1949. He played fourteen League games over three seasons, had four matches for Leyton Orient in 1954, and then realised he could make more money in non-League football. He played part-time for Ramsgate and Margate while working as a printer.

Frank was a natural teacher, delivering common sense, leavened by experience, to his two sons. At 82, he was afflicted by Alzheimer's. Alan, the elder by ten years, and Kenny radiated respect and a profound love for him when they spoke of his influence on their lives. Alan, a thoughtful, well-connected coach in his own right, was released by Luton, came close to a return to League football, but never quite made the grade. 'Dad was superb at putting football thoughts into a nutshell. He always said to me that Ken did the right thing at the right time on the pitch. That's what makes a pro I think, selection. I had a lot of ability on the ball but he said, "Alan, clear the ball from your own fucking penalty area, don't dribble it out." I didn't listen, Ken did.'

Frank, who had the same forensic approach to golf, his other passion, sensed Kenny's potential before any of us. He watched him from the age of eleven, and treated him with a subtlety alien to the Bad Dads and Mad Mums of the current Academy system. Football matches were tutorials, rather than mere entertainment. 'I grew up in an environment of analysis – following, watching, picking up the bits', Kenny recalls. 'I saw Alan play a lot. He had a really good spell at Enfield, when they were one of the top non-League clubs. He got real close there, as an integral part of a really

good team. I was in the bar with them afterwards. Not drinking with them, because I was a kid, but my Dad would point out their attitude, almost how not to do it. The things he said guided me in the right direction, really hit home. He spoke of attitude, approach, and the technical side of the game. What to do and when. We'd watch games, and he'd say, "You do this, you don't do that, you watch what he does". It was pretty clever – he was pointing out my weaknesses, but it didn't seem he was directly criticising me. He set up football as an education for me.' Between the ages of twelve and fourteen, Kenny unwittingly learned to think as a coach rather than a player. Saturday afternoons were spent in London with Frank, watching individuals, studying team shapes and systems: Steve Perryman at Tottenham, where Glenn Hoddle was coming through; the QPR team of Gerry Francis, Stan Bowles, Frank McLintock and Dave Thomas. Kenny admired Arsenal for the subtleties of Liam Brady, and 'for their dour professionalism, their never ending attitude'. At fourteen, he was entrusted into the tender care of his first youth coach, Tom Walley, one of the game's hidden heroes.

The coach's craft spans the generations. In one of those strange coincidences, life, in 2009, had turned full circle since Walley was the driving force of the Watford team that defeated Liverpool on that fateful February afternoon in 1970. In semi-retirement, at 64, he was now overseeing one-on-one coaching for my fourteen-year-old nephew Jamie, a promising centre forward. He saw a boy with latent talent and determination who refused to succumb to the remorseless setbacks of football life. He could have been looking into a mirror at Kenny Jackett, whom he remembered as 'the boy who was as white as a pear'.

Walley has the ferocity of an Army PTI, the warmth of an adoptive father, and the philosophy of a Jesuit priest.

Give him a boy at fourteen, and he will give you a man. He built FA Youth Cup-winning teams at Watford and Millwall, helped lay the foundations of Arsenal's development system. England internationals whose careers have been shaped by his strictures, like David James and Ashley Cole, revere him. Generations of apprentices have traipsed around to the house he shares with Pauline, a wife who refuses to obey the conventions of a football widow. They'd stay for tea – tomato ketchup with everything – and, in an age of innocence, even sleep over. They were eager to learn, awestruck to be invited. The crisp clip around the ear, designed to amplify his advice, was accepted without a murmur.

He told them stories of his childhood, of collecting firewood to sell from the age of six. He ran endlessly in the hills of North Wales, distancing himself from the rituals of village life. Contrition in chapel, following the Saturday night fight in the pub, was not for him. He lived right, took a bus to London, had a successful trial at Arsenal, and made something of himself. His catechism is the essence of simplicity: look after your body, be on time, do your work, and learn from every experience.

'When I signed a boy I was putting my job on the line, so I got into them, sorted them out. It was, "Right, let's see what bollocks you've got". I wanted them to relax around me, but when we worked it was proper work. I wanted them to take pride in themselves. I wanted them to shine their boots so they could see their faces in them. I wanted them to look at those boots and say, "They're mine – they will make me a life". I wanted them to take that feeling on to the pitch with them. I loved them, controlled them, gave them discipline.' The cardinal sin, for any apprentice, was failure to put sufficient vinegar on Tom's fish and chips, which they ran into the town centre to collect.

Tom's boys would take perverse pride in surviving the bin run, a series of 300-yard shuttles around a dustbin, set in a field at the bottom of his garden. The coach set an optimal time of 36 seconds for the run, allowed little more than a minute's rest in between, and probed for physical and mental weakness. He hadn't done his job until the boys were retching. Jackett hadn't made the county schoolboy side, because the hobby coaches who picked the team doubted his pace, but Walley sensed the warrior within: 'He learned quickly, had what you need. There was a mettle about him, a massive toughness. He'd want to win everything. He wasn't a cross country runner – he was useless, tailed off last. But you give him doggies, shuttles, and he'd be in the top lot. He was like his Dad, very quiet, but got what he wanted. You hardly heard his voice but his attitude spoke for him. He was busy, a nasty little fucker, exactly like his old man.'

Jackett beamed delightedly, when the description was relayed to him: 'Tom's a good football man, but he's more than that. He's a good man, full stop. He was tough with us but his bark was much, much worse than his bite. My Mum and Dad thought the world of him. He could have beaten me up and they would have said it was my fault. They trusted him. He had a really good heart. A kid would be struggling. He'd have him around his house, give him the best steak, and talk him through his problem. He would do that for any of us. He wanted us to succeed, maybe needed us to succeed. At five o clock most days I'd be in his front room, with cakes and biscuits. He'd be off and running.

'He'd talk about football, your game. Some of the things he tried to teach us about life, Christ. He once got a load of us in a room. He started telling us about women. "When you fuckers get married you've got to take her out, buy her a bunch of flowers now and again. Let her have a dance. Take her shopping, let her have a wander." One day we were

walking down Watford High Street, and saw his wife Pauline with Sarah, their youngest daughter. "Where's Tom?" we asked. "Oh, he's lying on the settee watching the racing!" That's football, big time. Don't do as I do, do as I say.'

Jackett was a reserve team regular before he left school at sixteen. He grew up fast in a dressing room that taught him the value of senior players, powerful personalities who developed into managers and coaches. Sam Ellis had a face that belonged on Mount Rushmore; Dennis Booth a viper's tongue that reduced apprentices to tears. John Ward was cerebral, Steve Harrison comical. Even as England's assistant manager, he would walk around the team hotel dressed as a tramp, or Quasimodo. When Kenny took his first team place, at eighteen, Harrison sought out Alan Jackett. 'That's me fucked', he told him. 'Your kid's there for good.' More of Walley's eager youngsters, like John Barnes, poured into the breach. Graham Taylor used them to build a team that rose from the Fourth Division, to runners-up in the First Division, in six seasons.

'When you're young you get used to opportunity. I was pretty battle-hardened. It wasn't a problem for me walking into the dressing room and getting changed. I loved the toughness of it, the banter, the competitive nature of the environment. That group took some holding. They were fucking fierce. It was full-on. Graham used to call Tom "the individuals man". He would do the big picture, the team structure and club ethos. Tom would get inside your head. We trusted him, in all aspects of our life.'

Taylor is an enduring influence: 'With Graham there was some distance. I learned a lot from the way he talked to the group. He had a collective approach, but pared down his analysis so you knew when he was talking about you. Graham was the manager, an authority figure. There was not that closeness, on a human level, that we had with Tom.

I can't really remember Graham giving me a bollocking as an individual, but if he called you upstairs you knew about it. His strength was standing up in front of the group and summarising what we needed to do collectively. He was brilliant at it. He could touch on things and not say it all, but leave the message there.'

When Taylor left, Walley was recruited by Millwall, where he ignored the first law of football and declined to look after number one. Jackett's enforced retirement, and installation as Watford youth coach, meant he was in direct competition with his mentor. 'Tom was still living in Watford. He'd started a centre of excellence, and I was thinking, "Fucking hell, he's gonna nick all the kids and take 'em to Millwall". I'd earned my badges early, but didn't know shit. He must have been 45, and in his prime. I'd sit in his front room and he'd tell me what to do: get the boy in, map out his future for his Mum and Dad. If the parents like you, and what the club has to offer, then he will go to you. I did six years as youth coach, and he was my first point of contact on training sessions, player issues, team meetings, principles of selection. He did nothing but help me. He taught me to be a coach and a manager. At that time Watford lacked stability and direction. We were drifting. Tom was there for me. I can still hear him: "Be steady son, fucking steady. Let it go."'

Jackett developed the habit of recording his professional life in a series of diaries. Taylor's traumas as England manager helped him to rationalise his principles as a manager, and his priorities as a man. He saw someone he respected reduced to the level of a cartoon clown. He understood the impact on Taylor's family, and the scars it has left on his psyche. One private exhortation in his diary, underscored for effect, stands out: 'You have to act and not react.' It's a simple mantra, which comes in handy when the Cold Blow Lane End is running hot.

'If you are a manager you are going to get criticism, so you'd better learn to take it. That's really important because when you react you give certain people the credence they are looking for. It gives them their niche in the market. I love my football but I know why I'm in it, and what I get out of it. I like the mechanics of the game, the planning, the whiteboard, the training. I like logging it, comparing what I did this year to last year. The witch hunts and the endless analysis bore me. Sometimes I watch games and leave the sound off. I want the information without the opinion, but I don't begrudge the whole media show. It generates the interest from which we profit. We can't have it both ways. We can't earn money that is perceived as unrealistic, and escape scrutiny.'

Watford went 22 matches without defeat in Jackett's only season as manager, but he struggled to come to terms with a schizophrenic existence. Taylor, elevated to the front office during his second spell at the club, was, simply, 'boss'. Walley, recruited to whip the reserves into shape, still cuffed Jackett around the ear. He reverted to being assistant manager, and when Taylor warned him that Gianluca Vialli was to take over, with disastrous consequences, Jackett understood: 'There's nothing worse than walking in dead man's shoes. Graham gave me time to sort myself out.'

He spent three years assisting Ian Holloway at QPR, then joined Swansea, another club with a distinctive culture. 'It was a hard one for us as a family. I wanted to be around my kids as they were growing up. They went to school just around the corner from the ground, and, in retrospect, I wish I had found a compromise. Living on top of the job added to its intensity. I got a lot of praise, and a lot of criticism. Swansea has such a small-town mentality. It's insular, but wonderfully passionate. You don't see any shirts in the town other than Swansea shirts. They think the world ends

at the Severn Bridge. Even Cardiff, 50 miles away, is a different land.'

He won promotion from League Two in his first full season, lost on penalties to Barnsley in the League One play-off the following year. Swansea's win in the Football League Trophy at Wembley offered minimal compensation and in February 2007, despite being in and around the top six all season, he left by mutual consent. Football's all-too-familiar euphemism for a messy divorce masked traditional tensions. Like many managers, Jackett was caught in a pincer movement between political opportunists in the boardroom and agitators on the terraces. Assisting Eriksson at City was a release, a return to the purity of life on the training ground.

Even in League One, a charnel house where the average life expectancy for a manager is fifteen months, Millwall redefine the notion of insecurity. Jackett understandably rejected their initial invitation to become their ninth manager in 28 months. The club was in disarray following the sacking of Willie Donachie. According to director Constantine Gonticas, 'We were in a death spiral'. John Berylson, their seventh chairman in five years, had a shortlist of a dozen potential recruits, but was convinced by Jackett's integrity and strength of character. He used Eriksson as a go-between, and eventually got his man with a simple promise: 'This club isn't a jail sentence. You are free to walk, when you want.' On the day he accepted, Jackett bumped into Everton's David Moyes, who told him: 'If you can manage that club, you can manage any club.'

Jackett sees no need for an agent, and sends his contract to the League Managers Association. They raise any subsequent queries with the club chairman or chief executive, and offer a modicum of insurance against football's traditional reticence to compensate the victims of its insanity: 'The pressure is there from day one, believe me, but it's not

unlike real life. You live from contract to contract. Once
you get that nailed you know that if your face ceases to fit,
you are due x amount. As a manager you have to identify
what works at a particular club. It's not a one-size-fits-all
approach. Millwall is a volatile club, which demands hon-
esty, commitment, integrity. Its underlying strength is its
grittiness. The fans want a going-to-work kind of guy. They'll
let him know, very quickly, if they're unhappy. That's fine.
I've learned you need to know about yourself before you
can impose your beliefs on others. You need practical expe-
rience to find your way around people. You have to be able
to find winners, back them, and invest your time in them.'

He rescued Millwall from relegation, imposed his work
ethic on a divided dressing room, and showed malcontents
no mercy. Redemption, for a team of over-achievers, beck-
oned on a sweltering Sunday afternoon, 24 May 2009. More
than 45,000 Millwall fans converged on Wembley for the
League One play-off final against Scunthorpe. The first of
Gary Alexander's two goals, a dipping 40-yard volley, was
one for the ages, but Millwall conceded twice in the last
twenty minutes to lose 3–2. Alexander's missed header, at
2–1, was crucial. When it was over, Jackett stood in the cen-
tre of the dressing room, surveyed a scene of devastation,
and said simply: 'Remember how painful this feels. Feel that
pain in each of the 46 League games we play next season.'

The memory was still raw when he did his first public
duty of the new season, a fans' forum at The Den. The Barry
Kitchener suite, named after the retired greengrocer who is
a Millwall deity, was stiflingly hot. The faces were muttering
that the lager was flat. Jackett took questions from 100 die-
hard supporters who defied the demographics of the mod-
ern, gentrified game. They were there for the long haul,
true believers. Predominantly bulky middle-aged men,
many had Lions tattooed on assorted body parts. There was

an unspoken sense that they could handle themselves in a ruck, but their respect was genuine. Jackett is regarded as 'a proper manager', which, in such company, is a symphony of praise.

The Big Man in the Pub evidently begged to differ. A grimy T-shirt, once an optimistic shade of salmon pink, hung limply over his belly. His three-quarter-length tracksuit trousers, flip flops, and 'No Surrender' tattoo were the essence of chav chic. As he moved closer to the front, a murmur rippled around the room. One solid citizen approached his son, who was leaning against the back wall wearing a Millwall baseball cap at an improbable angle. 'You still livin' at 'ome with 'im?' he asked. 'Poor bastard …'

The Big Man, oblivious to the derision, was determined to make the most of his annual opportunity to put the Millwall manager in his place. 'I stood here last year and told you we weren't going to get enough goals', he began. 'There's not enough goals in this team either.' The impact of his defiance might have been diluted by the shout of 'How the fuck did we get to Wembley then?', but he ploughed on regardless. 'That Jason Price is terrible. He's got nothing to give you. If you're the opposing manager, you're not worried. You're missing out on great targets. That Ibhere, who was at Walsall and has gone to Milton Keynes. He was a proper player. This lot are going to give you nothing. Your signings are poor. What are you doing? That Tony Craig. Crap. That Ashley Grimes. He's got no pace. He can't play.'

Jackett smiled: 'That's your opinion, and you are quite entitled to it. What's your question, please? I'm wondering if I'm going to have to sit here for the rest of my life.' The mocking laughter didn't go down well with the Big Man. He blurted: 'You might have 30 years in the game but I'll pit my knowledge against yours any day of the week.' Jackett refused to take the bait: 'The beauty of football is that it's all

about opinions. All I can tell you is that we are going to go at teams with a fury. It's about me grafting, doing it for you over the next nine months. If I thought I'd win by picking you, you'd be in the team.'

The Big Man convulsed with embarrassment and unrequited aggression, but stayed silent. 'Welcome to the world of being Millwall manager', Jackett said later. 'It's a no-win situation but you have to fight your corner, win your respect. Maybe Mark McGhee had the right approach when he was here. He grabbed one guy by the throat, and pinned him against the wall ...'

The Mark of Death

The silence was broken only by the tubercular rasp of four jet sprays, watering the main pitch at Millwall's training ground in the bland backstreets of Bromley. I'd got lost in the suburban sprawl, and had been informed by a bored battery hen at Directory Enquiries that the place did not exist. Thanks to a Crystal Palace-supporting postman – 'Why the fuck do you want to go there, mate?' – I was merely fashionably late for the start of pre-season training. It was 1 July 2009, a Paul Weller, 'Wild Wood' sort of day. Temperatures simmered at 31 degrees. The players' ice bath, a glorified paddling pool swathed in physio tape, refused to inflate. 'Not like this at Man United, eh?' giggled masseur Danny Fittler, who was privately negotiating his own transfer to West Ham.

Meanwhile, on another planet, the Glazer brothers had designs on the £80 million that United had banked that morning from the sale of Cristiano Ronaldo. His new Real Madrid team-mate Kaka, at the vanguard of another generation of Galácticos, was being introduced to 50,000 hysterical fans at the Bernabeu. Radio bulletins led with a year-long inquiry into football clubs being used to launder money, but no one really cared. Football wouldn't be football without its cosy assumptions of skulduggery.

In other news, Elton John nominated Graham Taylor for the National Portrait Gallery's 'Gay Icons' exhibition

because 'he made my dreams come true'. Dear old Reg Dwight cried buckets at Wembley in the 1984 FA Cup final, when Watford lost 2–0 to Everton. I still cannot bring myself to watch the VHS video of the match, which gathers dust as a symbol of the tyranny of technology and illogical emotion. My Mum, who sat next to Freddie Starr near the Royal Box and couldn't tell a midfield player from a meringue, probably had the best deal of all.

Kenny Jackett, who is rather more sanguine about his losers' medal from that afternoon, assembled his squad around four circular tables in the spare, functional dining room. The easy laughter about misdemeanours in Magaluf was deceptive. He had released ten players in the brief summer break, and wielded the authority of a new three-year contract. Unlike his Premier League counterparts, who must cope with insouciant teenagers who become millionaires before the acne of adolescence has cleared, he lived with the knowledge that his decisions could be life-changing. The PFA, the players' union, had nearly 700 unemployed professionals on its online transfer directory. Most would kill for a one-year deal. Many would sell their souls for a one-month contract.

'Guys in the Premier League are pretty much made for life', observed fitness consultant Jon Goodman, who had overseen the feared ritual of body fat testing, and was waiting to take the players on their first lung-scouring run. 'These guys are insecure. There's still the threat of the manager not giving you a contract, or dropping you. That brings bigger consequences. At this level players can't rest on their laurels, in the way they could in a large squad at a Premier League club. They can't hide in the system. What is the stick with which you can beat a Premier League player? There isn't one. If they're not self-motivated, they become journeyman millionaires.'

Goodman, a former Millwall striker, was sold to Wimbledon for £1 million in the declining days of the Crazy Gang, 'where the injured players would go out to do rehab, and come back pissed'. Think Fitness, his performance consultancy, is a vehicle for a secondary career in sports science. Jackett cannot afford full-time fitness staff, but he values Goodman, whose status as an ex-pro demands respect. He has an inquiring mind, an understated intelligence, and a keen insight into a singular trade.

'Football is a very insular lifestyle, which breeds streetwise, sceptical people. Players get so many people telling them what they think they want to hear, it's hard for them to cut through to the truth. They're not great at acknowledging criticism and looking at themselves first. The group mentality is changing. It's becoming a more individual sport. The smart young guys have an understanding of the underlying mechanisms of their physical, mental, tactical and technical approach. The older guys recognise if they can play for another couple of years, it's a few more quid in the bank. If they can maximise their individual careers it will help the team in the long term, but really it's all about them.'

Goodman understands that philosophy is a direct challenge to Jackett's ethos, which stresses consistency of purpose and collective strength. But the balance of power is inescapable: 'We have all to be aware of our strengths and weaknesses, and be on top of our game all the time. Kenny has got a ring of steel around him. He's tough, without necessarily having to be tough. He's approachable, but distant. He clearly knows what he wants. Some guys find it hard to accept his honesty because it is unusual. There is never anything personal about football. This is business. It's ruthless.'

Jackett lacks physical presence, and has an unconscious habit of smiling beatifically during conversations, which

he litters with occasional observations of 'Well done'. But he comes alive in the company of football people. He values men of substance, and, addressing those in whom he had placed his trust, spoke with characteristic earnestness. Wembley was history, he told them. They must concentrate on a twelve-game, three-month spell until the end of September, which promised to shape their season. 'Get over last season very quickly', he ordered. 'You've got to look forward. Believe in yourself. Respect and support the group. If you commit, give everything to the club, you will be successful. It will reflect well on you as an individual. Remember, your fitness and preparation is your responsibility as a professional. It's about having a fit body and a positive mind. You are all on the line together. You start equal.'

Well, almost. Two of his audience, Danny Spiller and Danny Senda, were in limbo. Victims of the summer cull, each persuaded Jackett to let them train through what was, effectively, one month's notice period. Each had endured debilitating long-term injury. They were both 28, a dangerous age for an unattached professional footballer. Jackett had made his risk assessments, balanced talent, character and experience against human weakness. In such circumstances, emotion is excess baggage: 'It doesn't do to get too close. I let the coaches form the relationships. Getting rid of players is not nice, but you get used to it, really. I owe it to them to be concise, decisive and honest. I won't play games with them.'

That formed the thought for the day on Monday, 6 July. As usual, Jackett was first in, as a bright dawn gave way to intermittent rain. His players began lapping the training ground at 7.30am. Goodman's runs were shorter, increasingly intense 1,000-metre pieces, and he allowed less time for recovery. Sprinting was frowned on. Stamina-building was aligned with core stability sessions, strength and conditioning circuits, boxercise classes and measured ball work.

Wednesday, the traditional day off, was assigned to a squad swimming session. Those who could swim did 24 lengths, alternating front crawl and backstroke. Midfield player Ali Fuseini, who couldn't, was given a float and told to work on his leg strength.

John Sullivan, a goalkeeper recruited on a free transfer from Brighton, took to the runs like a duck to liquid tarmac. He laboured at the back of the group, and made the rookie's mistake of observing, breathlessly, that 'All clubs are the same, really'. Subjected to a trademark tirade by senior goalkeeper David Forde – 'This is not just any fucking club' – he was suitably contrite when he entered Jackett's first-floor office. It was small, the size of a box bedroom, and the manager made the gesture of vacating his desk, and sitting opposite him. 'Just checking everything's OK', said Jackett. 'Is Beryl looking after you in the digs?' Sullivan mumbled sweet nothings, which suggested he couldn't have been happier had he billeted in Buckingham Palace. He was visibly eager to impress and vowed: 'I'll get better. I won't give up. I'll give everything.'

Jackett knew he was listening to the quiet desperation of a perpetual number two: 'Some players get to the stage where they spend too long, too far down the pecking order. They don't get as much attention as perhaps they should. Everyone's focus drifts. Their idea of a hard day's work becomes distorted. They don't put so much in, and there's a spiral of decline. They pay lip service to their talent. Sully's got a good character, though. I think we can make a good goalkeeper out of him.'

Sullivan was followed in by striker Jason Price, who had arrived to complete the formalities of a free transfer from Doncaster. A distinctive figure with Sideshow Bob hair, thick-rimmed glasses, and a distressed grey designer cardigan, he had held out, briefly, for the two-year deal that was

never going to materialise. At 32, a one-year contract was a lifeline.

'In the car since 5.30, gaffer', he announced, in a soft, strangely theatrical Welsh lilt.

'Well done. How's your fitness?'

'Been doing 2½-mile runs, steady pace, but did nothing over the weekend because I was moving house. I'm not going to buy, I'm going to rent and see where my career takes me.'

'You're in the hotel till Wednesday, then you'll have to sort yourself out. If you don't, you'll be sleeping here.'

Jackett smiled paternally as Price left for a medical with physiotherapist Bobby Bacic: 'He's a funny lad, but a genuine worker. The fans loved him when he was here on loan last season. Our players can't hide anything. The body language has to be right.'

He turned left out of his office and walked five paces into a bigger room at the end of the corridor. His assistant Joe Gallen, reserve team coach Richard Shaw, goalkeeping coach Tony Burns and Goodman were waiting. Goodman was worried about an apparent quadriceps strain picked up by the unsettled Zak Whitbread: 'I'm stretching them but not breaking them. I'm always conscious about damage limitation. I didn't think Zak did a lot. His running was fine. How did it happen? I don't know.'

Jackett sensed his discomfort and reassured him: 'It's got nothing to do with the programme. He's either thrown in the towel, or he's de-conditioned.' His fatalistic tone suggested he was resigned to an unequal battle to keep the ambitious American defender at the club. He had to make the best of what they had, and that involved effectively sealing Spiller's fate. 'It's time to get the goals out', Jackett announced to his staff. 'Don't fuck about keeping them happy. It only puts the inevitable off a week.'

Spiller was a diligent character who could, should, have been a contender. He was denied a £750,000 move to West Ham by the prevarication of Gillingham, his first club. They demanded £1 million, and ultimately lost him on a free transfer to Millwall. He started only seven games in two seasons, missing fourteen months with a hip injury, which was preceded by two hernia operations. It was a complex process. Spiller consulted five surgeons before a diagnostic injection in the hip finally identified the problem. He was officially released on 27 May, but Jackett's gesture in allowing him to train with the survivors fuelled the delusion that 'there's a contract on the table for me'.

Isolated by Gallen as the odd man out in the first major ball work session of pre-season, Spiller was as vulnerable as a wildebeest separated from the herd. He acted as a ballboy, stretched and sprinted across the width of the pitch, behind one goal, to keep up appearances, but was demeaned by the irrelevance of his enthusiasm. Everyone knew, instinctively, that he had been branded with the Mark of Death. He seemed to shrivel, physically. It took the longest fifteen minutes of his life for him to accept the inevitable. He trotted slowly to Gallen, quietly asked permission to slip away, and headed for the dressing room. 'Sure, the lads spotted it', confirmed captain Paul Robinson. 'It can be a cruel game. It's funny how quickly things change. Hopefully Spills will get fixed up, but it's a fickle environment. You're gone, and life goes on without you.'

Jackett was watching, impassively, from the touchline when Bacic ambled across. Price had passed the medical, with reservations. 'Whatever he told you was bullshit', Bacic smiled. 'He's been on his holidays. Hasn't done a stroke.' Jackett didn't miss a beat: 'I don't want him with the group. Get him out with Jon.' Within five minutes, Goodman and Price were clambering over a mountain of grass cuttings

and into an adjoining field. On their return Price plunged into an ice bath and pleaded: 'Can you get a Daiquiri here?'

Once he had changed, he wandered into the lobby and tried to make small talk with Karen Wilson, the youth development secretary. He could have picked better moments. Convinced she was suffering from swine flu, she was waiting for NHS Direct to return her call. 'Don't know what went on out there', said Price. 'I went all jelly legs. The next person who says footballers have an easy life is going to get a punch in the mouth. The flats they're sending me are three grand a month to rent. We're not all in the Premier League, you know.'

Karen playfully seized her opportunity: 'You footballers are all rich. We get all the stress.' She was diverted by the arrival of her stepson Paul, sent by kit man Adrian Wisson to ask Price what squad number he favoured: '28? Yeah. Sounds good. They sold some of those with my name on last season, didn't they? Hang on, though. Is 23 free? Like that. Give me 23, not 28. I'll be Beckham.'

Spiller's number, 17, was vacant. It took nearly an hour for him to join the scholars for second sitting in the dining room. Goodman confirmed: 'He didn't see it coming.' Bacic reflected sadly: 'Some would have been a bit cuter, and hidden the blow better.' The condemned man ate a last meal, of pasta salad, and left the club that afternoon. He was apprehensive, bewildered, yet defiant. He complained: 'I've been left in a very difficult situation. I've only trained for three days. How can you assess someone after that length of time?' Gallen, whose playing career was ended by a succession of injuries, empathised: 'It's hard. There are mortgages to meet, bills to pay. Everyone is worried about the money situation. He should still have a career, if he steps down the League and accepts less. But it will be difficult for him.'

When it came to danger signs, Senda had 20–20 vision. He prowled around the car park, muttering into his mobile

phone with his hand cupped over the mouthpiece. When he saw the chance, he made his pitch to Jackett: 'We've had a few days, anything doing, gaffer? I'm over the injury. If you want me to play a game to prove it, I will.'

Jackett offered no hostages to fortune, but understood the tension: 'He was fishing, really. This is the time where you see the anxiety. Everything in life is dictated by selection decisions. You see the little glances, read the body language. I can't blame Danny. He's got himself to look after. You may think you have recovered from a big injury, but once you lose that yard of pace, you're gone.'

Senda was popular with the fans, who identified with his work ethic and buccaneering runs from right back. He had not played for fifteen months, and adversity revealed the dimensions of a deceptive personality. Eleven years in the game had imbued him with the superficial swagger of a senior pro, but he could not disguise a child-like need for reassurance. He spoke, softly yet urgently, about the injury at Swindon, in the last game of the 2006–07 season, that sabotaged the old certainties.

'I was playing centre half for the first time in my career, funnily enough. I went up for a corner six minutes into the game, and scored. Then we had a free kick on the far right-hand side of the box, and they still weren't picking me up. I made the run, but the ball's gone over my head. I planted my right foot, heard a big crack, and then a crunch. I thought, "I'm going to look down on a broken leg". When I saw my knee was facing the wrong way I instantly went into shock. I'd never heard of anything like that happening in the game. I never knew the knee could move that far. That's why it frightened me so much.

'Neil Harris was the first to reach me, and I was asking how bad it was. He was the calmest person ever. He was telling me: "There's nothing wrong, I can't see where the

problem is." I knew it was bad, but to have him by my side was a comfort. I held on to him so tightly they had to prise my hands off him, to put me on the stretcher. I didn't want him to leave my side. People talk about Neil at this club, and he was absolutely fantastic for me. It wasn't just on the pitch, it was afterwards. The phone calls in hospital, the constant support when he could see I was a little down. He's just an amazing person.'

Jackett laid down a marker on the way home, ordering the team bus to divert to the hospital. It was a gesture of respect and solidarity. Senda had ruptured his patella tendon, and needed a complete reconstruction of the right knee. Surgeons removed a large fragment of bone, which had snapped under pressure, looped his hamstring through the top of the kneecap and pinned it to his shin. His cartilage was also torn as the kneecap dislocated. It was, to all intents and purposes, a career-ending injury.

'You play it back in your mind and you pause, because you can't believe it actually happened. It's just surreal. It's not supposed to happen to me. It's supposed to happen to someone else. It took me two months to get my head around the seriousness of it. I was on the phone to my family and I just broke down, to be honest. I thought this is it, this is the end. Where do I go from here? I had just got to the point where I was comfortable, confident, seeing the game in a different way. I was really quite excited. Suddenly, I felt robbed. I was in new territory.

'With rehab you have to be focused, selfish. Think about yourself, because no one else can help you. There are no corners that can be cut. I didn't feel lonely because the lads were incredible. They dropped computer games off at my flat, made sure I wasn't abandoned. They probably thought, "There but for the grace of God". You find players out as people when this sort of thing happens. How they

conducted themselves around me, as a group of men, was unbelievable.

'It's very rare you get a group like this. Most clubs have clear cliques. The southern boys stick together, the northern boys stick together, the black boys stick together. There might also be a couple of lads in the team you don't really fancy. But, with this group, there is no one I don't get on with. Everyone pulls everyone else through, and that's massive when you're tired and under pressure in the last ten minutes of a game. You can look to Neil, his stature in the game, his stature at this football club, the type of man he is. But we are a collective.'

His incorporation of a football team as a surrogate family had a powerful poignancy. He lived with his mother until the age of nine, and was ushered through a difficult adolescence by his father, who remains a pivotal figure in what is a complex personal life. Senda is separated from the mothers of his three children, Luke, ten, Bethany, nine, and Freddie, five. Without the anchor point of a game that has absorbed him since childhood, Senda was vulnerable – as were those around him.

'It's not just me I worry about. I have to pay for my kids, their lives. Everything hinges on football. It would be quite easy to let it consume you, but you can't let it rule you. You've just got to work hard and hope the manager can see how much you want it. You'd be a liar if you said you didn't think about it, every minute of every day. It's peak pressure, but you have no option but to deal with it. I don't have the convenience of those players who say, you know what, I've got so many million in the bank, I'll just pack up. I don't have that luxury. I have to keep going for the people around me.

'I'm happy here. I will do everything in my power to stay. This will be the biggest month in my career by a long, long

way. It could be life-changing for me. It has been so hard to get to this point. It's a big fight, down at this level. Look at the Sky Sports breaking news bar. Look at the names of the players who are on trial – they've played 30 or 40 games in the Premier League and they are at League Two clubs, fighting for their lives. That's how football is now. It's not a case of, "Well, we've seen you, you've played 200 senior games, here's a two-year contract". Even when you're in the side, it's not so much a case of "I've got to stay in the team", it's "I've got to stay at this football club".

'Six-month contracts are being handed out. It's opening up players' minds, because at the end of the year they could be out with hundreds of other players trying to fight for one job. It's then you start to realise you're running out of time. What can you offer to a boss in the real world? I turn up at, say, 30 years of age. He asks, "What experience have you had, what GCSEs have you got?" None. "Right. What have you been doing for the last ten, fifteen years?" Er, kicking a ball around a field. "Goodbye."'

Jackett was sufficiently impressed to double-check whether Senda needed to sign an insurance waiver, as he was technically out of contract. The defender took comfort from the pre-season tour of Ireland, where he played the first half of a 1–0 win at Shelbourne. He trained well, survived the psychological ordeal of his first block tackle, and continued his reintegration into the group as an unused substitute in a 2–1 win at Stevenage. Aware of his need for defensive cover, the manager gave him a one-month contract on 27 July.

Senda made his first start the following day, in a friendly at Dartford, where the kick-off was delayed fifteen minutes to accommodate a record 4,022 crowd. The rhythms and rituals of the dressing room felt good. He studied the set-piece routines, stuck to the wall with Blu-Tack, and listened

intently when Jackett called for 'a real fucking Millwall performance'. He settled quickly and, in the 35th minute, scored their third goal, a superb dipping volley from the edge of the box.

Lost in the moment, he had a thousand-yard stare during the half-time team talk, and absent-mindedly flexed his right knee. When the final whistle confirmed a 4–1 win, he punched the air and scanned the stand for his father. He lingered after the warm-down, taking off his white boots as he signed autographs and posed for photos. 'It's been a long hard road', he said. 'I want to draw a line under the worst year of my life. Now every day is a special day.'

Richard Sadlier was once sufficiently innocent to share such sentiments. But, worn down by pain and periodic disappointment, he opted to retire at the age of 24, following three abortive comebacks in eighteen months. A degenerative hip condition soured a career in which he scored 34 goals in 103 starts for Millwall, and made a solitary appearance for the Republic of Ireland. His benefit match, staged at The New Den on 1 August after a six-year hiatus, offered a belated chance of closure.

Gareth Southgate used the game as a culture shock with which to remind his relegated Middlesbrough squad of the realities of Football League life. 'They want a taste of what's to come for them', Jackett told his players. 'Lads, don't fucking disappoint them. Let's hit 'em with everything. I'm looking for an intensity of attitude, almost a desperation to compete. Close 'em down. Win your tackles. Lay down the law. Show them what runs through this club, and this team.'

Millwall took a first-half lead through Gary Alexander, but a back injury to Tony Craig led to Senda coming on at the interval as a makeshift central defender. Fate dutifully responded to temptation, twenty minutes into the second half. Senda launched into an innocuous aerial challenge

with Jeremie Aladiere, and collapsed with a sharp scream on landing. He was beating the ground in pain and frustration when Bacic arrived. Bacic saw the fear in his eyes and suspected, correctly, that he had ruptured the Achilles tendon in his right leg. An equalising goal, nine minutes from time, didn't seem to matter.

Senda had been helped into the dressing room by assistant physiotherapist John Alty and club doctor Imtiaz Ahmad. Shock gave his skin a waxy pallor, as if he had aged prematurely. His team-mates gathered silently around him as he lay face down in an ante room leading to the changing area. Harris kissed him, and, as Jackett threw a consoling arm around him, he mouthed 'How long?' to Bacic, who extended four fingers, then six. Four to six months out, minimum. On the other side of the wall, Sadlier, who had come on for the last ten minutes, sat alone, deep in thought. He knew, at that moment, why he had grown to hate the game that had once promised him so much.

Jackett retreated to his office to observe professional courtesies with Southgate, who was trying to change the culture of a club that required rebuilding from top to bottom. He had attempted to make a point the previous evening, when he took his players to watch the musical *Billy Elliott* at the Victoria Palace Theatre. Alan Smith, Middlesbrough's director of football, explained: 'It's a football-type story, about a council-house kid, pursuing the dream. It's about dedication, teamwork, fellowship. Did they get it? It went a million miles over their head. We have kids on £35,000 a week, not trying a lick. We've got some on £45,000 a week who haven't realised that no one wants them. Ridiculous.'

Senda had a stark choice. Sign on, live off his savings, or rely on the goodwill of friends. He would be unable to earn a living until the New Year at the earliest. The mournful realism of Harris captured the mood: 'That's why you argue

over an extra £50 a week', he said. 'Where is the bread for the table coming from?' Bacic's diagnosis was confirmed the following day, following a scan. Jackett promised to pay for the operation and oversee his rehabilitation, in an emotional telephone call to him on Monday morning. 'God', he said, sinking back into a chair after ringing off. 'That was horrible, absolutely horrible.' The surgeon, who invited Bacic to watch the operation, knitted two detached pieces of tendon together, and was encouraged by the lack of damage to the knee joint. He was also struck by Senda's determination to wear his Millwall shorts during the procedure.

He did so as a gesture of desperate defiance. He wanted to remind himself what he was fighting for.

Collateral Damage

Martin Kelly. Mark Little. Ryan Shotton. Hogan Ephraim. Alex Nicholls. Jordan Rhodes. David Amoo. Elliot Omasuzi. Dorian Dervite. Nicky Adams. David Bell. Wayne Brown. Jake Livermore. John Bostock. Max Gradel. Jason Puncheon. Tamika Mkandawire. Neal Trotman. Chris Smalling.

Twenty names, as intriguing in isolation as any on a village war memorial. Twenty stories, individual yet inextricably linked by the common thread of human potential. Twenty young men, marketed as fresh meat for the grinder. Twenty intangible assets in a business that is slavishly short-term. Twenty reasons to believe. Twenty players who could, just could, make Millwall a better team. They were all on the first page of a long list of possible signings, discussed at the first recruitment meeting of the new season.

It was brisk, businesslike. Kenny Jackett was looking for a right-sided defender, a right winger, a central midfield player and a centre forward. Youth, strength and character were key criteria. They would be unfinished articles, possessing the drive and discipline to respond to development work on the training ground. Jackett, Joe Gallen and chief scout Stuart Murdoch spoke in shorthand that carried echoes of a bloodstock sale. When Murdoch announced, 'Not for us: long body, short legs, unbalanced', he could have been talking about a broodmare rather than a wannabe who was nowhere near their top 200, never mind their top twenty.

Millwall are well down football's food chain. They rummage through the recycling bins of Premier League clubs, offering a slice of real life in exchange for raw material on the loan market. They scan the fringes of Championship squads for players who have been eased towards the margins. They trawl lower Leagues for the unsettled and unfulfilled. 'We're looking for those flying below the radar', acknowledged Jackett. 'We offer a structured training environment, and a unique challenge. This is a place for men, a League for men. If they do well here, they say something about themselves.'

Jackett, like many at the club, defers to Adrian Wisson when he considers the consequences of its culture. The kit man is a confessor figure, a warm character whose superstitions extend to shaving during the season only when Millwall have won. First taken to The Den by his father in 1968, aged eight, he is a former postman who was training to be a driving instructor when offered the chance to chauffeur former chairman Peter de Savary: 'I'm not saying I coveted this job, but I'm like a pig in shit. It's the dream job, for any fan. People of all types get the Millwall bug. It's a hard place, but honest. Players have to put it in, otherwise the fans kill them. We had a player here, Bas Savage, who had played half a dozen games when he said to me, "Adrian, I don't think they're having me". I told him to look at one of the great Millwall heroes, John Fashanu. He put his head in, put himself out for them. Give everything, and they love you.

'Players do get scared. It's a tough place to play. They hate posers. Take Teddy Sheringham – they despise him, despite everything he achieved here. Everyone loved it when Chopper broke his goal-scoring record. Now there's a hero. They've seen through Teddy. When he said he was a boyhood West Ham fan they went mad. That they will not

forgive. They see players as their representatives, what they would want to be if only they were good enough.'

Martin Kelly, a principal target, moved out of range when he played full back on Liverpool's Asian tour and was given a squad number for the initial stages of the Champions League. A cheeky attempt to loan back winger David Amoo, a product of the Millwall youth scheme sold to Liverpool for £400,000 two years earlier, was compromised by the ruthlessness of Rafa Benitez's restructuring. No one blamed Dave Moss, chief scout of the UK element of the Anfield Academy, for deflecting such a politically sensitive approach. 'He's survived by his fingernails', Gallen rationalised. 'He doesn't answer any knocks on the door these days.' Stoke manager Tony Pulis stalled about Ryan Shotton, and then failed to pick up calls. Even the affable Roy Hodgson refused a favour. He offered no apologies for intending to accelerate the integration of the quick, strong Chris Smalling into his first team group at Fulham. A £10 million transfer fee, agreed by Sir Alex Ferguson in the subsequent January transfer window, to the intense irritation of Arsène Wenger, justified such pragmatism.

Mick McCarthy, looking to balance his newly promoted Wolves squad, was true to his Yorkshire roots when asked about Mark Little: 'I'd give him the keys to my house. He's tough, won't get beaten one-on-one, but you'll pull your hair out because of the selection of his passes.' Jackett summoned a wan smile at the bluntness of the sales pitch: 'Not a bad statement, eh? Mick speaks well of him. Wants to sell him, not loan him out. He's got to get moving. Big, strong, powerful, energetic. Indisciplined in his passing. Fifty grand might do it. He's twenty years old, let's put him in the jigsaw.'

'Can handle this League, without doubt', Murdoch stressed. 'Injury last season. Let's make sure there's no hangover from that.'

'Powerhouse', observed Gallen, but when Jackett suggested, 'Maybe it is time for a signing', he was cautious: 'Fifty? He's still a right back. No more.'

Bids were in for Jason Puncheon – 'Plymouth will be whipping him about' – and Tamika Mkandawire, a Malawian defender who would eventually be priced out of the market by Leyton Orient. Gallen admired Walsall striker Alex Nicholls – 'Slip of a lad: like his movement, athleticism, pace' – and Ipswich's Jordan Rhodes: 'He's gettable. Got class, going to get better.' Murdoch concurred: 'Intelligent footballer, but they're wary of committing. It's all change there. Everyone wants to keep their job.' Jackett cut to the chase, and called Roy Keane, who promptly sold Rhodes to League One rivals Huddersfield for £300,000, double Millwall's entire transfer budget.

Courtship rituals are well established. Everyone lies about their financial situation. It's known as 'talking skint'. No one admits to tapping up a player, but conversations are littered with such euphemisms as 'the word is in motion'. One phone call you are the hunter, the next you are the prey. Agents are white noise in the background. Jackett was worried about losing Paul Robinson – 'Of course he'll go, he'd double or treble his money' – but relieved when Cardiff instead chose to spend £200,000 on Anthony Gerrard, Steve's cousin. 'We need winners', he told his staff. 'This is a unique club, and a unique group. We have to consider that. We have to be careful, respectful of the group. If you can get us a world beater, who doesn't drink, for 500 quid a week, that would be handy.'

He returned to his office, where the names of a putative first team, in 4-4-2 formation, were on rectangular cards attached to a whiteboard. With only 22 professionals, he knew he could not afford too many entries in adjoining columns earmarked for short- and long-term injuries: 'Injuries

kill you in the lower Divisions. Sides do well early on in the season, but you see them at Christmas, with five out and the kids in, and they collapse. The team is dead, the kids can't handle it. Everyone loses confidence and morale. The only way is down.'

That was no reason, however, to compromise standards: 'It's easy to get journeymen pros. There are a lot of players kicking around who are not necessarily better than what we've got. That wasn't the case when I came in. We needed new players, any players. I've weeded the weak out. I've got at least average players in every position.'

He was cautious about triallists, fearing too many would be a distraction. He initially assessed Andy Holdsworth, a former Huddersfield captain released after protracted contract negotiations. He was neat, nimble, experienced, but not exceptional. 'I'll keep my money in my pocket. It's going to be a no. Maybe this time last year, I would have taken a chance. He's got a good reliability record, but he looks a lower Division footballer. It's his stature, the way he holds himself. He'll get a club, but he's not for us.'

No room for argument, you might think, but Holdsworth inhabited a parallel universe. He returned to Yorkshire, where the local press claimed he had turned down Millwall's offer of a contract, and hinted he was about to sign for Bradford. 'That's what they're saying, is it?' said Jackett, who has long been inured to football's petty deceits. 'Good luck to the lad.' His wry grin led to an admission he had just recommended Holdsworth to Dave Penney, who signed him for Oldham 48 hours later.

Managers perform a scorpion dance dictated by mutual trust. They use each other as sounding boards, accept professional judgements at face value. Unemployment is the universal truth, the game's great leveller. Like many, Jackett was particularly appalled by Tranmere's summer sacking of

Ronnie Moore, who was a minute away from taking them into the play-offs. He had immense respect for his knowledge, team-building ability, and straightforward approach to the absurdities of his trade. He planned to offer him occasional coaching sessions as a gesture of solidarity, if he needed a release.

Murdoch, a familiar figure in a grubby white Astra estate, managed Wimbledon when the franchise moved to Milton Keynes, but has largely operated as a freelance goalkeeping coach. He worked with Jackett at Watford, where he was struck by his combative instincts and clarity as a coach. Murdoch's wary, watchful nature identified him as one of life's survivors. Ten days into pre-season, he stood in the sun, his shorts emphasising a squat, stocky frame. He agreed to take me on a nightmare scouting trip – 'Hartlepool in December, you drive' – and seemed utterly at ease: 'This is the nice part of the season. No one's made a mistake. No one's been blamed for anything. It'll change …'

He was sacked the following week, and the club released an anodyne three-sentence statement, thanking him for his efforts over the previous seventeen months. There was no time to dwell on the consequences of the decision. Jackett had other lives to shape. Zak Whitbread had rejected a new contract, citing his need to find a bigger platform from which to push for a place in the USA's World Cup squad. He was placed on the transfer list, but it was not that simple. The American was running at 70 per cent capacity, and after twenty minutes was pulling up in pain. 'It might be his old hernia', cautioned physiotherapist Bobby Bacic. 'Not a good scenario. If it's not a hernia, and it's his hip, we're in trouble.'

Deliberations were interrupted by the arrival of Simon Walton. A product of the Leeds Academy, Walton was involved in two £1 million transfers before Plymouth

gambled a club record £750,000 on his temperament. At 21 he had a reputation for ill-discipline, the obligatory Page Three girlfriend, mother of nine-month-old Poppy, and the security of a £1million, four-year contract. He had been ostracised by his manager Paul Sturrock after the summer break.

'Record signing, training with the youth team, sent on trial. Some come-down, eh?' laughed Jackett.

'Sometimes they wake up, gaffer', observed goalkeeping coach Tony Burns, his world-weary air amplifying his doubts.

'Sturrock just hammers him', said Gallen. 'The assistant is saying he's a great lad. Who do you believe?'

Jackett sided with Sturrock: 'They can get lazy on those long-term contracts. They can stand there, telling everyone what to do, and rub everyone up the wrong way. Still, it's a free look for us. That's the market we're in.'

'Can't wait', said Gallen, rubbing his hands together with theatrical glee. 'Looks like a case of too much too young but you never know.'

The players went out to train at 11.15am, after signing a wedding card for Joanne and Steven, Millwall fans who were getting married that weekend. The verdict on Walton was instant, withering. Gallen retreated to the laundry room, and exclaimed: 'Awful, just awful. Overweight, and not a player.' Jackett concurred: 'I'd made my mind up about him by twenty past. Let's give him a couple of days and see if we feel any differently.'

For Walton, pleasant and surprisingly reserved, given his advance publicity, rejection was a troubling experience, but hardly terminal. Jordan Anderson, meanwhile, was being eaten alive. The youth team triallist would not survive the biggest opportunity of his life, created by a chance comment by head of youth Scott Fitzgerald. 'He's been with

Birmingham for twelve months, but they don't want him', he reported. 'We can take over his scholarship from them. He's 6'4", seventeen, stick thin. He's just got no power in his body. But he can play. He's better than what we've got. Mentally he sees things early, and he can pass. He had five years at Spurs, released at sixteen. He's homesick, and lives just down the road.'

Jackett acted on impulse and promoted Anderson into the team for the following night's friendly at Dartford, which was to offer such false hope to Danny Senda. 'Why don't we just play him?' he said. 'Give the kid a proper trial, put him in with the pros and see what he's made of.' His misplaced lightness of tone was an appropriate epitaph for a boy who found himself in the right place at the wrong time. Anderson's solitary training session with the first team squad deserved the scrutiny of Amnesty International. It was tortuous, uncomfortable to watch.

'Body language doesn't look good', murmured reserve coach Richard Shaw as he prowled along the touchline. 'What's his name?' hissed goalkeeper David Forde, who used it incessantly as he barked orders to his defence in a ten-a-side practice match. 'Squeeze Jordan … left shoulder Jordan … press Jordan … line Jordan … fuck's sake Jordan … show him inside Jordan … runners Jordan … JORDAN …' It was a running commentary from hell, punctuated by an irritated intervention from Gallen. 'This ain't real', he complained. 'It's all too fucking nice. We need more aggression, without topping each other. We've had ten minutes of nicey nicey bollocks. Now let's play football.'

Anderson was betrayed by physical immaturity, and the false conventions of the football fairytale. He struggled to change direction with sufficient speed, lacked the body strength to compete. Reality burned at the back of his throat, as he attempted to catch his breath. 'He doesn't

look fit', said Shaw, with surprising tenderness. When the session was over he took him to one side and went through some basic defensive drills. It was a compassionate gesture, from a decent man, in an occasionally inhuman business. To the players, Anderson was a body, a human mannequin, collateral damage.

See ya later, kid.

Jackett had already posted his team on the notice board in the dining room. It was quietly revised that afternoon. Anderson was replaced by second-year scholar Chris Hegarty, and sat through the game, doe-eyed and bewildered, as an unused substitute. He was released the following weekend by Fitzgerald, who eased the blow slightly by arranging a trial for him at Charlton. 'It's harsh, but we haven't got time to wait for him to grow into his body', he said. 'That'll probably take five years. I might not be here then, and the odds are that the manager won't be here. For Jordan's sake, you hope he's one of those kids who comes through in his early twenties, and everyone wonders why he wasn't picked up earlier.'

Jackett had a responsibility to ensure the production line kept rolling. He took a call from the father-in-law of Colchester central midfield player Johnnie Jackson, who claimed to be acting as his agent. He checked the legitimacy of the situation with manager Paul Lambert, and received permission to speak to the player, who had never fulfilled the promise he once showed at Tottenham. It was a one-sided conversation from the moment it became clear he was looking for 50 per cent more than Millwall's weekly basic wage for a senior pro, £2,000. Jackett told his staff: 'I wished him good luck, but there's not a lot of three grand a week out there.'

Jackson eventually leapt on the Notts County gravy train. He was last seen clambering out of the wreckage, joining Charlton after it hit the buffers at warp speed. Jackett was

more secure with the diligence of Jack Smith, who refused to take no for an answer. He had given him an initial two-day trial as a favour to his father Dave, whom he knew as an age group coach at the Watford Academy. Smith had been released by Swindon, looked sluggish, and was manifestly unfit. Yet there was something heroic about his single-mindedness. When Jackett told him he had nothing for him, he shrugged and kept reporting for duty, regardless. 'I'll keep coming until they tell me to fuck off', he said. In football, that attitude was as eloquent as any mission statement, as convincing as a lavishly-embroidered CV.

Smith was living with his prospective father-in-law, Richard Fetherston, a marketing man retraining as a ski instructor. We had kept in contact after meeting at the Rugby World Cup in Australia in 2003. 'Jack's had nine managers', he said. 'What he really needs is someone to believe in him.' Fate duly went to work on his behalf. Jackett noticed Smith's ease on the ball, the increasing confidence of his distribution, and his unflappable nature. His body fat percentage was decreasing, and an expanding injury list emphasised the value of his defensive versatility. He excelled on either flank, and in a central role.

He took to wearing Danny Spiller's old training kit and, a week before the start of the season, his perseverance was rewarded. Jackett called him into his office at The Den, sat him down on a low-slung chain store sofa, and offered him a month-by-month contract. His only reservation concerned his dress sense: Smith was wearing a dark three-piece suit, patent leather shoes, and no socks. 'Sorry gaffer', he said. 'I was late for my lift this morning and couldn't find any.' It was a heavily incentivised deal, lubricated by gentle humour and the fact there was no agent agitating for his 10 per cent.

Recruitment is rarely so simple, or the process so innocent. Jackett lost out to Derby on Jake Livermore, a powerful

midfield player he had seen score for Tottenham against Celtic at Wembley. Dorian Dervite, a French recruit to the Tottenham Academy, had lofty ambitions of a move to Ajax. As Jackett feared, Plymouth refused to reduce their asking price of £250,000 for Puncheon, and cut their wage bill by sending him out on loan to MK Dons. Millwall received a measure of compensation when Sturrock allowed Mattias Doumbe to play in Richard Sadlier's benefit match, as a trial.

Jackett recognised Doumbe's quality as a quick, intelligent defender, and was buoyed by a character reference from Ian Holloway, back in football at Blackpool after a year out of the game. Doumbe made encouraging noises to his friend Jimmy Abdou, the Millwall midfield player, and his agent suggested he was ready to accept a lower basic wage, if offered a two-year deal with a bonus for reaching the play-offs. But something didn't ring true. Deadlines were missed, and Jackett began to suspect he was being used as a bargaining chip. Sure enough, three days before the start of the season, Doumbe cancelled his Plymouth contract, by mutual consent, and joined MK Dons.

Paul Ince, who had returned to Milton Keynes following a sobering sojourn in the Premier League with Blackburn, had the transfer strategy of a schoolboy let loose in a sweet-shop. No one doubted the quality of his signings, but he was storing up trouble by accumulating a bloated squad of 34 players. The frustration of those inevitably isolated in the reserve group would be corrosive. Money, as ever, would be a catalyst for dissent.

'Football clubs are famous for imploding', Jackett said, justifying his strict wage policy. 'We haven't got the budget of a lot of teams in this League. If someone walks into our dressing room on four grand a week, it could easily blow up. You have got to get the pecking order right, but, as a rule, you generally try to create parity. At Chelsea, a player on

100 grand a week will whinge when he's changing next to someone on 110 grand a week. At our level the difference is measured in hundreds of pounds, but the effect is the same. Team spirit suffers.'

League One is not immune to football's alms race. Wealthy chairmen were throwing money at clubs like Brighton, Colchester, Huddersfield and Swindon. Charlton and Norwich were prepared to risk financial meltdown in a bid to buy an immediate return to the Championship, where turnover increases by 50 per cent. Leeds had a budget beyond anyone, with the exception of Southampton, who intended to act with the restraint of a crack addict celebrating an unexpected inheritance. History, in the form of a five-year decline that left them on the brink of ruin, was bunk from 8 July, when they were bought for £12.5 million by DMWSL613 Limited, an acquisition vehicle for Markus Liebherr, a 61-year-old Swiss billionaire.

Southampton began the 2009–10 season with a ten-point penalty imposed for having been in administration, a new manager in Alan Pardew, and a home game against Millwall. Liebherr, a portly figure waving to the great unwashed from the directors' box, had his shot of Caligulan adrenaline. Sky, recognising the strength of the storyline, sent the cameras. They missed an intriguing sub-plot, the presence of Stuart Murdoch on the Southampton bench. Jackett had followed the Masonic traditions of management by recommending him for a job that combined the roles of goalkeeping coach and scout.

'Stuart's better off', said Jackett. 'It's a good thing, from his point of view, that he's on the training ground every day. He'll be on the bench, involved. It's hard to get chief scouts. It's a lonely job. They live separated lives. While most of us get up and go to work, they're hanging around during the day, and are out at night. I'm glad it has worked out for him.

Alan phoned me, asked if there was anything he should know. I just told him that Stuart wants to coach. He'll give him no problems. He's a good lad.'

Opening day is soccer's summer solstice, a time of ritual and renewal. In Millwall terms, that means monitoring message boards that provide a platform for pond life like the Southampton fan who cowered behind the pseudonym Let's Be 'Avin It. His balsa wood bravado – 'Come and av a go if you think you ard enuff u millwall scums' – was treated with appropriate contempt: 'Does your Mum know you're on the computer?' Another respondent, perhaps favouring the traditional pre-match diet, several Stellas and a spliff, decided to veer towards the existential: 'To say that these men paid their shillings to watch twenty-two hirelings kick a ball is merely to say that a violin is wood and catgut, that *Hamlet* is so much paper and ink. The rules of soccer are very simple, basically it is this: if it moves, kick it. If it doesn't move, kick it until it does. I am a member of a team, and I rely on the team, I defer to it and sacrifice for it, because the team, not the individual, is the ultimate champion.'

Makes a change from 'You're gonna get your fucking head kicked in', I suppose.

The match was a microcosm of Millwall's season. They recovered from the setback of falling behind, missed a penalty, hit the post through Steve Morison's header and should have won after Abdou equalised. Jackett was concerned about a lack of cohesion in possession, the durability of a makeshift defence, and the limitations of winger Dave Martin: 'He had a good season last year, but he can't see a picture on the ball. He will graft, but he hasn't got what I call football intelligence. Basically he's out of non-League. He will chase anybody one-on-one if I play him up on the full back in a 4-3-3, but in a four he's got to be in the right place at the right time, making the right angle.'

He had replaced Murdoch with Jamie Johnson, who took a pay cut 'to try and make a go of football, full-time'. Mick McCarthy, for whom Johnson had worked at Sunderland, agreed to loan left back George Friend. 'We're waiting for someone to buy someone, or have a few bad results, and decide to shake things up', Jackett explained, as his mobile phone buzzed. 'Four messages', he said, to everyone and no one. 'C'mon. Four centre halves.'

The best prospect was Neal Trotman, surplus to Preston's requirements despite the public faith of his manager Alan Irvine. He had initially rejected Millwall's interest, but texted his number to Gallen after watching the Southampton game on TV. 'We've got a big chance', Gallen reported. 'We had a bit of a crack on the phone. He won't say yes right now but has obviously got people round him he trusts. It could be a go.'

His optimism was drowned in the shriek of money making itself heard. Southampton spent £1 million on striker Rickie Lambert, and made him League One's best-paid player, reportedly on £12,000 a week. They invested £400,000 in central midfield player Dean Hammond and paid Preston to take Trotman on loan.

'They've got fortunes', Jackett reasoned. 'For all my work out there on the training ground, their fella can suddenly go bosh in the marketplace, and he'll have the advantage. Southampton have gone for a guaranteed goal-scorer, an experienced midfield player, and a big centre half. Right down the spine of their team. That is the equivalent of about three years coaching. That's OK. I know where I am. I'm no different to a mate of mine in the insurance game. It's about putting the hours in, making the calls, gaining the intelligence. It doesn't matter what people think. I know what I'm about.'

With that he turned to another list. More names, more stories, more opportunities.

Chapter 5
Legend

It's True Confession time. Boys do gossip in the toilets, especially when they're in front of the mirror. Neil Harris was teasing his lightly gelled hair with a comb, in preparation for a personal appearance on behalf of Everyman, his cancer charity. He had nicked himself shaving, and was in a reflective mood, knowing what was to come. He would pose for photographs with desperately optimistic patients and their parents. He would see the fear in their eyes, summon familiar emotions, and spread the word that diagnosis is not a death sentence. He would repeat the tale of his survival, and gloss over the days 'when you can still feel the radiotherapy, deep in your bones'.

Zak Whitbread walked over from the urinals, having taken care to avoid the one closest to the door, which had been out of order for as long as anyone could remember. He washed his hands, and idly ran them through his short, bottle blond hair. As he listened to Harris, he bared his teeth at the mirror, his flared nostrils giving him an uncanny resemblance to the winner of the 2.30 at Kempton. 'The papers going to be there?' he asked. 'If they are, tell 'em I'm available. 350 grand.' Harris laughed, and shouted at Whitbread's retreating back: 'That's a footballer for you. We're talking life and death, and he's looking to get a move.'

Even in a training ground toilet that had the faint aroma of diluted disinfectant, he exuded an air of authority. Harris is what Italian managers call a *trascinatore*, a player

who pulls the group together. He puts people at ease with a ready smile and kind words, but has a politician's instinct for influence. He's a diplomat in the boardroom, a shop steward in the dressing room, a folk hero in the pubs and playgrounds. He has that distinctive mixture of unforced empathy and professional detachment that marks him as managerial material. At 32, he was completing his coaching badges in the company of Gianfranco Zola, and keeping his options open by strengthening his links to the PFA, the players' union.

His survival of testicular cancer has given him the sense of purpose that unites those who feel they have been given a second chance in life. He is conscious of his status, accustomed to being judged for his human qualities as much as for the records he has set as an intelligent, mobile forward. His charity work is low-key, effective, and defines his character in greater detail than his achievements as a footballer. He is the antithesis of the Premier League icon who adheres to brand values dictated by an image consultant. He's known by his nickname, Chopper, and lends a little credibility to that trite title, man of the people. He can be manipulative, but is sensitive to his surroundings and, above all, accessible.

'I have seen good players, big personalities, go into their shell here', he reflected. 'I say to every new player: "If you fall below what the fans expect from you, you will dig your own grave." Our fans graft from day to day, and they come here with every penny they've earned, legally or illegally. If they spend their money on a luxury like football, you have to give them what they want, everything you have. They see you as one of them, and have a huge respect for loyalty. Fully grown men come up to me, call me a legend, and say, "I'd do anything to be you". I laugh, and thank them. Why would I want to be anyone else? We look after our own at Millwall.'

But even a band of brothers has its limitations. There are few lonelier places than an oncologist's consulting room, when the news is bad. Harris was there in June 2001, after a championship-winning season in which he had scored 28 goals. He had noticed one testicle was bigger than the other, as he watched television with his hands resting in his shorts. An ultrasound scan confirmed the cancer. His first question was, 'Will I live?' His second was, 'Will I be able to play football again?' The doctor could not give a definitive answer, although he took encouragement from CT scans and X-rays that confirmed the cancer had been caught early, before it had spread.

'As a footballer you think you cannot be touched. It's all too rosy. You're earning a lot of money, with not many out-goings. Then, suddenly, life grabs you by the throat. I knew nothing about cancer, apart from the fact it killed you. I tried to be very strong-minded. I went on a footballer's instinct, isolated the problem, and dealt with it as quickly as I could. Within two days of the diagnosis, I'd arranged radi-otherapy. Within three weeks I'd visited the sperm bank, which was as bizarre as it gets. I'd conditioned myself to the fact I'd have a testicle chopped off. I had sex once between the operation and the radiotherapy treatment, and my wife conceived. A miracle. I'm blessed.'

That miracle, Cameron, occasionally tags along to train-ing. He's an earnest boy in Millwall kit who practises his shooting, with both feet, into a small-sided goal. When he was six, Tottenham put their trust in his bloodlines, and tried to sign him. 'Come back in ten years, and ask me again', Harris told them. 'I'll let him play with his mates, and coach him one-on-one. If he's good enough, I'll know.' Such reliance on family values was another tribute to his father, Roger, who died of cancer in 2006. His first gesture was wearing a T-shirt bearing the legend 'For You, Dad',

when he equalled Millwall's goal-scoring record at Walsall on 13 December 2008. He broke the record, held by Teddy Sheringham, a month later, at Crewe.

Roger Harris saw no need to assuage his ego through the talent of his son. Neil was a shy boy who needed to be persuaded to play in colts football. His father offered him £1 a goal, a reward quickly capped at £3 when Neil scored all ten goals, from central midfield, in a Cubs Cup final. His individualism was a by-product of his education, at the same independent school as Frank Lampard. Neil was fourteen when he scored in a trial for Southend. He was asked back, but repelled by the impersonal nature of the experience. He was one of 25 kids herded into a small dressing room by a manager who knew no one's name. 'Not for me, Dad', he said.

That instinctive suspicion of the false glamour of professional football resurfaced when, at the age of sixteen, he was offered a YTS contract by Leyton Orient. He lasted the first day of pre-season training, where he cleaned boots and baths after running up and down the terraces. His father picked him up, wondered how the day had panned out. He knew the answer – 'Awful' – from his son's face, which was skewed with disappointment. 'Do you want to go tomorrow?' he asked. 'No Dad, it's not for me.' It was a brave admission, because questions would be asked by friends and family. Roger respected his judgement, gave him room to breathe, and applied the emotional compress of complete faith. 'Son', he said, 'if you're good enough to play pro football you will play it, one day.'

Neil took the scenic route through the non-League game, where he loved the lack of pretension and the honesty of men who played for pin money. His first fee, £15 a match, plus a £5 win bonus, came in a brown envelope supplied by Great Wakering Rovers in the Essex Senior League.

He signed his first contract, worth £45 a week, plus a £5 goal bonus, at Maldon Town, who sold him to Cambridge City for £4,000. For two years, his life settled into the rhythm of the wage slave. He would rise at 6.00am and take the commuter cattle truck to London, where he worked for a Japanese insurance company. He endured the reverse journey before jumping into his car and driving from Rayleigh to Cambridge for training or a mid-week match. He would not be home until after midnight.

Kenny Jackett, then managing Watford, sent a scout to watch him, but was discouraged by the negativity of the assessment. Harris instead joined Millwall for £30,000 in March 1998. He listened to his father, and began to invest in a pension. His first goal, at Northampton the following September, was a curling right-foot shot, on the run, into the top corner. It was to become a trademark. His ambition was fierce, his acceptance of personal responsibility unusual. He cherished the privilege of being paid to play full-time, relished the pressure of public expectation. That underdog mentality suited the club, and sustained him when illness threw a shadow across his life.

'People treated me differently at first. I was Neil Harris, cancer sufferer, when all I wanted to be was Neil Harris, goal-scorer. The lads wanted to give me a cuddle, and I wouldn't accept them feeling sorry for me. I needn't have worried. Marc Bircham, a good friend, said, "Come on, then, show us your bollock". I dropped my trousers, in the middle of the dressing room. They all had a look, and started giving me stick about being unbalanced, and having to run in circles. They were soon stealing my car from the car park. I was out for six months. Maybe I was not honest enough with myself. It took a lot out of me. I've become a lot less naive since then. The more people ask you about cancer, the more you think about it. Will it come back? I got it when I was 23. Will

I get to 80 without getting it again? That's very unlikely. But you can't live your life with fear.'

He keeps football in perspective, without considering it a triviality. He entered his thirteenth season as a professional still bothered by the brutality of defeat in the May 2009 play-off final at Wembley. 'I had no vision of us ever losing that game', he admitted. 'Five minutes of football, two deflections, and it's gone. You go through the rituals, the piss-up afterwards, but you're in shock. Everything's numb. The first thing you do the next morning is switch on Sky and keep seeing that Newcastle, Middlesbrough and West Brom are coming down into the Championship. Instead of going there, you're going to Wycombe, Exeter, Brentford. With the greatest respect, it brings home what you've missed out on.'

He came on as substitute for the last eight minutes of the opening day draw at Southampton on 8 August 2009, and three days later scored the seventh hat-trick of his career, in the 4–0 Carling Cup win over Bournemouth. It was textbook stuff. His first goal, a flash of opportunism at the far post, testified to the speed of his brain. The second, a clinical finish after he had exchanged passes with Chris Hackett and Gary Alexander, rewarded a five-man move of speed and simplicity initiated by Alan Dunne. The third, a dipping right-foot volley from the right-hand angle of the penalty area, deserved a better stage. Even referee Grant Hegley couldn't help himself saying, 'Great goal'.

Referees do funny things down at The Den. It's a forbidding place for any authority figure, never mind anyone armed only with a whistle and a call-centre headset. Most arrive in macho mode, determined not to be intimidated. Unpopularity is a campaign medal, to be worn with pride. The atmosphere doesn't encourage logical thought or optimal decision-making. Just ask Darren Deadman, who

controlled the dour goalless draw with Carlisle on 15 August, the following Saturday. He was the subject of an official complaint to the Football League by Carlisle player-coach Graham Kavanagh, who heard him shout 'Get in, Harris', as the Millwall striker closed in on goal during the second half.

Confronted by Kavanagh, the referee initially ignored him. He then denied he had made any outburst, before finally admitting he was instinctively congratulating himself for playing advantage. Deadman eventually apologised after the League, assisted by referees' manager David Allison, completed its investigation. The circus of the absurd, however, had not left town. Three days later, Andy D'Urso, the referee whose career never recovered from his pursuit by a lynch mob at Old Trafford led by Roy Keane, excelled himself. Jobsworths the world over would send their congratulations, in triplicate, at his surreal sense of order.

Millwall were leading Oldham by a close-range Dave Martin goal when, midway through the first half, D'Urso bought a dive by Andy Holdsworth, the former Millwall trial-list. The Orcs in the upper tiers stirred. Stewards scrambled, and a lighter was thrown in the referee's general direction. Even the guard dogs in the surrounding scrapyards cowered at the guttural howl of triumph generated by David Forde's penalty save from Pawel Abbott, low to his right. The Monk's chant, 'Mmmmmmmmiiiiiiiiiiiiiiiiilllllllllllllllllllllllllllll', repeated at *Spinal Tap* volume until the lung and larynx explode, echoed in the darkness, which was emphasised by the red lights on the chimneys of the adjacent incineration centre.

D'Urso, blinking with the ferocity of an adolescent discovered downloading internet porn by his granny, almost got away with it. Then, four minutes before half time, Steve Morison pulled a hamstring, sprinting to track back. A straightforward substitution degenerated into a farce when

fourth official Philip Knight spotted that Harris was wearing a taped-up wedding band. D'Urso refused to allow him on, insisting on its removal. Harris plunged his hand into a tub of Vaseline, but it wouldn't budge, despite the attentions of most of the Millwall bench. Even Martin Gray, Oldham's assistant manager, pleaded with the officials on the striker's behalf. Word was sent to the security staff: find a hacksaw; we might have to cut this ring off.

Harris was hustled into the home dressing room by club doctor Imtiaz Ahmad when the half-time whistle blew. Jackett and his coaching staff were outside the referee's room, on the opposite side of the corridor. The door was open. D'Urso stood a step back, as his fellow officials surrounded him like an over-nourished, under-trained Praetorian Guard. 'Let's have some common sense', the manager said. 'It's a small band. It will be really well taped. It won't hurt anyone. He's played the last three games with it on.'

D'Urso was unrepentant: 'If the club have an issue about this, they should have made representations to the League before the match. This is the first I have heard about any problem.' Jackett, perplexed, appealed to his better nature: 'C'mon. You're going to look very silly. He's got a bump over his knuckle. He's never going to get that ring off.' He might as well have saved his breath for one of the more challenging team talks of his career. Jackett spoke softly when he began to express his thoughts – 'Keep working hard. Raise the tempo. We have to find that balance between urgency and calmness' – and took time to find the right level of intensity.

Everyone was all too aware of the drama being played out in the toilets. Harris had plunged his hand down one bowl, and flushed repeatedly. He then held his ring hand under icy, fast-running water. Ahmad applied soap,

manipulated the finger, and flinched as Harris bit his shoulder to counteract the pain of the band being wrenched over the knuckle. Harris was sweating profusely as he sat down on the bench with a bag of ice over his left hand. The hacksaw, which looked as if it had been requisitioned from a child's DIY set, was mercifully unnecessary.

Ahmad smiled bashfully and whispered, 'I do it all the time in A&E'. His reward came in injury time, when Harris' clever movement enabled him to convert an unchallenged header from three yards out. Jackett was appeased by the 2–0 win, telling his squad: 'We missed a couple of good chances early in the second half and the game came back to us. The ref just lost it. Some of his decisions were a fucking joke. You did well. Remember, this is the learning time in the season. We take this into the next game.' Victory is never enough in this business. One win demands another. Two wins require a run. A run of wins must be sustained, or, at the very least, protected. It's not about what you did in your last game, but what you will do in your next.

Harris was on the agenda for the next management meeting in a spare room furnished by four MDF desks, a filing cabinet, and a promotional poster that eulogised the nirvana of 'Real Football. Real Passion. Real Talent.' Jackett wanted feedback from his coaches about whether Harris could cope with the conveyor belt of Saturday–Tuesday– Saturday football. Joe Gallen set the tone by suggesting: 'There are times he looks dead in his legs. We might have to move him in and out, because of the build-up of games.' Tony Burns added the rider that 'his work rate is unbelievable. He knows himself really well.' Richard Shaw agreed: 'Neil knows he is going to have to step out for some games. That's OK with him. He seems to know how to play at home, and what the crowd wants.' Everyone nodded when Jackett summed up: 'Some man, isn't he?'

The pair have history. Harris was part of the fixtures and fittings Jackett inherited. His legend was woven into the fabric of the club. He had left after falling out with Dennis Wise following the FA Cup final in 2004, but had renewed his career at The Den after two insubstantial years at Nottingham Forest. Manager Gary Megson, an abrasive personality, hadn't been a fan. Jackett could not envisage building a team around Harris once he had saved Millwall from relegation in his initial season, but was sufficiently pragmatic to change his mind. Harris is a proud man whose brain has the setback stored for future reference.

'I've had some dark days. The insecurity is always there. We're in a short-term business. Rejection is fine, as long as it's honestly done. I have pride in my ability as a player, and my principles as a person. Sometimes I have got angry and said, "Why aren't you fucking picking me?" It's not nice. It takes you back to being the kid who's the last pick in the school playground. Any player who says competition for places is good is only half telling the truth. It's fucking horrible for players, and good for managers and clubs. As you get older you realise managers don't do things by accident. Changing the gaffer's mind, when he told me he probably wouldn't be offering me a new deal, is one of the biggest achievements of my career.'

Harris is not physically imposing, but projects his personality. He has the self-assuredness of a political leader in party conference season. Flesh is pressed, brains are engaged, and key messages are delivered. He doesn't flaunt his authority. It's unspoken, yet omnipresent. It goes beyond the basics of team selection. It reflects on his intrinsic value to the club. I can think of many managers who would be unnerved by having a senior player with such a strong emotional pull on those around him. Harris knows the score, understands the agenda set by his reputation:

'I appreciate that, on and off the field, body language is extremely important. Off the field everyone associates me with the football club. To a certain degree I'm an ambassador, even though I'm a player. I'm proud to be so. On the field I know the other players look to me for inspiration. It's fundamental that I share the experience of playing here for more than ten years with the boys.

'The make-up of a Millwall fan is different to any other fan in the country. Sharing how they think, and act, is so important, especially with new players. It takes a certain time to settle in here. Fans can be perceived in different ways, not just by the media and other clubs, but by players as well. You might think they're having a go, when you hear them swearing at you, but it's their way of trying to encourage you. There's a very fine line which everyone treads.

'That word, the c-u-n-t word, is an ugly word. But it's a word used quite a lot at Millwall. It's part of the vocabulary. Fans are not necessarily using it to have a go at you. To thrive here, you have to be extremely thick-skinned or bright enough to let it go over your head. Take it in, get annoyed, but think about it. Work out why they are doing it, and come back stronger. The alternative is to be completely brain dead, and don't recognise they're having a go. That works for some. If you look at us as a group, the one word that sums us up is honest. They're a good set of lads. Strong, tight.

'A group of football players in a dressing room is similar to a group of friends anywhere. You have the leaders, the outgoing, normally older ones, who have experience and are not afraid to say what they have to say, but respect each other. You have the lads who will be like that one day, and the younger ones who keep themselves to themselves, and just get on with it. You have to have a strong bunch, because in a dressing room one bad egg can sour things

if he's allowed to get away with it. I've been in teams like that. Every footballer would have played with someone who doesn't want to be there.

'They are the ones who are happy to pick their wages up without trying a leg. They're happy to lead the life of a footballer, without having the bollocks to put it in on the pitch. They love being down the nightclub, telling every bird they meet who they play for. The leaders of the group have got to try and manage that, be the go-betweens. We have to talk to a player, keep his head up, and ensure he doesn't go to the dark side. If he's a good lad he will respond.'

A dressing room is a paradoxical place. Compassion goes hand in hand with casual cruelty. It requires strength for a player, coach or manager to admit to weakness. In such a macho environment, it takes courage to open up, emotionally. Getting hammered for a dim or dubious comment is a daily occurrence, but there are limits. When they are ignored, tribal instincts take over. The line was crossed, for Harris, at Swindon, in a melee that followed the dismissal of Andy Frampton.

Its origin was a simple mistake. Frampton chested the ball down, lost control, and lunged in, studs up, on Jon Paul McGovern. He was angry with himself at such a basic error, and exacted self-destructive retribution on anything in his way. He was still on the ground when the red card loomed out of the red mist. Frampton had torn his ankle ligaments, yet Swindon's Kevin Amankwaah was trying to yank him to his feet. The ritual handbag-swinging, traditionally prompted by such disrespect, acquired an additional dimension when Harris exploded with rage for no apparent reason. He had to be hauled away by his team-mates, as both benches got involved.

Amankwaah, who had played for Jackett at Swansea, initially denied abusing Harris. His eventual apology, for

taunting him about the consequences of his cancer operation, was accompanied by a promise that he would make a donation to the Millwall striker's charity. However, following reports he had been ordered to apologise by his teammates, Amankwaah complained, retrospectively, that he had been physically and racially abused. Harris dismissed the accusation as 'frankly laughable', before the PFA brokered an unconvincing peace.

'We both wrote a letter saying we didn't want it to go further', Harris said. 'There was an argument, following Framps' sending off, and he made a comment regarding my lack of a testicle. That's why I lost my head. It was the first time anyone had mentioned it to me on the pitch. Anyone who knows me, and knows my reputation, knows what was said. It was an argument on the pitch over a game of football. It was very distasteful but does it affect my life? Nah. Was I calm enough not to slap him in the face? Yeah. But in football senior players in particular have a way of dealing with things, and it's not through the press or the FA.'

Harris may be mild-mannered, but he's a product of a hard school. He was suddenly oblivious to the background hum of canteen conversation and commentaries on the contents of the Sky Sports News feed. He stopped pushing a piece of chicken around his plate, fixed me with a cold stare, and spoke softly, yet urgently. Mr Nice Guy had left the building. 'He won't play at our place this season – no way. I don't think his manager will pick him. But you know what I'm talking about, Mike. Next time there's a ball to be won, smash. He'll have to take his chance in the tackle. That is the other side of me. That's how football is. It's how life is. You have to stand up for yourself ...'

Chapter 6
The Guvnors

'I'm not being funny, Dave, but if I ever see you bottle it like that again, I'll fucking chin you. I promise you. Don't ever do that again.'

Only Andy Frampton could make such a threat sound like an invitation to tea and biscuits. The warning was all the more menacing because of the measured way in which it was delivered. Millwall had dropped two needless points at home against Brighton, and, as stand-in captain, Frampton exercised his right to apportion blame. Dave Martin looked crestfallen and stared into space. Kenny Jackett cringed inwardly, even though he had responded to Martin's act of self-preservation by quickly substituting him. He had to balance his respect for Frampton with the impact of the defender's controlled anger.

'I understand the frustration', he said, twisting his body to the right to address Martin directly as he stood in the middle of the changing area. 'Dave, I know it looks hard, going off at you like that, but he's right. He's the captain of this team. I thought the same thing. The crowd thought the same thing. Do you know why he said it? It's because he knows, Dave, that you can win a tackle.' It was like listening to a primary school teacher delicately disciplining a highly-strung child. Jackett was concerned about making Martin a scapegoat, but understood the dynamics of his dressing room. Rather than immediately stress the need for sensitivity, he would have a quiet word with Frampton when the time was right.

Frampton is one of the Guvnors, the senior pros who shape the team's personality and gauge its intensity. The others are goalkeeper David Forde, skipper Paul Robinson, defender Tony Craig, and strikers Gary Alexander and Neil Harris. In a football sense, they have made their bones. The group is self-regulating, and membership must be earned. They are experienced players who set high personal and professional standards. They help weed out the weak, and are intolerant of lapses in character.

Frampton is a deceptively aggressive, deeply impressive man, who adheres to the motto of Lancing College, his alma mater.

'Beati Mundo Corde' – Blessed are the pure in heart – may be an incongruous notion on the mean streets of Bermondsey, but a public school, set in 550 acres of the South Downs in West Sussex, demands its own form of resilience. Lancing was founded in 1848 with the aim of providing education 'based on sound principle and knowledge, firmly grounded in the Christian faith'. Chapel attendance is compulsory, regardless of religious belief, and sporting excellence, in everything from football to Eton Fives, is admired.

'I was a boarder', Frampton recalled. 'You learned, straight away, that you have to look after yourself. You weren't molly-coddled. You were bullied a little. I suppose that kind of toughened me up. You have to be self-reliant, take the flak as it comes. That's moulded my character. As a kid you look at the bright lights of international football, but you soon realise your capabilities. You can make an OK living at my level, so dreams do come true, to a certain extent. I got to be that professional footballer I craved to be.'

Frampton earned a scholarship, though the principles of Victorian austerity on which the school was built do not come cheap. It costs a basic £27,000 a year to board, and the

Framptons personify the understated ambitions of Middle England. His father is a chartered surveyor with a decent property portfolio who lives in semi-retirement in Purley. They are an artistic family – his sister is a theatre designer and his older brother is completing a music degree – but Andy can draw nothing more complicated than a stick man.

Give him a striped blazer and a silly cap, and, with his broad shoulders, he could be a varsity rower. Put him in a uniform, and he could be a fresh-faced subaltern on his way to the killing fields of Helmand Province. Give him a dog collar, and he would be condemned to a lifetime eating marble cake in the company of over-attentive spinsters. Parenthood has increased his awareness of the sacrifices his parents made to give him the best chance in life. His children, Dominic, five, and Eloise, three, are an escape valve.

'My parents gave me every opportunity and I'd like to feed my kids self-belief, through my own experiences. I want them to be able to stand up for themselves. They're still at kindergarten, and I don't know if I'd send them to boarding school. But you try and instil values in your kids as early as you can. I don't want them walking around with swagger and arrogance.'

That is precisely the template of the modern footballer. There is something old-fashioned about the values the Guvnors enshrine, and enforce. The dig at Martin struck a familiar chord. 'When I first came to this club I wouldn't have been able to get away with saying something like that', Frampton admitted. 'It's a privilege you have to earn, and that takes commitment to your job. You have to show you mean it, in your gym work, in your preparation, in the way you train. The way they behave, the way they give something of themselves in their personal lives, gives probably three-quarters of the team the right to have a go. It's a good mix. If the younger lads have a pop back at us, it's respected.

You have to be a certain type of professional to be around this football club. You find out very quickly about people, because of the nature of our training sessions. They're full-on. You get to know the ones who will pull their weight, who won't sulk, moan, or drop their head. They see what they have to do to be accepted. It's not something we talk about. The strongest rules are never written down. Everyone just knows. Somehow or other there's a connection between us. We have had players here who haven't quite fitted into the group. I'm not saying they're bad players. It's just that there are certain types we'd like to be in a team with. They're the ones who are ready to fight for you.'

At the landmark age of 30, Frampton appreciates his limitations. A left back by inclination but a central defender by expedience, he gets by on aggression, anticipation, and concentration. He has been what he calls 'a shouty' player since his schooldays, when he led Lancing to victory in the Independent Schools Cup final at Craven Cottage. He played for Crystal Palace youth teams during the holidays, and abandoned his A-levels after earning a professional contract. He accepted a free transfer to Brentford after playing 35 times in four seasons. He joined Millwall in the summer of 2007, and endured the traditional trial by hanging jury before being named Player of the Season in 2008–09.

'That award meant a huge amount. It was absolutely massive, because when I came to the club I had a difficult first few months. I wanted to come here to test myself. I always knew I'd settle in because I'm the style of player they like to see. One thing they do love – you can feel it from the crowd – is someone who gives 100 per cent. It's more intimate here than at other places. They voice their concerns more than at any other club I have been at. They say it as it is. They don't beat around the bush. You have to take it at face value, and deal with it.'

Players are not inanimate objects. They hear the insults, are occasionally able to isolate their abusers in a sea of distorted faces, but can rarely afford the luxury of an honest response. One jibe, among many, has never left Frampton. It was spat at him during a 2–2 home draw against Swansea on the day Jackett joined Millwall: 'Fuck off back to Brentford, you cunt.' It was the sort of empty-headed slur that doesn't deserve rational discussion but somehow eats away at the victim's subconscious. 'It was one single person. The rest of the crowd were quiet when he yelled it, and then they laughed. There's no answer to that. I looked at him and thought, "Yeah, you're probably right". I wasn't playing particularly well. My hunger had gone a tiny bit. I felt under pressure. The timing, the gaffer's first game, was great. I thought, "That's it, I'm down the job centre". I broke my toe that night and didn't come back for two months. I had a long time to reflect, and look at it from a fan's point of view. I knew I needed to come back mentally stronger, physically tougher.

'I had to move down to League One to kick-start my career. Through doing that, I realised that going to a club where you don't have everything put on a plate for you is a good thing. You have to grow up quickly, take more responsibility for yourself and others, on and off the pitch. I have to scream and shout. It gets my concentration up, gets me out of my shell. I'm a thinker. That might have been the undoing of me when I was younger. Sometimes one sentence used to eat away at me for a couple of days. It would affect my confidence. Now I've got it in perspective. It's an opinionated game. You have to get on with it.'

That doesn't stop him occasionally telephoning assistant manager Joe Gallen the day after matches, seeking assurance about the validity of his contribution. Forde, also 30, is another kaleidoscopic character whose insecurities are fil-

tered through the prism of instinctive anger. In his case, Dr Jekyll is a reflective, intelligent man who could have been a teacher, and is planning to resume a business studies degree. Mr Hyde is a tyrant with a hair-trigger temper who thinks nothing of grabbing a team-mate by the throat when his mood has been soured by frustration, or a deep-rooted pressure to make up for lost time.

'Everything I do is professional, not personal', Forde explained. 'My missus says that, off the field, you couldn't meet anyone more laid-back, but once I cross those white lines I come to work. If we have a barney, or a bit of a ruck, we shake hands and get on with it. I don't want to fall out with anyone – it's just how football works, and how I work. This has been a massive second chance for me. I have been very lucky. I've had to leave the magic circle of English football. I've gone back to Ireland, where the domestic league is not really recognised. I had to re-establish myself, get back in love with the game. The experience gave me a real hunger. I don't want to be sitting in a pub with my mates in years to come, saying I could have done this or that. It's about having no regrets.'

Scrape away the veneer of manhood and the dark-haired boy from the west coast of Ireland blinks back at you. Forde is the dreamer whose father teases him about his habit, in Under-10 matches in Galway, of making sandcastles in his goalmouth when the ball was up the other end. He's the warrior whose confrontational nature was developed, together with his handling and kicking skills, in Gaelic football and hurling. He's that soap opera staple, a tough guy with a tender touch. Beware the tungsten fist in a padded goalkeeping glove.

His personality has been refined by rejection. He began with Galway United, played in the Champions League for Barry Town, and, in hindsight, regrets joining West Ham

instead of Millwall in 2001. He spent three seasons without a first-team appearance, learning from the perfectionism of David James, and listening to Raimond Van der Gouw, the long-term understudy to Peter Schmeichel, his hero. He was released, retreated across the Irish Sea, but salvaged a career from the debris of disillusion. Two rehabilitative seasons at Derry City earned a move to Cardiff. Loan spells at Luton and Bournemouth brought him to the attention of Tony Burns, who engineered his free transfer signing in May 2008.

The relationship is pivotal. Burns is 65 going on 26, a cross between a regimental sergeant major, an eternal schoolboy and a doting grandad. He's as likely to be prancing around the training ground, answering a forfeit with his bare backside hanging out of his tracksuit trousers, as he is to be setting standards of behaviour for his group. He's impossible to miss, difficult to dislike. His eyes are bright, and his opinions are sharp. He's the alpha male in a breed apart, which purges itself with hard work.

On this particular day, Yusuf Mersin, an improbably imposing schoolboy of Turkish extraction, was taking life lessons. Forde, John Sullivan and the scholars Wayne Drummond and Jamie Farmer looked on, appreciative of the magnitude of his mistake. 'Get your fucking boots clean', growled Burns. 'Don't ever come out here, to work, when they're dirty. Ten press-ups. Come on, get up on those hands. Get that body down low. Have you ever had a bird? With that bugle of yours, I doubt it …' The youngster, insulated by talent and ambition, took his punishment wordlessly. 'They're all trying to nick him', confided Burns with revealing pride. He led the other goalkeepers in volleying balls at the kid from close range. 'Don't back off', he ordered. 'The ball will not hurt you. Remember. Elbows in. Stand big. Hands narrow.'

Burns was distilling the lessons of a twenty-year playing career that took him from Arsenal to Plymouth, via South Africa and the United States. He managed Tonbridge, his original non-League club, in three spells between August 1980 and May 2002, and spent seven years in charge at Gravesend and Northfleet. Inevitably, this being Millwall, he took his turn as caretaker manager, alongside Alan McLeary at the fag end of the 2005–06 season. He quietly cherishes the wisdom of his wife, who sensed his restlessness and suggested he mothball a successful decorating business to devote himself to goalkeeping coaching.

'Football has never been a money thing for me', he explained. 'It keeps you young, coming out to work each day. This club is different. It loves being as it is. Fordie's chucked five years of his earning career away. He's had his knock-backs, but I liked the way he responded. That's Millwall. These next seven or eight years are his time. He's an intelligent boy, a grafter. He's made himself a 20 per cent better keeper since I've worked with him. He's got good technique, and a manly character.'

Forde understands the culture into which he has bought: 'As a young goalkeeper you have to be battered from pillar to post. That's what makes you strong, tough physically and mentally. If you chuck one in, you're on your own. The quicker that is bred into you the better. Teaching you to be thick-skinned is part of what Burnsy does. You know you're taking stick during games, but you try not to listen. Once you react they know they're on to you. They're like a shower of leeches. I've had a couple of pops back out of naivety, quite silly really. As Burnsy says: "The more you mature, the less you allow things to get to you."

'As a goalkeeper it's important to have organisational skills. You have to motivate, breed confidence. It's important to have that understanding with your back four. If we're hav-

ing a bad time, or being sloppy, it's up to me to be focused. All good sides have that core, leaders who replenish that hunger to be the best. Football always finds you out, sooner or later. That's the great thing about it. It all comes down to looking after your family. You win, you get the bonus. If you see someone threatening that by not putting it in, you have a word. If they don't listen you make sure they're shipped out, and replaced by someone who will put it in.'

Robinson is more considered, no less authoritative. When Soccer AM filmed the Crossbar Challenge sequence that is required viewing in dressing rooms across the land, he introduced himself, simply, as 'captain of this shower of shit'. That rustled the crinolines of the producers, earned him an on-screen bleep, but strengthened his street cred immeasurably. The crew did not hang around long enough to burrow beneath the bravado. They would have found an understated leader who accepts, without rancour, that 'there is a bit more realism at this level'.

Robinson first came into contact with Jackett at the Watford Academy, where he spent five years before being released at fifteen. Without football, he would have probably used his A-levels in PE, English and Economics, and gone to university. Instead he graduated through Millwall's YTS scheme, and absorbed the club's values through the osmosis of experience: 'It's unique, and once you find yourself inside the club, it's infectious. They will let you know here. Some people say it's hard to play for these fans, but I find it easy. All they demand is that you give everything you have got.'

He had trained throughout the summer recess to compensate for the break, in the fifth metatarsal bone in his right foot, that had kept him out for the final three months of the previous season. He was driven by the 'sickening' memory of the Wembley defeat in which he made his comeback as a late substitute, but, ten days into pre-season train-

ing, was struck by what he described, with unintentional irony, as 'a bolt from the blue'. The internal screw, inserted in the initial operation, could have been compromised by an awkward challenge. Jackett and Bobby Bacic had a stark choice: allow the pain to settle, and gamble on his vulnerability, or sanction an operation involving the application of a new, thicker, longer, high-density screw. It would blow Bacic's budget, which had been stretched by surgery to Danny Senda and Zak Whitbread, but was a no-brainer.

'Fucking hell, we love an operation at Millwall', mourned Jackett.

'There's no money left after this', confirmed Bacic.

The manager grimaced: 'Any more, and I'll have to do them myself.'

The physiotherapist smiled: 'It's not a bit of sewing your granny could do. I'll send your regards to the surgeon as he drives off in his Aston Martin.'

X-rays were taken, from every angle, during the procedure. No fracture was found. Robinson spent the following month in plaster and an airboot, but pushed himself through the rehabilitation process with typical single-mindedness. He swam, did aerobic work in an altitude chamber, and followed a stretching programme with religious zeal. He changed to a sturdier, wider boot, modified by a specialist to limit the rolling motion of his foot.

'I was genuinely worried', he admitted. 'The longer you are out the harder it is to come back. You tell yourself to believe, and keep working, but when you stop, and you're on your own at home, the doubts crowd in on you. We haven't got a safety net. You start to wonder what you will do with yourself, when football isn't an option. You begin to plan ahead. It can be scary.'

He lasted 37 minutes of his comeback match, a surreal 2–0 defeat at Barnet in the Football League Trophy on

1 September. Coming a week after the West Ham riots, it was a culture shock, a leap from urban unrest to suburban apathy. A group of twenty or so juveniles, who went under the banner of Barnet Bovva, chanted, 'You're not scary any more' from behind a soothingly large police cordon. The lights were on in the terraced houses that overlooked one end of the ground, but no one appeared to be at home. The lines were crooked, the pitch was bumpy, and the slope, running down to the left-hand corner, was pronounced. The hapless former FA press officer, who compiled the programme, refused to give out team sheets 'because they're already allocated'. Four under-powered floodlights, each containing five bulbs, lent a strange sheen to the scene. It would have taken a power cut to hide the discomfort of George Friend, whose embarrassment by the pace of winger Albert Adomah effectively confirmed the failure of his loan spell.

True to the bizarre nature of the game, Robinson was initially treated by Barnet physio Mark Stein. Sold short by a pass, he landed awkwardly after being clattered on his left ankle. Bacic, who was tending to a facial injury sustained by Jimmy Abdou, summoned an ambulance at half time. Robinson was accompanied by his father, who lives ten minutes from Underhill, and, still in his kit, took his turn in the queue at Accident & Emergency. He waited for 90 minutes, behind a boy who had been hit full in the face by a cricket ball, instead of the advertised three hours. 'Thank God it wasn't Friday or Saturday night', he said, grateful to have avoided the drunken dregs that form the department's customer base. An X-ray revealed there was no bone broken, but subsequent scans confirmed he had suffered ligament damage to his ankle. Vivid bruising, yellow black and blue, gave his lower leg the look of an artist's palette. Not pretty, not clever. 'I'm sick for him', said Jackett, with convincing force.

His renewed absence threw more responsibility on Craig, whose complex mixture of assertiveness and insecurity characterised the goalless draw at Southend. He had come through the ranks with Robinson, and had been forgiven the sin of spending a season discovering whether the grass was greener over at Selhurst Park. Roots Hall, raw, claustrophobic, and as basic as carbolic soap, was more his scene. Bacic and masseur Chris Harvey worked from a partially-erected bench set up in a sunken bath, no more than four feet square, as garage music from the home dressing room filtered down the narrow corridor. Forde lost himself in a cocoon of concentration. He closed his eyes, bowed his head, and intertwined his gloved fingers as if in supplication. 'Don't go fucking quiet on me', Craig ordered. 'Winners. Every fucking one of us. Everyone in their faces.'

A frantic first half of misplaced passes and sprints down blind alleys did little to ease his mood. 'We're making them look fucking good. We're ten times the team they are. We haven't fucking turned up.' Jackett, toying with the counters on a whiteboard propped beside the corner peg, let the storm abate before making decisive changes. Substitute Harris almost scored within seconds of the restart, and although Alexander hit the woodwork, a draw was about the right result. 'There's nothing wrong with your effort, commitment, and spirit', Jackett summarised. 'We were absolutely balls out. If we can add to that the selection of the next pass, and recognition of your best option, it'll be exciting. It's never a bad point here.'

Craig seized the floor: 'We need to be a bit cute, boys. We have to kill games off a little better. If we win ten games ugly, I don't give a shit. If we can turn these draws into wins we'll have a good season.' Speech over, he suddenly seemed spent. He was confronted by weakness, real or imagined. He stretched his legs out under the ancient wooden table

that dominated the room, and sought reassurance. 'Did you think what I said was OK, Joe?' he asked Gallen, in a stage whisper. 'Listening to you talk tells me how far we have come', he replied. 'Your disappointment shows me who we are, and where we are going.'

Craig leaned back, satisfied, and shuffled on the wooden bench. He was still in his kit when most of his team-mates had braved the tepid showers and changed. 'I'll be awake until four in the morning, you know', he confided. 'I always am, after night games. The adrenaline is ridiculous. I'll get home and watch Sky Sports News on the loop, with the odd sneaky look at the Babe Channel.' He chuckled at the absurdity of the image he had created. He knew Fantasy TV couldn't be as alluring as reality. His back hurt, his legs ached, but he was replete.

Alexander, meanwhile, was being warned by Frampton that 'they're after you'. His full and frank exchange of views with fans in the main stand, which involved him grabbing his shirt, and thrusting its Rampant Lion badge at them, had not gone unnoticed up in the rabbit hutch that passed as a press box. Whatever. Alexander is still, at heart, the eleven-year-old boy who was entranced by his first away trip as a Millwall fan, to Oxford on a rainy Tuesday night, 27 February 1991. It was a goalless draw, watched by 4,570, but it had the primal power to end a flirtation with the Liverpool of Ian Rush and John Aldridge. He loved the late night, the memory of the crowd scenes that enlivened the reverie of first lesson the following day. He wanted to be Real Wall, even though he crossed into enemy territory to begin his career in the YTS programme at West Ham.

He cleaned John Hartson's blue boots, aware of the probability of disembowelment if he left any polish on the sponsor's logo. His other job was to clean the treatment room, where the physio would leave a tea stain under

a piece of equipment to check his efficiency. If the stain remained, every apprentice would be forced to stay behind until Alexander had left the place spotless. It taught him self-discipline, the value of self-respect, and the wider importance of his responsibility to the group. It might have gone against the modern principles of an enlightened workplace, but the culture of the good pro had taken root. It has sustained him, in a career that has taken him to Swindon, Hull, Leyton Orient and, finally, the club to which he remains devoted.

'A good pro is someone like Robbo. He's here early, working constantly. He's in the gym, trains hard, and doesn't want to lose. Good pros do their work, look after themselves. If they've had a night out they come in the next morning and work twice as hard, to sweat it out. There are times the gaffer loses it, but he knows he has a lot of good pros here. There's going to be rows. We argue because we care. He calms it down. He will get the hump if we toss it off, but sometimes there's no need to shout. If he wants to give it you, he'll have you up in the office, one-on-one.

'The senior lads speak up. There are times you've got to hammer someone, and be there to pick them up if they need it. Certain characters could go under. I'm not as loud as some in the dressing room, but I make myself heard on the pitch. Some lads know if they're having a stinker – others need telling. If I get bollocked, I might argue back, knowing, deep down, that I'm in the wrong, but I will go out there to prove them wrong.'

Jackett knows what he has on his hands. He calls the Guvnors 'black boot men', in homage to their no-nonsense, back-to-basics approach. They are loyal, driven, yet dutiful. Whitbread, whose immediate future was compromised by his hip operation, agitated for a transfer. This meant he had forfeited his membership of the inner circle. His

House of Fun

PA announcers at football grounds aren't exactly prize exhibits for the evolutionary process. Trapped in permanent pre-pubescence, most babble incomprehensibly, as if matron has sprinkled crystal meth on their chips. They've got a captive audience, a cause to champion, and lingering fears of insignificance to address at maximum volume. They deserve to be garrotted by their microphone leads, or, at the very least, locked in a padded cell with James Corden, Chris Moyles and the cast of *High School Musical 3*.

But, just occasionally, a renegade avoids the obligatory lobotomy and acquires a personality with more than one dimension. John Hall, in charge of the tannoy at Princes Park Community Stadium in Dartford, has the dry humour of those tube drivers who serenade commuters with sub-Wildean observations on the meaning of life. On any given Tuesday, he can be found trumpeting the delights of curry night – a pint and a chicken tikka masala for £6.95. If he's lucky, he's got Millwall Reserves to add to the sense of drama.

This was the biggie, a local derby against Crystal Palace in the totesport.com Combination. The £6.5 million stadium, with its living grass roof, rainwater recycling system, and environmentally-friendly floodlights, was a tree-hugger's delight. Just to make sure the locals knew whom to thank, the advertising hoardings proclaimed: 'Built by a Conservative Council.' Hall looked out on the pristine

pitch, which the council website suggests is the equal of those 'at Real Madrid and Ajax', and was suitably inspired. 'Evening everyone', he said in his best late-night DJ drawl, 'welcome to the House of Fun'. The strains of Madness, the Nutty Boys of sainted memory, echoed around an empty arena, where Millwall were warming up with little apparent enthusiasm.

Reserve team football is where cynicism meets idealism in a vacuum of indifference. The scholars, fighting to preserve the dream of a professional career, are thrown in alongside fringe players who have every right to fear for their future. 'They hang themselves', sighed Richard Shaw, the reserve team coach. 'No matter how many times you try to tell them that people will be watching, some of them won't try a leg. Reserve team football is a state of mind. Scouts will be looking for the senior pro who puts himself out, talks the kids through the game. He doesn't have to play well, only show the right character.'

Scott Fitzgerald, Millwall's head of youth, nodded assent. The pair are the same age and have a similar mentality. They are former central defenders whose professional instincts, ingrained over long careers, are intermittently offended. 'They're mad if they think we won't give the gaffer honest answers when he asks us what we think', he said. 'A potential buying club will watch and wonder – will this guy put himself out when we're in the shit, looking at relegation? Good characters will find work in the game. The ones who find it all a little beneath them will struggle, big time.'

Lewis Grabban, uncommunicative but by no means unintelligent, had the most pertinent questions to answer. Tall, lithe and quick, his attributes as a natural athlete led to Kenny Jackett spending £150,000 to sign him from Crystal Palace in January 2008. At 21, he had reached the cross-roads of a career compromised by the complexities of his

character. A devout Muslim, he had just endured a difficult Ramadan. He had taken the advice of James Collins, the club's part-time performance nutritionist, and taken fish oils, multi-vitamins and anti-oxidants to supplement his diet during the hours of darkness, but tiredness radiated from his red-rimmed eyes. He had refused the discreet offer of Bobby Bacic, who suggested he rehydrate during matches and training by sipping surreptitiously from a plastic cup placed in the shower area. Jimmy Abdou, the club's other Muslim player, agreed to compromise his faith by doing so.

Grabban had been Millwall's best player for the first half of the previous season. The tipping point came at Hereford, where, according to team-mates, he was abused as 'a lazy black cunt' by his own fans. He was alienated by media coverage of the incident, which generated initial sympathy. His form matched his depressive mood, and dipped alarmingly. He became increasingly diffident, played a peripheral role in pre-season matches, and was marginalised in the dressing room. 'He presents differently', observed Collins. 'He's aloof and doesn't respond when you discuss things with the group. But he is listening. He is interested. He'll come back later, when no one is around, and almost surprise you by asking the right questions.'

Bacic agreed: 'He plays on the image of being a loner.'

Jackett is, by nature, pragmatic. 'No one condones the abuse Lewis took, but football is about mental strength', he rationalised. 'This is a big year for him. He can learn from Jimmy. Our fans love him, because he gives everything of himself. Lewis is a talented lad but he's way out there, without a doubt. It's going to be difficult for him. He needs backing to an unbelievable degree. Most of my group are men. Their lives are sorted.'

Jackett dispenses with the niceties of selection – if you don't feature in the pattern of play training sessions 48 hours

before a match, you're not in his team – and gives short shrift to those seeking explanations. 'I don't encourage it. You can spend all your time talking, say too much to them, and then have your words thrown back at you later on. Actions speak louder than words. They know, deep down, why they're not in the team. They shouldn't need to be told, but if they need to know why, I'll be blunt and to the point.'

Shaw, conditioned to picking up the pieces, was much more at ease with the blind fury of Alan Dunne, who responded to being dropped by driving away from the training ground without bothering to change. 'I can understand that. I've felt that way myself, as a player. When I was at Coventry, Gordon Strachan dropped me for a game against Chelsea after I had played well in a win against Tottenham. I was hauled out of my car by Colin Hendry, and told not to do anything rash. I was fuming, and was going to absolutely batter the manager. I got up to Gordon's office, banged the door down, and found him waiting with two cups of tea and two bits of cake. We sat down, but before I could start he was off. An hour later we were best mates. Gordon had told me all the Man United stories, given me insights into his career. It was great man-management, an object lesson in how to defuse a situation.

'There's no right and wrong way to deal with players who are not in the first team, but any coach will tell you it's the worst job in football. I study body language, which tells me everything about their character. Players like Adam Bolder and Marc Laird are an absolute credit to themselves. They have a positive mindset and respond well every time I have them. They'd be the first I'd recommend, if someone asked whether we had anyone worth a punt. Lewis hasn't helped himself. He's on the edge of the group. It's a close-knit dressing room. No troublemakers, no one speaking out of turn. How you can't fit in here is beyond me.'

Shaw is a quietly-spoken character who has the escape valve of a wife, Paula, who has no interest in football. There's nothing in his home to suggest he had a model professional's career, which ended two months short of his 40th birthday. His football mementoes are in the attic, and he can live with his principal regret, that he never acquired the habit of swapping shirts with stellar opponents in the Premier League. 'Being a black player, I wasn't too sure about coming to Millwall', he admitted. 'I talked it through with my wife, and told them if I heard any abuse I'd walk. The crowd have changed my philosophy about this club. This is the real world. It's a family. If you are one of them they will be behind you 110 per cent. These players have an affinity with the working man you'd never find in a million years in the Premier League.'

Respect, the legacy of 656 senior appearances over 22 years, has eased the transition into coaching. It earned him the right to silence in a dressing room that would have struggled to accommodate the average family saloon car. 'Whatever level this is, remember it's a local derby', he told his players as kick-off approached. 'Have pride in yourselves. Ability-wise, you are fucking good players. If you weren't you wouldn't be here. Let's not question your attitude or application when this is over.'

Hall, his ironic instincts unleashed, was playing The Jam's 'Town Called Malice' when the teams emerged. There were 26 fans behind one goal, eleven, including Millwall goalkeeping coach Tony Burns, behind the other. He sat on the steps, rather than in the dugout, because he wanted to hear how John Sullivan communicated with his back four. The goalkeeper could have whispered sweet nothings and still been understood, such was the lack of atmosphere. Whoever came up with the eventual attendance, 356, must have had the beer goggles on.

Professional footballers are not used to the indignity of climbing over the fence to collect the ball. When they have to ferret around at the feet of a 5.5-metre wooden statue of a supporter celebrating a goal, the ordeal is surreal. With wisps of fog shrouding a deserted stand, and Bolder's high, reedy voice echoing encouragement, football's Undead were on the march. Play was disjointed, disrupted by elementary errors and a collective lack of confidence. Within twenty minutes, Grabban was asking the Millwall bench how long was left in the half. Jackett, concerned by the indolence of young forward Kiernan Hughes-Mason, moved menacingly from the stand to the dugout. At least Marcus Bignot joined Bolder in cajoling the youngsters.

At 35, Bignot's career was petering out. 'I've frozen him out', admitted Jackett, forcibly summarising the consequences of a contract dispute that involved Eric 'Monster Monster' Hall. In the days before *Big Brother* turned theatrical vulgarity and shameless exhibitionism into an industry, Hall was the pantomime dame of football agents. A gaudy refugee from Tin Pan Alley, he attached himself to Terry Venables and the anti-heroes of Wimbledon's Crazy Gang. He marketed himself as a cross between Alan Sugar, Ben Elton and Albert Steptoe, and was generally received as warmly as a skinhead in a seminary. He looked after Bignot for old time's sake, as a diversion from his weekly nostalgia show on BBC Radio Essex.

Jackett's logic, in pushing Bignot to the margins, was impeccable. He had played only a single game the previous season because of chronic tendonitis, which trapped him in a vicious cycle of painkilling injections, rest and rehabilitation. Yet there was a degree of latent respect. Bignot had trained well, after labouring pre-season, and was responding to the supportive gesture of being allowed to help Fitzgerald coach the youth team. He was energetic and

empathetic to the youngsters around him. He was the last of Shaw's worries as the half time whistle blew and John Hall announced, over the PA, that the gates had been opened 'in case you're gasping for a fag'.

Grabban locked himself in the toilet and had little apparent inclination to reappear. This was not the time to reflect on social alienation, or investigate the digestive problems of an athlete emerging from the rigours of religious devotion. Shaw had a team talk to give, and its principal target was in no mood to cooperate. 'Lewis, we're waiting', he announced, as Jackett moved from the shower area to a place on the bench in the middle of the room. Grabban unlocked the door, but remained in trap two, out of sight. 'Thank you, Lewis', said Shaw. 'You, and the entire front three, need to work harder. You must close down more. There's no out ball. You're too deep. Stay higher.' The coach was in an impossible situation – how can you give a bollocking to the Invisible Man, especially when everyone has a mental image of him sitting, scowling, with his shorts around his ankles?

At that moment a mobile rang in someone's kitbag. This was blasphemy, as offensive to a professional footballer as skateboarding naked around St Peter's is to the Vatican Guard. Eyes widened at the horror of it all. Shaw paused, rummaged around, and disgustedly lifted a holdall in the air as if it were a month-old sock found beneath an adolescent's bed. Instinctively, I grabbed it and headed for the door. As I did so, Jackett began to lay into Hughes-Mason: 'Call for the fucking ball. Your body language is too timid. Get after them. You've hardly shown.'

Outside, in the tunnel, disgorging the contents of the bag on to the floor, I felt slightly unclean, like one of David Frost's undercover sleuths on the game show *Through the Keyhole*. The bag had all the accoutrements of a teenager's

bathroom: Rubber Shine hair gel, aloe vera shampoo, Paul Smith Extreme Men eau de toilette spray. Only the bog standard Lynx anti-perspirant disappointed my inner style consultant. The mobile was at the bottom of a side pocket, with an MP3 player.

It had been switched off. Shaw had selected the wrong bag. Right on cue, the door opened, and a disembodied arm threw a smaller holdall, containing the offending implement, out into the walkway. All it needed, to make a bizarre cameo complete, was Basil Fawlty to wander by, cuffing Manuel with a hairbrush the size of a tennis racquet. We had to make do with Jackett, spilling out of the dressing room in agitated conversation with his coaches. 'I don't care if he's got the shits', he said. 'He's doing nothing. He might as well be in the fucking stand with me.'

Intriguingly, given the faith placed in him, Hughes-Mason was more of a worry than Grabban. It had seemed so simple on 3 August, when Jackett had summoned him to his office for the sort of conversation that spawns schoolboy fantasy. Fitzgerald had mentioned, in that morning's management meeting, that Fulham and Chelsea had sent scouts to watch him in an Under-18 match at Swindon. 'Kiernan was bright', he reported. Jackett was decisive: 'We might as well sign him now, protect the club a bit. Parents?' Fitzgerald was unequivocal: 'Good people, nice people. There's no agent that I know of.' This was what Jackett wanted to hear. No apparent complications. 'Right. There's no reason why we can't give him this year, and the next. I'll speak to him before training.'

Hughes-Mason had been picked up by Millwall when he was released by Tottenham at sixteen. He seemed diligent, even though his initiation ritual on the pre-season tour of Ireland, a song and dance routine he christened the Migraine Skank, hinted at hidden depths. Now he was

sitting on his hands opposite the man who had the power of dreams. Jackett spoke quickly, softly. He had the air of a country curate, attentive and reassuring, but he meant business. 'You've done a year with us', he said. 'Would you be interested in a professional contract?' The youngster convulsed and blurted 'Yes' almost before the manager had finished posing the question. It was impossible not to smile. This was the freeze-frame moment any aspiring footballer should take to his grave.

'Don't think too much will change', Jackett cautioned. 'But you could be in and around the first team group. That's the major advantage of being at this club. Three out of my four forwards are 30 or over. Now I've got you coming through. You can learn a lot from them. We want to settle you down, give you the message we believe in you. If there are injuries I'd put you on the bench. If you play the last twenty minutes, you've got it in you to cause problems. But never forget. You've got to work at it. We'll get your Mum and Dad in, and I'll tell them anything they need to know.' The boy walked out, convinced that he was The Man.

He signed the contract, on the pitch, before the 2–0 home win over Oldham. He acquired a squad number, 31, and swapped the light blue training kit, assigned to the scholars, for the dark blue of the seniors. Jackett was as good as his word, and gave him a seven-minute debut, as substitute, in the 1–1 draw against Brighton on 28 August. But, with bewildering speed, Hughes-Mason was drawn towards the centre of a force-field of negativity. 'The gaffer's obviously got him on the brain', said Fitzgerald, as he attempted to get his head back into the reserve team game. 'There's no doubt he's not played well since signing as a pro. He's got to learn that perceptions and expectations change, immediately. There are so many factors involved. I'm asking myself whether he understands what a big thing this is.'

Fitzgerald had been confronted by the consequences during training. The nine remaining second-year scholars were unsettled, calculating that Hughes-Mason's promotion drastically reduced their chances of being taken on. Aware of the delicacy of the situation, Fitzgerald had gathered the youth squad around him and asked everyone to share their deepest fears. He was torn between his principles and duties as a coach and his responsibilities as an adult in charge of a group of impressionable, uniquely vulnerable boys.

'I thought Kiernan signing might spur the rest of the group on', he confided. 'It had the opposite effect. They came out, one by one, and said how nervous it made them. I've had to reassure them that we don't operate a quota system, but they're coming in and saying they feel under pressure. Pressure? Playing football? Pressure is worrying about feeding your kids, not being able to pay the mortgage. It's being out of work for three years, and having beans on toast every night. I've got mates who haven't got a pot to piss in. Football's a lovely pressure. It's their get-out-of-jail card and I'm not having it.'

Hughes-Mason, oblivious to such realities, failed to respond to Jackett's entreaties. He was substituted immediately after Palace took a 75th-minute lead, when a missed header by Chris Hegarty allowed Kieron Cadogan to score. Simon Thomas rolled in a second goal before a scrambled third, in stoppage time, completed the rout and gave John Hall an opportunity to remind us of his omnipresence. 'Put your hand up if you scored', he boomed over the PA. 'I can't work out who got the final touch.' Nathaniel Pinney, a stocky midfield player, obliged like a bashful schoolboy as he trotted back towards the halfway line. No one on the Millwall bench was inclined to join in the hilarity.

Jackett was concerned about full back Scott Barron, who had pulled up sharply with a hamstring twinge in the

build-up to the final goal. He lay on the dressing room floor with an ice pack borrowed from the Palace physiotherapist. Shaw towered over him as he addressed a dispirited team. Grabban, kept on for the duration despite his discomfort, had the common sense to try to look inconspicuous, settling down at the far end of the room's left-hand bench.

Shaw spoke deliberately, yet wistfully: 'I'll see you young ones individually on Thursday, when I've gone over things in my mind. I'm not going to say much now, but I'm unhappy with little things I'm seeing.' He was obviously tip-toeing through a minefield of destructive emotion, and paused before turning to Hughes-Mason: 'Kiernan. Remember this. Your first contract is the easiest you will ever earn. It's the second and third ones that are the hardest to get. Don't be like those know-alls who get in late and go home as soon as possible. Do your weights, get in the gym, and learn from the senior pros who are a credit to themselves.'

Hughes-Mason stared blankly at his stockinged feet. Blood was congealing around a stud wound on his ankle, and he lacked the courage to make eye contact with Jackett as the manager took the floor: 'We've got to move on from tonight. Senior pros: that was a good workout. Young lads: keep listening to Richard and Scott. This is about your development.'

With that, he strode purposefully away into the night. Shaw was denied such respite. He taped a video interview with Deano Standing, Millwall's press officer, before we sat together amid the detritus of the game in the away dugout. The floodlights had been extinguished. Reflected light from the bar picked out half empty bottles of water, soiled adhesive tape, and torn team sheets. Shaw exhaled deeply: 'I'm steaming. I didn't want to say too much in there because sometimes, in the heat of the moment, you say the wrong thing.

'I was looking around and thinking, "What way are you going to go?" Without the attitude and application I talked about, you are not going to be a player. You don't want the ones who turn up and play for themselves. Players are judged on their character. Can you handle it? Are you going to hide? Are you going to go through the motions? The majority of our senior pros are excellent, but some of them ...'

His words were almost too weighty, and carried the conversation beyond football. We talked of the perfectionism of the champions I had worked with. I summoned images of frighteningly intense pre-dawn training sessions with Steve Redgrave. I tried to describe the primitive pain felt by Bradley Wiggins in physiological tests where he rode a stationary bike to the edge of consciousness. I recreated the final ritual of Colin Montgomerie's working day – 100 three-foot putts that had to be made in sequence.

Returning to football, I recalled Gabriele Batistuta keeping me waiting in the rain for three hours while he practised free kicks, over and around a wall of mannequins placed precisely seven metres from the ball. Train as you compete. Give your talent due respect. Never sell yourself short. It takes 10,000 hours of practice for a learned skill to become automatic. These are the eternal truths of elite sport.

Shaw understood: 'I've watched Kiernan closely since he's turned pro. NO. You can't rest once you get that contract. People don't miss much around here. We've all had careers, we've all played. We know you have to work. I talk to people at other clubs and the youngsters are the same. They think they've made it, too soon. They put cars and bling before the basics. The top boys, your Ryan Giggs and Paul Scholes, deserve it all, because they've won ten championships. They live their lives the right way. They have an overwhelming work ethic. I don't begrudge them a single

penny. Eric Cantona dragged the kids out every afternoon to help him be the best. That sort of commitment should be a given.

'I stand in the car park and see some of our younger pros going home as soon as they can. You tell them, over and over, that you only get out of this game what you put in. If you're out on the practice pitch until four in the afternoon, practising free kicks, you're going to get rewarded. I can't accept Joe Gallen putting a shooting session on, after training, and Lewis walking in. I'm thinking, "Hey, just a minute". I just shake my head in disbelief. If the best players in the world can do it, why can't players in League One? I will never ever understand that. I tell them, "If you want to carry on playing at this level, carry on doing what you are doing. If for whatever reason you don't make it higher up, but you put the work in, you can at least look yourself in the mirror and say I gave it my best shot." Too many young pros blame everyone but themselves. It's not just our club – it's everywhere.

'I have said from day one what I think about Lewis. What do you do with him? He said he had stomach ache tonight. Whatever. Sometimes you just lose faith in players. You think you're banging your head against a brick wall. I don't think lads like Lewis are in love with football. I don't think they watch games. I don't think they can be bothered to study their trade. I have had my day – Scott's the same – and I'm really conscious about coming across as some grumpy old man. But when I was making my way in the youth team, or reserves, I was forever watching the first team, trying to get a game in their five-a-sides.

'I don't see that today. I think Scott's group is really good, in terms of attitude. They all want to learn. Wayne Drummond, the goalkeeper, has improved ten-fold. Chris Hegarty has something about him. I have no problem if

they have a bad game because they're trying to get better. It's the younger pros, aged eighteen to 21, who worry me. They really do. I will never work out footballers, however long I'm in this game. I can't understand the mentality of anyone who misses the obvious. Why ignore what you need to do to get out of this level?'

Stuart Pearce, England's Under-21 coach, had encapsulated the issue perfectly at a performance seminar: 'As a manager one thing you find soul-destroying is seeing real talent wasted. Sometimes you say that's a product of society, or parenting. You know there is someone else with less talent who will roll their sleeves up and come through. Sheer effort gets you there eventually. Mental toughness will drive players to the top. Maybe it's in their breeding, or maybe they are products of the environment they live in.'

Grabban is at the confluence of two cultures. Educated at Cumnor House prep school in Croydon, like Andy Frampton he seems to strive to avoid being defined by his middle-class background. Modern football understands the success stories of the Premier League, multi-millionaire players with cliched mock-Georgian mansions and self-serving retinues. It struggles to deal with non-conformists like him. He lives in Peckham, immerses himself in the rituals of his religion, and has a defiantly different peer group.

Grabban was feeling ghastly that night. He was emotionally constipated, physically compromised. It takes courage to be true to one's core beliefs, but in football it's all too easy to lose the privileges of personal and professional respect.

Shaw had taken him to one side in training and told him he envied his talent. The praise bounced off the protective layers of Grabban's personality. The proud old pro, a true role model, smiled bleakly, shook his dreadlocks. He had done all he could. As The Specials, those other titans of Two Tone, sang: 'This town is coming like a ghost town …'

Fragile

Bobby Bacic dealt with death on a daily basis in an NHS intensive care unit. He has never forgotten the terrifying tenderness required to cradle the broken body of a car accident victim, knowing that a momentary lack of coordination could result in paralysis, or worse. He was humbled by the experience of helping to retrain stroke sufferers to walk, in awe of the dignity of those denied the quality of life they once took for granted. Football has its moral dilemmas, its recurrent physical traumas, and its acutely personal tragedies, but it can never match the bitter truths of the real world. In the grand scheme of things, Millwall's inability to select more than three outfield substitutes was an irrelevance. Crisis, what crisis?

The answer to that perennial question was provided by Kenny Jackett's decision to devote his weekly management meeting to the injuries that had deprived him of eleven players. The season was in danger of stalling before it had barely begun. As head physiotherapist, Bacic was a key figure in the debrief about prevention techniques and personality issues. He sees players at their most vulnerable, and is a conduit for their anger, fear and frustration. The autonomy he is given by Jackett testifies to an enduring mutual respect. The pair worked together for six months at QPR before Jackett left to manage Swansea. Bacic was discarded the day after John Gregory arrived at Loftus Road, renewed his career at Preston, and, wishing to return south to be

close to his seriously ill mother, accepted Jackett's invitation to help rebuild Millwall's reputation.

'This is a progressive club, but when I came here it was a carnival, an absolute disgrace. My department was all wrong, dysfunctional. Without being rude, the whole club was like that. It just showed the scale of what the manager has achieved here. I'm aware I only get autonomy if I earn it. He's my boss, and if he has something to say I listen. I like the fact I head a team within a bigger team. I want to make a contribution. Football is very fast-moving. I don't believe in keeping a player in the dark. It's important to explain your reasoning, get their trust.

'A lot depends on the personality of the player, and the nature of the injury. There are players here who are on the phone if they have a blister, and insist on giving you a blow by blow account of it. You've got others who are very strong and self-contained. With long-term injuries you expect the odd moody episode. Generally, players know the nature of the game and just get on with it. I have had a few in tears – it's not nice seeing a grown man cry – but usually it's a flare-up, and bang, it's done. I try and avoid arguments, because they are not conducive to a good working environment.'

It's easy to dismiss Bacic as dour. With his dark-ringed, deep-set eyes, high forehead and sombre demeanour, he would make an ideal funeral director. Yet his humour is sardonic, his warmth is genuine, and his social conscience is tinged with militancy. His air of detachment is a defence mechanism. The experience of hospital work, undertaken alongside a part-time role at Fulham in 2002 after he had completed his Master's degree in Australia, was pivotal, both personally and professionally.

'It makes you a bit more human, you know? Let's face it, sometimes this game is complete bullshit. You can lose yourself in the bubble. You need to experience life. In hospital

you see people trying to rebuild their lives. You see people dying on the wards. You are there to be strong. You do as much as you can. It's the same when I run on to assess an injury. Sometimes it's ugly. You want to preserve the player's dignity and prevent others seeing something nasty. You see someone you work with, someone who is part of your team, in pain. As much as you try and detach yourself, it's difficult. Even I feel for people.'

Self-deprecation would get him only so far on a bright morning when the first fallen leaves of autumn skipped across the training ground on a gentle breeze, like school-girls let loose at the local rec. They were hot bunking in the treatment room, which was organised around three well-worn benches, one of which was torn and losing its stuffing. Some of the case studies were summarised in a single sentence. Zak Whitbread was in the initial stages of recovery from his hip operation. Danny Senda was beginning his rehabilitation at Lilleshall. Paul Robinson had suffered a collision injury. 'We've had a heart to heart', reported Bacic. 'That Barnet game was right for him. He was a sitting target. He got clattered, end of story. There's nothing we could have done.' Tony Craig, whose back seized as he stooped to get out of his car on the afternoon of the West Ham Cup tie, was another matter entirely.

'He knows the sports car has to go', said Bacic, who reported that Craig was in the market for a family saloon. 'It encourages the sort of extreme movement that caused him problems. He knows he's got to be more aware. I'm trying to educate him, and have given him strengthening exercises. He'd been painting and bloody decorating at home. He might as well have gone the whole hog, and dug the garden. He's a million miles away from an operation, but he needs to up his game.' Jackett, who had been taking notes on an A4 pad, looked up. 'It all comes down to being

diligent', he said. 'Keep on top of him. If the player doesn't buy into the process, it doesn't matter what you do.'

Chris Hackett, one of the quieter members of the squad, had refused to come off in the latter stages of the Bournemouth match after suffering heart palpitations. He had been given the all-clear by the doctor, but had a weakness in the groin area that required ice baths on recovery days. 'Works his nuts off in the gym, but never seems to be able to give us a run of games', reported Bacic, who organised tests that suggested a problem with his adductor muscles. Jackett was concerned at his lack of explosiveness.

'He's been our main set-piece taker, especially in training', observed Joe Gallen. 'That must put the adductor under pressure.'

Bacic agreed: 'Biomechanically, he's got a very heavy whip.'

This was the sort of insight Jackett had been hoping for. He immediately changed Hackett's training regime: 'We've got someone here who is a very good pro. Anyone disagree?'

Gallen shook his head: 'He's always in very early.'

Bacic concurred: 'He eats birdseed, is keen, and never wants to show a weakness.'

Lewis Grabban was out with an indistinct back problem, which instinct suggested had a psychological dimension. Jackett was concerned at his lack of focus, and his recent habit of doing his strength and conditioning work in a private gym, away from the training ground.

'We pay his wages. He's got to do his gym here', stressed the manager.

Bacic replied: 'His personality is difficult. He doesn't mix. He wants to do things at his own pace, and on his own terms. I half trust him, but he's a bit too cool for his own good.'

Jackett was unequivocal: 'I don't give a fuck if he's a moody fucker. I'm not seeing a burning desire. He's giving

us 70/30 at best. He needs to be told, "This is what you are going to do". We can't let him wander on like this.'

Steve Morison – 'a real pro, he'll do anything you ask', said Jackett with telling alacrity – had a more sympathetic hearing. Bacic suspected his hamstring injury was a warning sign, that he required time to adapt to the rigours of League football. 'He does a lot of work in the gym, to develop quick feet', he reported. 'He looks a little tense. He's developing his aerobic capacity, but he's got a good physique, without having real strength. He's not like Gary Alexander, who can look all over the place but is as strong as fuck. We've got to watch him, because that tear was in a dangerous area.'

Bacic took the responsibility for Neil Harris injuring a calf in the warm-up before the Brighton match. Ironically, he had allowed himself to be influenced by the intensity of the striker's determination. 'I'm annoyed with myself', he admitted. 'I had him walking and jogging on the warm-down day after West Ham. I shouldn't have sent him out to train the following day. He told me he would have come knocking on your door if I'd have said no.' Jackett made allowances for an understandable error of judgement. He recognised that the strength of character that makes Harris so formidable could also be a weakness.

Jackett was more concerned with Jason Price, who had damaged his hamstring at Barnet, where the Football League had rejected his request for dispensation to field a weakened side because of the length of Millwall's injury list. The Welshman's initial jauntiness had proved illusory. He was a clever player, a striker whose intelligent movement brought others into the game. But, at 32, he was coming to terms with the fact that 'sometime soon, no one will want me'. He was in constant touch with Alton Thelwell, his closest friend in football, who was searching for a club with increasing desperation after being released by Leyton Orient.

Price was going through the motions of taking his coaching badges, but admitted he had fallen out of love with the game: 'To be honest, I prefer to watch rugby. Football has been running around my brain all my life, and I need a break from it. I'm starting to wonder just what I'll do with myself.' The way in which he had exacerbated the injury revealed his state of mind. Too many miles on the motorway had taken their toll. He had poured his slender 6′4″ frame into a battered six-year-old Renault Megane, snatching every opportunity to see his partner and young son, who had remained in the Doncaster area. 'He's got half his house in the back of that car', observed kit man Adrian Wisson. A cursory glance confirmed that it contained half-opened bags, a duvet, assorted footwear and the slurry of service station cuisine.

'He looks tired', said Bacic. 'It must be hard, living away from the family.' Jackett was sympathetic, but firm: 'I'll have to speak to him about his lifestyle and preparation. Jason has been one of those lucky ones who has just been able to turn up and play. He's now at the stage of his career where he has to think, work, and plan. You can't do at 32 what you did at 22. We've got to get right on top of this fucker, otherwise he will drift. I'm not saying he can't see his little boy up north, but we've got to find a better way. I'm looking for him to show he has the diligence and professionalism to do the job.'

The solution was relatively simple. Price subsequently agreed to fly up to see his family from Gatwick, instead of taking the car. Bacic summoned the courage to mention the elephant in the room, the legacy of defeat at Wembley. 'Last season we had a longer break, and people could heal naturally', he said. 'The recovery time this summer has been condensed, because of the play-off. Everyone was knackered after the final. Hand on heart, that has to be a

minus.' No one disagreed, but as Jackett said: 'We can only go from where we are this morning. Look back, learn lessons, and move forward.'

He had invested a lot of faith in Marc Laird, whom he had coached at Manchester City. Bacic read more into his lack of durability, and physical presence, than was comfortable. 'This is his third or fourth soft tissue injury', he said. 'I've been mollycoddling him, and now it's time to get him by the scruff of the neck.' The threat was implicit, but powerful, when Jackett responded: 'This is a big year for him. His contract is up.' Richard Shaw interjected: 'I don't think he does enough. Every time I'm in the gym I see him there, posing, doing nothing.' Bacic nodded sadly: 'It's bollocks, just rubbish. He needs some tough love.'

Jackett lightened the mood by referring to his notes. 'That takes us nicely into double figures. Who's the lucky boy who makes up the team?' Pat O'Connor, given his first professional contract in April, was struggling in the early stages of his rehabilitation from a cruciate injury, sustained while training on his own during the summer. They had to judge his character in the context of his medical condition. Bacic was concerned that there was still swelling on the afflicted knee, eight weeks after surgery. 'It should be better than it is', he said. 'I'm not happy with him.' Jackett wanted to believe that O'Connor was guilty of nothing more than naivety. As someone schooled in the intricacies of youth development, he knew the perils of transition from scholar to young pro. Some, like Kiernan Hughes-Mason, find promotion, and attendant praise, as toxic as mustard gas. Others succumb to their eagerness to make an immediate impact. Jackett suspected O'Connor had been impatient with the injury, rather than negligent, but would reinforce his responsibility to himself and the club. 'I'll tell him what I expect', he said. 'To put it mildly, the injuries aren't help-

ing us. In this League if you are 5 per cent below capacity you can lose three on the trot. That might be the equivalent of losing two players.'

His words were to prove prescient, but the mundane chores of management took precedence. He gave Gary Alexander, whose wife was due to give birth, permission to drive to training at Bath University on the eve of the Bristol Rovers game. Shaw offered to act as the striker's chauffeur 'as long as he sorts out the insurance'. Danny Spiller had impressed Dagenham and Redbridge manager John Still, who sought a character reference from Jackett before signing him on a short-term contract that rewarded his resilience. Spiller had endured an unsuccessful trial at Brighton in mid-July, and had been released by Wycombe Wanderers after playing for a month without pay. His comeback was under way.

Jackett's brain filtered conflicting priorities as he sat on a ball and watched Gallen and Shaw take training. He was looking at a bigger picture than a light-hearted session designed to ease the depleted squad into their work. 'As a manager I'm there to lead, to set the precedent', he rationalised. 'There's nothing worse than being a coach and to have a manager who doesn't let you be one.' He circulated inconspicuously, pulling individuals for beguilingly casual conversations. He feared, correctly, that his makeshift team would lack the necessary pace and power to compete. It was time to suppress his anxiety, affirm his faith.

'You are the group who matter to me', he told the survivors, gathered around him in the centre circle of the main training pitch. 'You have to fight every day to prove yourself, every fucking day. If your body language says you can do nothing for me, that is exactly what you will get from me. Nothing. Don't sulk. Don't give me that "but I'm a good player" bollocks. Prove it to me, the coaches, the group and,

most of all, to yourself. Make sure you show that hunger, that fire and fight.' Later, in the privacy of his office, he would be more reflective: 'You've got to give some of them the benefit, even if you don't believe they are capable of it.'

Bristol Rovers won comfortably, through a Jeff Hughes penalty and a spectacular Chris Lines volley. Ominously, Alexander aggravated a deep-seated heel injury. He took painkillers at half time, but was forced off within four minutes of the restart and replaced by scholar John Marquis. 'We need bodies', admitted Jackett, who took winger James Henry on loan from Reading. It was a rare success – his adherence to the wage structure had led to more than twenty such deals breaking down in the previous month. Darren Ward, and Danny Schofield, an industrious, technically adept wide player picked up from Yeovil at a bargain £25,000, were still settling in.

The hysteric who campaigned for Jackett's replacement by Martin Allen was encouraged by another bad 2–0 defeat, at Gillingham the following Saturday. Henry's debut lasted 70 minutes before he suffered a hamstring injury, and Harris limped off after 64 minutes with cramp in his other, previously unproblematic, calf.

Defeat, in isolation, is like the death of a distant relative. It demands decorum, but cannot be allowed to dominate. 'The next game is very important', counselled Andy Frampton. 'We win that and you will notice a big difference. We will come in with an extra spring in our step, an extra urge to excel. We will have added to that brotherly belief in this group of players. There's no need to panic. I don't think I can remember so many key players being out. It's a very odd situation. We'll probably ride it out, and push on.'

Others were not so sanguine. One win in their first seven League matches challenged the consensus, which suggested a play-off place was a realistic goal. Directors Constantine

Gonticas and Trevor Keyse joined chief executive Andy Ambler for their monthly informal meeting with Jackett, at the training ground, 48 hours before Huddersfield arrived at The Den for a critical test of nerve. They valued the manager's gesture in welcoming them into his domain, and had learned to respect his judgement. But they were fretful. 'Momentum', said Gonticas, enunciating the word with reverential clarity. 'We earned that with blood, and now it's gone.' Keyse was rather more prosaic. 'A massive game, Saturday', he said, with the wistfulness of the true believer.

They stayed for the start of training, and were enraptured by the sounds of the schoolyard. 'I'd give everything I have to do this', said Gonticas with a sweep of his hand towards a circle of players noisily re-establishing their pecking order in the one touch warm-up. 'Do they realise how lucky they are? Their peers are working in tiny cubicles, manning production lines or wasting their lives in the pub.' Keyse was less voluble, but intimately involved. The archetypal local boy made good, he was a throwback in an era of leveraged purchases and boardroom narcissists. The training ground was his baby. He had funded, and supervised, the building of new changing rooms, the installation of new flooring, and a new pitch. He had also purchased gym equipment and two Portakabins for the youth team.

It was his down-payment on an emotional debt that had been accumulating since 1958. Then, aged eight, he perched on a crash barrier on the halfway line and watched his first Millwall match, at home against Walsall. The colours of the crowd, blue scarves and bobble hats set against a grey backcloth of humanity, have acquired a nostalgic lustre. The clack of wooden wartime rattles echoes down the years. Keyse has been on the board since 2006, and has retained the schoolboy's habit of storing carefully annotated match programmes in a series of suitcases. Success in

the timber trade highlights an affinity with the lost world of the Thames barges, in keeping with the club's traditions.

Keyse was a promising centre forward, and worked on the canals around New Cross after leaving school at fifteen. The dockers were fierce, garrulous, Millwall to a man. He unloaded wood from barges owned by club director Bill Nelan, who named the fleet after Millwall players. The exception was one that chugged along bearing the legend *Promotion*. He rejected £4 a week to sign a professional contract at the club, in favour of the extra 35 shillings (that's £1.75, kids) on offer on the Thames. His father, enraged, chased him out of the house.

'That's the only time he ever frightened me', Keyse recalled. 'He thought, as fathers do, that I was going to play centre forward for England. I knew, deep down, that I was never going to be quite good enough to play in the Fourth Division. It's sad, really. Millwall is my only club, the only one I will ever want. I absorbed it so easily into my bloodstream. I loved the collective excitement, the comedians in the crowd. It became a way of life for me. My wife became a football widow. My mother handcuffed me at home on the day my daughter Sarah, my first child, was born. Good thing, really. I was going off to watch Millwall play QPR. Sarah turned up at 3.00pm, right on kick off.'

Jackett was at ease with his attentiveness, but preoccupied with the weaknesses he had confirmed during a study of the DVDs of the three successive defeats. 'You've got to show some leadership', he said. 'I've been right through the club. Everyone has got their own story, but I know football. I don't mind a meeting, but it gets to the point where I don't listen. My missus might tell you that's a bad thing, but it isn't in my world. I am my own judge and jury.'

He made four changes, and was rewarded with two goals inside the first fourteen minutes. Harris set up Hackett to

conclude a 50-yard sprint with a fierce drive past highly regarded goalkeeper Alex Smithies, and scored the second, a diving header from Dave Martin's cross. Morison's first League goal for the club, a header from Hackett's corner four minutes into the second half, was neutralised by a late consolation goal from Jordan Rhodes. It was a timely win against a well-funded team of similar quality and ambition, which had a surprise bonus. Huddersfield's management team were so disoriented by the conclusive nature of the defeat that one of them left his private scouting report in the away dressing room.

This was a largely symbolic lapse in professionalism, which allowed Jackett to see his side through the eyes of a rival. The report, based on Millwall's defeat at Bristol Rovers, contained no blinding shafts of insight but should have been kept in-house. 'Start is crucial', it read. 'After 20 minutes crowd will react and be hostile to home players.' Under strengths, the scout had listed: 'Do things quickly. Alexander draws free kicks. Central midfield will win the ball. Frampton's strength in the air.' He identified Millwall's weaknesses as: 'Slow centre halves. Full backs don't provide cover. Give away free kicks in own half. Overplay in defence. No height in centre midfield.'

The individuals were judged as follows:

David Forde C
Confident claiming crosses. Looks to get them playing quickly.

Alan Dunne C
Anticipates game well. Makes good options to receive the ball wide. Will leave foot in and go two-footed into 50/50 challenges.

Scott Barron D
Looked unfit. Poor positioning. Gave players too much
room and had very poor game.

Andy Frampton C
Very good in the air. Does not like being turned as he
is slow. Would struggle with a quick striker running at
him with the ball.

Jack Smith D
Slow. Takes too many touches on the ball in poor areas.
Heading poor under pressure, didn't mark man for
man tight enough.

Jimmy Abdou B
Poor in the air but good understanding with Fuseini.
They work well together winning the ball back and
giving simple passes. Made options to receive the ball
in open play.

Ali Fuseini B
Very good at closing down and winning the ball back.
Likes to take two touches to beat his man. Good first
touch under pressure.

Dave Martin D
Game passed him by. Looked disinterested.

Danny Schofield C
Set pieces clipped and floated with the inside of the
right foot. Tracked back in defence. Opts to go outside
the full back.

Gary Alexander B
Link up man. Very good at drawing fouls in good areas
where he is going nowhere. Will play off the defender's
shoulder and win headers. Will also drop deep to
receive.

Ashley Grimes C
Didn't stop running. Good energy.

The faceless, nameless scout didn't particularly like them,
and you can bet they cared. The coup de grace was supplied
by the question: 'Anyone frightened of a fierce challenge?'

With cruel inevitability, a white feather fluttered in the
direction of Dave Martin.

A Hard Day's Night

Andy Ambler scrolled through his iPhone and retrieved a text message from his wife. 'Smile and enjoy the challenge, or walk', it read. His reflexive grin ebbed away, like a weak wave soaking into sand. 'It made me think. What am I doing this for? Why put up with all the aggravation? I took stock of the issues, the people involved, and there was only one answer. Sod it. Stand and fight.'

It was two hours before kick-off against Yeovil Town, on an unseasonably warm Tuesday evening, 29 September. Ambler walked around the perimeter of the pitch at The Den, away from a group of stewards undergoing pre-match instruction. The low sun, glinting off high-visibility jackets, lent a strange softness to the scene. Suddenly aware of the sprinkler system, Ambler recoiled, leaned against an advertising hoarding, and took a call from retired FA councillor Alan Turvey. The former elite Football League referee, chairman of the Ryman League for 25 years, was sympathetic. He promised to keep his eyes and ears open.

Ambler thanked him, and warmed to his theme: 'We've got friends in the game and a lot of people are questioning why we've been charged. They're saying, quietly, there but for the grace of God go I. The politicians are at work. The word we're getting is that they want to use us to make a statement. I've got a chairman who's going nuts, threatening to sue the FA. He's a fighter, and he's seeing things through a keyhole. He's back in the States, monitoring the

media and listening to sound bites from his mates. They know nothing about football, and have no idea of the environment in which we work. He lives in a litigious world. He won't roll over.'

John Berylson had made a flying visit from Boston to London to take in the 1–0 defeat at Leyton Orient the previous weekend. He assured Kenny Jackett of his support, but the tension was tangible. Ambler, promoted to chief executive six weeks earlier, was attempting to reconcile an ambitious board, a pragmatic manager, volatile fans and a vengeful establishment. It required sensitivity, street wisdom, and survival skills honed while working for Mohamed al-Fayed as Fulham's chief financial officer.

Just as Ambler won't have a word said against the idiosyncratic Egyptian, he's at ease with the emotional intensity of his American owner. 'John speaks to me differently than he does to Ken. I get the frustration, the complaints that "it's not good enough". I'm happy with that, because it means Ken can get on with his job. I've told him he needs to manage upwards better, towards the boardroom, and by his own admission, he's learning all the time. Football has always been about two things – politics and results.'

He called into Jackett's office, where assistant manager Joe Gallen was transcribing set-piece routines on a flip chart, to wish him good luck. Millwall had lost at Brisbane Road to the sort of goal that bedevils teams bereft of confidence. Right back Alan Dunne, lured infield to make an injudicious tackle, retreated, and had not recovered sufficiently when he lunged at Andros Townsend. The Orient substitute, only on the pitch for two minutes, was advancing diagonally into the penalty area. His right-foot shot threaded between Dunne's legs and those of Jack Smith. It evaded diving goalkeeper David Forde and nestled into the far side of the net. Cue anger and introspection.

Millwall shaded possession, but crossed poorly, lacked penetration and creativity. In Jackett's words, 'It was like watching fog'. He had worked on team shape in training, to no avail. Now was not the time to succumb to frustration. 'There is a confidence issue with lower League footballers', he explained. 'Consistency is generally what keeps you in a job as a manager, but you have to cope with a very wide range of performance level. They can look like Championship players one day, and would struggle in the Conference the next. The longer you work with them, the more you suss them out. Go a little bit deeper and you realise they want it so badly there's a real fear of failure. You have to get your pitch right. You can't accuse them of not wanting to be the best they can be. There are times the frustration is almost physical, a huge knot in your chest. But if you let it burst, and slaughter them in front of their peers, you will lose them. The chances are they have lived their whole life, the way I did, to become a professional footballer. You have to suck it in, and point them in the right direction. It's not about liking players, as people, but getting through to them, as professionals.'

There is a balance to be struck. Footballers crave order, a simple delineation of emotion. Perversely, some are comforted by the rituals of recrimination. 'Orient was poor', reflected Neil Harris. 'Not a Millwall performance. Too nice. No passion, no response. Framps tried to have a go afterwards, but the gaffer said he didn't want to hear that stuff. I don't mind a tear-up. If I'm not doing it, I'm big enough to put my hand up and accept the stick. We used to have a right go, as a group, but now we just sit there and wait for the gaffer to analyse things.'

Dressed in a brown suit with striped shirt and sober tie, Harris had the air of a junior solicitor. His eyes followed Jackett as he entered the dressing room, 90 minutes before kick-off. The briefing was methodical, a synthesis of the

manager's experience and Steve Jones' scouting report from Yeovil's two previous matches, a 2–0 defeat at Southampton and a 2–0 home win over Brentford. Jackett had decided to revert to 4-4-2 against a side that retained the ball well but lacked penetration and a physical edge at the back. 'I'm telling you, lads, we've got enough to get on a run', he told his squad. 'We get our game right, we win.'

Ambler left him to it. He was walking down the narrow corridor past his office when he was confronted by Marc Elliott, development manager for Millwall's Anti Racism Trust. One of the first schemes of its kind, MART was formed in 1994 and works with schools and community groups across Southwark and Lewisham. Elliott is the embodiment of the club's defence against the FA, that they do all they can to combat the racist element in their support. He is obliged to balance cynicism and idealism, and perceptions of prejudice make his job extremely difficult. 'Sometimes, it seems as if the world is against us', he sighed.

Kick It Out, the organisation set up to salve the game's conscience in the name of social cohesion, had just cancelled a key training session for club staff, scheduled for the following day. This was the second time this had happened, and it prevented Millwall becoming the first Football League club to meet their Racial Equality Standard. Ambler shot me a glance. 'I'm thinking out loud here, and shouldn't be saying this, but this feels like a stitch-up. If we get that award it would be inconvenient for certain people.' He threw a consoling arm around Elliott – 'I know how hard you've worked to get us to this position' – and asked Ken Chapman, the club's head of security, to verify the situation with Lord Herman Ouseley, Kick It Out's chairman.

Ambler was working through the conspiracy theory when he entered the boardroom, where he noticed that three empty Guinness bottles, good luck charms from the

previous season, had been removed from a shelf behind the bar. Since there was no point in tempting fate, they were quickly reinstated. 'The problem with working for Millwall is that you are conditioned to thinking the worst. It stinks. There are people who would be quite happy for this club to go out of existence.'

Football's disciplinary system is opaque and encourages a persecution complex. Laws of natural justice are held in abeyance. In effect the FA, prosecutors of the case, appoint judge and jury. Hearings are held behind closed doors without independent scrutiny. Clubs must bear the cost of legal representation, regardless of the verdict. Inevitably, the grimy conventions of the gentlemen's club lead to resentment, and a sense of resignation captured by Millwall director Constantine Gonticas: 'There's some goodwill towards us, but we are generally seen as the blemish on the golden egg that is English football. The powers that be would much rather we'd descend into the depths of non-League, or disappear altogether.'

The issue was crystallised in the match programme, which carried a message from Berylson and supporters' representatives. Entitled 'Our Club, Our Behaviour, Our Future', it outlined why Millwall had been reported to the FA twelve times the previous season. It promised sanctions against any fan invading the pitch, throwing missiles, or indulging in racial abuse. 'Missiles can and do hit anyone, including children. Racial abuse is unacceptable; illegal and hurtful to the club, staff, fellow supporters, players and the wider community. For Millwall Football Club to achieve the success we all desire we cannot afford the potential financial penalties or ground closures associated with these offences. This is our club – help us protect it.'

Millwall fans had hurled three seats onto the pitch at Orient, where Harris lived up to the obligations of a folk

hero at the final whistle by cuffing opposing centre half Ben Chorley, who appeared to be taunting the away support. To Ambler's relief, neither incident was in the referee's report. Gonticas, a Greek-born financier whose love for English football was nurtured by week-old TV highlights in the seventies, is realistic about the culture into which he has bought.

'It's a time warp, a bit like Iceland in the purity of its DNA. There are very few floaters welcomed into the family. It has genealogical purity, which can be traced back to the stevedores who worked on the ships. The fans are largely white disenfranchised working class. They've been downtrodden, but insist they can be bigger and better than they are. They are saying: "The world has passed us by, but we will not change. We will not accept you. This is our mentality. We're special, strong, resilient. We are Millwall."

'On the positive side, there is a particularly passionate love for the club. On the negative side the fans, every now and again, feel compelled to show some cultural fundamentalism. That's when West Ham happens. They want to remind the world of their cultural identity, their history of misbehaviour. Even the vast majority, who never cause a moment's trouble, tolerate and even take quiet pride in our reputation. They want people to die for the shirt. They see players as themselves, as they would wish to be. I don't see Arsenal fans having that affinity with a Diaby, or even a Fabregas. Our lot have a clear self-image. They pour everything into the team, and occasionally at them. If it doesn't go well they take it as a personal insult. At Gillingham they were around the players' tunnel screaming, "Shit, shit, shit". They hammer people because they care.'

The sentiments triggered a bleak smile when I relayed them to Jackett. 'We're all just passing through', he said. 'This club is what it is. Raw. You won't knock off the rough

edges. The fans have always behaved like this. They always will. I can't change that. All I can do is get the results which keep them happy.' Half an hour remained until kick-off. He had returned to his office to meet Reading coach Nigel Gibbs, his former Watford team-mate. Gibbs was monitoring goalkeeper Alex McCarthy, on loan at Yeovil, and James Henry, in his second spell at The Den. He has an easy affinity with Jackett, dating back to infamous Monday training sessions where apprentices were expected to sprint up the terraces with team-mates on their back.

Like many football men, Gibbs is scarred by the casual brutality of his trade. He spent 23 years at Watford, but was summarily sacked just before the start of pre-season training in 2005. It was a dehumanising process, which justified the old pro's lament that loyalty is what they screw you with. It took him a year to find another job, under Steve Coppell, and the bitterness endures. 'Ken's a fantastic coach, and such a strong man', he said, when Jackett left to oversee preparations. 'He helped me when things were tough, and he will be good for James, who I've known since he was a kid. Everyone was after him at the time. He was the best thing since sliced bread, and being mentioned in the same breath as Theo Walcott. He had a couple of cruciate injuries, but he's showing signs of settling down as a player and as a person. This could be his year.'

The players returned to the dressing room, a sheen of sweat on faces reddened by exertion and expectation, with ten minutes to go. They were fuelled by fruit pastilles, carbohydrate gel, and Jaffa cakes. Their intensity was claustrophobic. I sheltered at the entrance to the showers, but they sought me out, drew me in. Fists were clenched, hugs were exchanged. I found myself repeating 'Have a good one' as if it were a religious incantation. Jackett and his coaches circulated, issuing urgent instruction – 'Get forward, Jimmy,

there'll be some weak-hearted cunt who won't want to go with you' – and quiet encouragement. Then, in the final minute before the buzzer sounded, the Guvnors seized the floor. Their stream of consciousness, bellowed breathlessly, formed the script of a familiar passion play:

> Harris: 'This is our place, our team. Let's hit 'em hard. Get the disappointment out of the system.'
> Forde: 'Fucking right. No backward steps.'
> Andy Frampton: 'Together. Fucking shoulder to shoulder. All the way through.'
> Gary Alexander: 'We push on.'
> Harris: 'Teams expect us in their face. Let's not disappoint them.'
> Darren Ward: 'Fucking team. Yeah. Compact. Tough. Hungry.'
> Frampton: 'Let's go, lads. Fucking give it to them.'

With that, they filed into the tunnel, leaving a vapour trail of testosterone. 'Wait till all my men are here', confided Jackett. 'The hairs will stand up on the back of your neck.' The words of Gibbs echoed in my brain. 'All you can hope for, in this game, is that the strong survive. It's a cruel business, but the dressing room is a fantastic place. There's nothing like it.'

Yeovil find ways to punch above their weight. It's a small, geographically-challenged club, reliant on loan signings and young players on low wages. At 34, Terry Skiverton was a novice manager. A self-confessed journeyman player, he owed his promotion in February to a combination of promise, diligence, opportunism and financial expedience. He no longer socialises with former team-mates, having grasped immediately the importance of distance and delegation. He finds match days as a manager much more tiring because of

the emotional toll: 'The highs are ten times better than as a player, but the lows are ten times worse.'

With his pale face and long, lank blond hair, he could be a surf dude or a roadie for a struggling indie band. A small group of home fans, to the left of the Yeovil dugout, were on his case before the last welcoming strains of the anthem 'Let 'Em Come' had subsided. Skiverton was subjected to cartoon homophobia, recycled jibes about soap in the showers and KY jelly in the kit bag. Following play from the edge of his technical area, he responded to the abuse by hanging out a limp left wrist, without a backward glance.

Game over. Playground Bigots 0, Cool Dude 1.

The truce wasn't entirely good news for Dave Martin, winger and whipping boy of choice for a certain section of the crowd. He earned an appreciative growl by sprinting 40 yards to chase a lost cause by the corner flag, but was condemned as 'a fucking bottler' when he put in a half-hearted tackle three minutes later. Wide players at The Den need a rhino's hide, an actor's stage presence, and a test pilot's courage. Martin's shoulders sagged as the insult hung in the air on a still evening. The undercurrent of unease was threatening to suck the life out of a side struggling with itself. Millwall were playing with no conviction or imagination. Yeovil, as forecast, lacked belief and pace at the back. They should have been reduced to ten men when striker Sam Williams elbowed Forde, but survived comfortably. A looping Steve Morison header hit the top of the bar and, right on half time, he wasted the best chance of the game: a free header from eight yards out.

Forde, booked for retaliating, rampaged through the dressing room. He screamed 'fucking pussies' at no one in particular, volleyed a bottle of water against the wall, and stalked into the physio's room where club doctor Imtiaz

Ahmad inserted three stitches into a gash beneath his right eye. Jackett retreated to his office to confer with Gallen, leaving Harris to break an oppressive silence. 'I've never known a Millwall team, at home, so fucking quiet. It's not just one of us – it's all of us.' He stopped himself, allowed the bile to rise. 'Fucking Yeovil Fucking Town!', he yelled. 'What the fuck is going on?'

Harris sat down as Jackett emerged, rubbing his hands together. Martin was empty-eyed. Morison licked his lips like a nervous cat. Frampton, stripped to the waist, leaned forward expectantly. Smith, the sort who would light a cigar before fleeing from a burning building, lounged back as if he were in a deckchair. 'There's a lot about our game that's right', said Jackett in firm, even tones. 'We're looking for a bit of confidence. Don't get over-anxious. I know there's no one in this room who doesn't want it, but we have to work for it. We need real purpose in our play. We need to pin their centre halves. Don't stop doing the simple things. We've got these by the bollocks, lads.'

Everyone knew a change was coming. Alexander had been called in from his one-touch session with the substitutes. Jackett turned towards Morison and put him out of his misery. 'Steve, you have a bath. Gary, it's all about forcing our ways on them. The expectation levels are different this season, because everyone knows how good we are. Lads, we've got to find more venom, more thrust. Joe?'

Gallen, more emotional and accessible than the manager, is the perfect foil. He's been there as a player, anxious and unfulfilled. The situation needed a light touch rather than a cold dissection of technical and tactical shortcomings. 'Football's about crosses and shots', he announced, as if he'd come up with a cure for the common cold. 'If you mess up, who gives a fuck? Take a chance, have a go. It's a skimmy pitch. Make sure you retain your belief in the final

third. Don't be afraid to make a mistake. It will drop for you. It will come for you.'

Jackett's interjection – 'it might be a set-piece game' – broke the flow, invited individuals to go through their own private rituals. As Adrian Wisson handed out fresh shirts and Bobby Bacic attended the walking wounded, Gallen followed Alexander to the toilet. He instructed him to pull on to Steven Caulker, a callow centre half on loan from Spurs. 'Bully him. He won't handle the aggression very well.' Tony Burns sat Forde down, in semi-darkness, on the edge of the bath. 'Settle down', he ordered. 'Keep your mind on it.'

Everyone ignored Morison, who slowly peeled off his kit, shin pads and socks first. By the time the buzzer sounded, he stood naked, nonplussed. When his mind cleared, he would remind himself that rejection demands resilience. He cried bitterly when he was released at sixteen by Tottenham. He was instructed to listen for his name, which never came, corralled into a group, and told never to return. Instead of being crushed by more rejection by Northampton Town, he salvaged his career in suburbia at Potters Bar, Bishop's Stortford and Stevenage, where he scored 89 goals in 157 games. That earned him a £130,000 move to Millwall and a reprieve from the drudgery of 4.00am starts at a shredding company.

Like all strikers, Morison defines himself by the number of goals he scores. His first for Millwall had come ten days earlier, at home to Huddersfield, but he was still adjusting to the pace and intensity of League football. Memories of his debut at Southampton were vivid. 'It was, like, wow. There were a million things going on. It was so manic I couldn't catch my breath. Gradually, though, the games are slowing down. I know I can play at this level.'

Such realities were beyond the first- and second-year scholars clustered behind the home dugout. They were lost

in adolescent fantasy, oblivious to the value of the lesson unfolding before them. Their principal topic of conversation, as the match resumed without changing its pattern, was whether they would rob a bank, if they were guaranteed to escape punishment. Inevitably, given football's selective morality, all were comfortable with the prospect of living with their consciences.

Yeovil had ambitions beyond nicking a point. They hit the bar twice in three minutes, and the mood turned ugly. Wannabe hard men showered the 156 travelling fans with posited promises of retribution. Their elders were more menacing, and mocked the manager. When Henry over-hit a right-wing cross, they were on their feet, spewing venom. The winger took the bait. He dropped his arm to his side, responded with the universal 'wanker' sign, and then turned and told the South Stand to 'fuck off'.

Respect. They don't like their victims to die quietly at The Den, even if Jackett spoiled their fun by quickly substituting him and Martin. Bereft of ideas, Millwall were reduced to relying on a succession of diagonal long balls by Dunne, aimed in the vague direction of Alexander. The goalless draw was a self-fulfilling prophesy. Dunne and Alexander are close friends but were raging at each other when the dressing room door was locked. Eyeballs blazing, veins throbbing in shaven skulls, they were a pair of pit bulls straining at the leash. Most managers would have been overwhelmed by anger, turned the inquest into a free-for-all. But Jackett stayed calm, deliberately sat beside Alexander, and began to speak with convincing intensity.

'I know there's a lot of frustration there', he said. 'There's a lot of frustration in me, too. I will do whatever it takes to get us through this. I will work and work and work, because I know we have a team to get going in this Division. I look at the players in this room and I tell you we have enough.

I know you care. Stick together. There's no question we've not done enough tonight, going forward, but it will come. I'm ready. I expect you to feel the same. Now, go on. Get in the showers.'

Eye contact was avoided for 90 silent seconds, before Ward led the substitutes out to warm down. As flaccid pizza slices were served from tin foil, the search for positives began. 'We didn't fucking lose', said Frampton. 'We'll put it fucking right on Saturday', promised Forde. Jackett sat impassively, making notes that he would later transcribe into a hard-backed A4 desk diary. He would pull players privately, after their day off, to remind them of their responsibilities. Hysteria and humiliation were counter-productive.

Dunne simmered with resentment and moved into the physio's room, where he made his own recovery drink. He knew his place was under threat from Smith's arrival and the impending return from injury of two of the Guvnors, Tony Craig and Paul Robinson. Instinctively, he gravitated towards fringe players like Lewis Grabban and Ashley Grimes, who paid him due respect. 'What else could I do?' he asked them. 'I must have hit fifteen diags in the last ten minutes. No one else was doing anything.'

Henry wandered in and slumped onto the spare bench. 'One bad ball all night and they're calling me a cunt', he exclaimed. 'Unbelievable.' Frampton, cutting away his ankle strapping, sensed the danger of disaffection. 'Forget it', he ordered. 'They've forgotten it, almost before the words are out of their mouths. Remember, at this club any sentence ending in the word "cunt" is not worth worrying about. Get over it. Get on with it.'

Alexander was pulling on a pair of black Calvin Klein underpants in front of the closest peg to the doorway. 'We're going to have a fight soon, Dunney', he said with a smile. 'Let's have one on Saturday, when we've won.'

Normal service was being resumed. Footballers are conditioned to walking away from car crashes with eyes fixed firmly on the horizon. Millwall were fifteenth, two points off the relegation zone but four points away from the play-off places. They had missed Jackett's official performance target, twenty points from ten games, by nine points.

This had to be the lowest point of the season. Accept it. Deal with it. Move on.

In the boardroom the talk was of the pressure for promotion. The consensus was that the next cataclysm, a restructure involving a 36-club, two-tier Premier League, would hit in 2013. Being stranded in League One wasn't an option for men like Berylson. Gallen reassured the directors that Millwall would be promoted through the play-offs. 'They looked at me as if I was mad', he reported. More immediately, Ambler's mind was put at rest by Chapman, who reported that the facilitator appointed by Kick it Out had, indeed, fallen ill. No need to worry about conspiracies.

Yet.

Jackett completed the formalities of his media duties, addressing five local reporters while seated behind an incongruously small circular table. 'Nobody gives you anything in this game', he told them. 'The players have to learn that.' He understands the mechanics of journalism, and his honesty commands respect from the press corps, but it was a chore, a necessary evil.

Unusually, his wife Sam and two sons were not there to greet him when he returned to his office for the last time. Home life, and school homework, took precedence. He was at ease with Skiverton, whose lemonade, without ice, was poured by Gallen from a two-litre plastic bottle. 'Well done, mate', Jackett said. 'A better point for us', Skiverton suggested. 'It got a bit too open at times, but we closed it down.' Jackett smiled: 'Yeah, you kept the natives quiet.'

Up to a point. As midnight approached, the House of Fun, Millwall's principal message board, was in meltdown. Cyber warriors, sheltering behind pseudonyms, proclaimed that Jackett had lost the dressing room. He was angling for a pay-off on his new three-year contract, and should be sacked. It was gibberish, standard fare in a parallel universe in which any fantasist with an agenda can dribble deceit and disrespect. No wonder Jackett, like the vast majority of managers, treats such ramblings with unconcealed contempt.

He drove home, watched the DVD of the game, and went to bed with a clear conscience. He awoke with a plan that would effectively end the managerial career of a close friend.

Chapter 10
The Hardest Game

John Barnes arrived early at The Den, eager to see a friendly face. He left his Tranmere players to the tender mercies of assistant Jason McAteer, knocked on the home dressing room door, and waited while it was unlocked. It was a minor breach of protocol, easily excused, but untimely. Kenny Jackett had launched into his detailed team talk, 90 minutes before kick-off, and was in no mood for interruptions. 'Hang on a bit, Barnesy', he said, man-marking a flip chart that detailed Tranmere's team shape and personnel.

Jackett sensed his former team-mate's discomfort, but he had his own problems to address. He feared, initially, that Darren Ward had sustained a season-ending cruciate ligament injury when he landed awkwardly on hard ground in training the day before. A scan offered grounds for optimism, but he would be out for at least six weeks. Jackett's limited resources were further depleted in the same session, when midfield player Ali Fuseini damaged medial ligaments in a block tackle with youth team player Kemal Tevfik. 'What's going on?' he asked his coaching staff, feigning ignorance to an obvious answer. Millwall were meeting the bill for a culture of commitment.

Barnes was paying the price for a reputation acquired as a quixotic winger for Liverpool and England. He was being bracketed alongside Bobby Moore and Bobby Charlton as lavishly talented players who lacked the empathy, guile and patience to make a successful transition into management.

He had lasted 29 matches at Celtic, and waited six years for another chance at Tranmere. He had walked, eyes open, into a surrealist fantasy. The club had been put up for sale on eBay, fans had taken to applauding opponents' goals, and the management team of Barnes and McAteer were being derided as Dumb and Dumber. Ominously, chairman Peter Johnson was becoming inextricably linked to the story. When that happens in football, the result is usually a gore-fest worthy of Quentin Tarantino.

Johnson had fired Ronnie Moore, Barnes' predecessor, for supposedly lacking the charisma to halt a 19 per cent decline in attendances. When Jackett called to sympathise, Moore had the gallows humour off pat: 'Trust me to find a chairman who blames his manager for the fucking recession', he said, with a hollow laugh that failed to hide his sense of betrayal by a club he had served over three decades. Johnson's cunning plan, that Liverpool fans would happily pay £1.40 to go through the Birkenhead Tunnel to support an Anfield legend, would have insulted Baldrick's intelligence. An online petition calling for Barnes to be sacked had acquired a life of its own. Gates were in freefall. Six first-team regulars had been allowed to leave because of budget cuts. The usual suspects peddled rumours of dressing-room unrest.

Barnes spent half an hour in Jackett's office before the game, rationalising his plight. Their relationship, formed as graduates from Watford's youth scheme, transcended the duties of the day and the managerial conventions of inconsequential gossip. The years had taken a toll. Barnes' once boyish face was fleshy, and, though he remained broad-shouldered, his stomach had the comfortable contours of middle age. He saw himself as a victim of a peculiarly English disease, an instinctive mistrust of free spirits and significant achievement. He knew that managing Tranmere

would not embellish his profile or add to his prestige, but was staggered by the virulence of the criticism. Jackett was impressed by his understanding of League One as a remorseless test of physicality. Private doubts about the wisdom of coming to a place like Millwall with a 4-4-2 system that placed a premium on flair, width, and individual discipline, were left unspoken. Jackett was in thoughtful mood when, in a change to his normal routine, he supervised the pre-match warm-up.

Barnes had approached Graham Taylor, who accentuated the few positives of starting his career at Grimsby by winning none of his first eleven games. Tom Walley, another mentor he shared with Jackett, crystallised the problem: 'Barnesy was a thoroughbred as a player, but you have got to have something extra about you to become a manager. It's not about how good a player you were. It's about how you cope with people. Can you find that little bit in them that others have missed? Have you got the coach's eye, to see what you've got? Can you ask, "What have you got to give me?" without killing them? It's not just about working hard.'

Jackett understood the eternal truths expressed by his old taskmaster: 'Management is not as easy as it looks on the telly. If a player at the top level has a bad game, he has the intrinsic confidence to know he has only to wait a week to put things right. If things don't go well at a lower level, players start to clutch at straws. They're balls-out. They want to do well, and when it doesn't, they worry about what comes next. There's a time to bollock them, but if you hammer the life out of people you'd better not do it too often. They've a habit of turning around and saying "fuck you".'

That, in so many words, was the afternoon's message to Barnes. Tranmere played without a vestige of professional pride, and were 4–0 down inside 27 minutes. Neil Harris

thought their first-half performance the worst he had seen at The Den in a decade. Marlon Broomes was dismissed five minutes from time, allowing James Henry to complete his hat-trick from the resultant free kick. McAteer had earlier rewarded his tormentors by being sent off for inciting the crowd. Jackett observed: 'If our punters see you bite, you've got no chance.' Johnson watched the psychodrama unfold from the front row of the directors' box with the grim functionality of a *tricoteuse* knitting in the shadow of the guillotine.

Barnes returned to Jackett's office after the match, but, with respective families present, the wine was out and conversation was deliberately low-key. It was his eleventh and last League match as Tranmere manager. He was sacked the following week, and, in a gift to headline writers, was pictured packing his bike into the boot of McAteer's black Range Rover. Five days later he filed for bankruptcy, describing his profession, in court documents, as 'a provider of media services, lately a footballer'. He was alarmed by the avalanche of publicity – *Strictly Come Dancing* Star on Skids – and included Jackett in a round robin text: 'I'm not bust', it read. 'Just dealing with tax issues.'

It was a thought-provoking moment. Jackett had ruthlessly exploited the naivety of Barnes in sending out a team that was far too open. A more pragmatic coach would have flooded midfield, compressed time, space and opportunity to dwell on the ball. The ease of victory had lifted the mood at Millwall, but its human cost was inescapable. 'It's a tough world, a hard, hard game', Jackett reflected. 'Not too many people in football go out consciously to do you harm, but they look after themselves. It's difficult to play against a friend, but you simply have to put the friendship to one side.'

Joe Gallen watched Barnes closely, just as he had another inexperienced manager, Huddersfield's Lee Clark. It helped

put his managerial ambitions into perspective. He sensed their bleakness, saw the strain, recognised the referred pain of their struggle on those around them. Clark, in particular, was visibly vulnerable, wildly emotional. 'I don't want to end up like that', Gallen confided. He was comfortable with his role as Jackett's number two, without being complacent. They had a common background in youth development and were complementary characters. Good Cop, Bad Cop. Little Brother, Big Brother.

A self-made man from an extended football family, Gallen made the transition into coaching ten years earlier, at the age of 26. An injury-ravaged playing career left him with one leg marginally shorter than the other. He had two major back operations as a teenager, broke his leg twice, and suffered more than 30 separate hamstring injuries. He earned £50 a week running QPR Under Nines, studied for a Masters' degree in Sports Coaching Science, and worked his way up, over six years, to be head of youth at Loftus Road. He worked all hours as the club imploded around him, and received the traditional reward, his P45.

'I hadn't done anything wrong', he said, his naturally sunny disposition clouded by bemusement. 'I'd made them millions out of players they sold on, but the place was a madhouse. To be honest, the sack was a relief. In one six-month spell I'd had one of my players murdered, another killed in a car accident, and four more kids on murder charges. Then we caused an international incident with a mass brawl in a friendly with China's Under-23 team. Crazy.'

He was recruited by Jackett from Exeter, where he had spent three months assisting Paul Tisdale, another under-valued talent toiling in the lower Leagues. 'Above all, I thought Joe was a very good coach', Jackett explained. 'The way he structured his sessions, and his influence on the players around him, was impressive. A number two has

to be strong on the training ground and have good man-management skills. He sees people from a different perspective. Players are different in front of Joe than they are in front of me.'

Gallen's lightness of touch makes him an ideal emissary. He wins trust, gathers intelligence, and disseminates information. His immediate priority, following the Tranmere win, was to do the rounds in the dressing room, stressing the need for greater resilience away from home. He also did some subtle work on the psyche of midfield player Marc Laird. The manager's impact would be made later in the week, with a pattern of play session designed to make compactness second nature. He called it 'middle third football'. Defenders were encouraged to use possession intelligently, and wide players were drilled within a tight midfield four.

Jackett was influenced by the tactical astringency of Roy Hodgson's Fulham, and the selflessness of Frank Lampard in Carlo Ancelotti's subtly reshaped Chelsea. 'Lampard has basically been playing on the left wing', he explained, as Gallen busied himself in preparation for a possession session. 'A player at our level would say, "Fuck that, he's not playing me in my best position". But Lampard gives it everything. What a team player. He's not scoring, not getting the limelight, but fuck me, what a man.' Adversity had stimulated Jackett's sense of humility, which led him to admit to his players: 'I've got to give you better direction.'

Laird, a pale, quiet Scot, was almost too eager in the tackle. He lacked the upper body strength to get his shoulder into the challenge and win the ball. Instead of staying goal-side, and putting the emphasis on the decision-making quality of his opponent, he was over-anxious and tried to second-guess the flow of play. Jackett ordered Gallen: 'Have a conversation with him. He will wobble if I start coaching him this week.'

Gallen understood: 'If Ken even hints he's a tiny bit disappointed or worried, Marc takes it really seriously. He really looks up to him. They had a close relationship when Ken ran the reserves at Man City, but when he brought him here that relationship had to change. With most of the players it's easier for me to filter information. I have my own style, but I do exactly what the manager asks. It's easier for me to talk to Marc – he would take it the wrong way if the manager said the same thing.

'If Ken feels there's something major that needs to be addressed, he will follow it through. But sometimes the player finds it easier to talk to me on the phone. They're at home, in their own environment. It's easier for them to say what they feel. I've lost count of the conversations I have had, when they have opened up. They wouldn't have done so if those conversations had been around the training ground, or in the dressing room. Some are uncomfortable making eye contact. Others don't like to be seen in deep conversation.

'A lot of players phone after the game. They talk about everything apart from what they really want to talk about – what the manager thinks of them. They are wary of Ken, very wary. I try to judge the moods of most people, and that includes the manager. I tend to have an optimistic outlook. I think things are going to go well, regardless of the problem. But recently, Ken's been frustrated. He's been a bit down, and it's my job to make him feel better.'

Gallen nibbles away at problems like a pony gently grooming its companion as it begins to shed its winter coat. Emotional rescue is part of an assistant manager's job spec. 'In time, we'll find out whether I'm a natural number two', he said, with a laugh. 'I started at the bottom, as low as you can go. Do I want to be a manager? I think so, but I'm in absolutely no rush. Two reasons. One: I have a job, and so

I've got to try and keep that. Two: I'm in a great position. The manager is so good it would be wrong to move on before I pick up all the knowledge he has got.

'I learn loads from him, more on the training field than from anyone I've ever known. His clearness of direction and ability to say what he wants in very few words is incredibly difficult to match. I have seen many a coach make things extremely complicated. Ken has a good mix of simplicity, directness and straightforwardness. It's funny, because without even realising it, I have become the same way. If you hold your hand up when you make a mistake you are actually saying to the players, "I want honesty in return". The worst thing you can have is a problem you refuse to admit to.

'It's definitely unusual for a manager to be so honest. Players respect someone who is confident enough to admit weakness. It's a big sign of someone who totally believes in himself. I can see when Ken's come to a decision and stopped listening. It's "Click, this is irrelevant to me now". He's very good at pulling things back to where he wants to go. He's not a screamer. He feels that's just not the way to do it. It makes the situation worse. It enhances nothing, invites a negative response. It must be incredibly difficult to keep a lid on it and come up with accurate observations. On that night, against Yeovil, he absolutely nailed it. He knew how people were feeling. That is so hard. It's experience, and natural ability, coming through.'

The work on the training ground was rewarded. The subsequent 4–0 win at Stockport was Millwall's best, away from home, in eight years. Paul Robinson marked his return from injury by heading in Chris Hackett's nineteenth-minute corner, and Harris could afford to miss a second-half penalty in the process of scoring his second hat-trick of the season. He offered to pay for the match ball, because of Stockport's

parlous financial state, but the administrator told him to donate £50 to his cancer fund instead. It was a small, affecting gesture of humanity that bore the hallmarks of Harris' ability to connect with people at a basic level.

Like Gallen, Harris was struck by the brutality of Barnes' ordeal. A fellow professional, a man he admired, was suddenly as disposable as a supermarket sandwich past its sell-by date. The howls of the lynch mob led Harris to challenge the assumption that, one day, he will manage Millwall: 'Would I want to be manager here? I love football. I love this club. But anyone, anywhere, who loses six games in a row is in trouble. We would be going back to that c-u-n-t word again. Look at John Barnes. People don't care about the manager's status or reputation if they're not winning games of football. Why put my status on the line for that? There are lots of things I want to do – I might eventually go abroad. I have family in Australia. They are crying out for qualified coaches in America. They are throwing money at football in Cyprus. I'm still young enough to vary my lines of direction in football. I'm very conscious of the importance of making the right decisions, and doing what you enjoy doing.'

Jackett had isolated Harris, Paul Robinson and Andy Frampton as potential managers, but looked beyond his own dressing room. He was quietly mentoring David Connolly, the former Republic of Ireland international striker who had just joined Southampton from Sunderland. He thought nothing of such split loyalty, and counselled all four with revealing passion. He weaned them on the realities of his trade, warned them to ignore media myth. 'First and foremost, you have to love the game', he told them. 'Without that, it's pointless. Make sure it won't be financial Armageddon if you lose your job, because a lot of wives have a problem with insecurity, and then go for it.'

Emotional security was another matter. Frampton was taking his coaching badges while wrestling with the innate pessimism of the older pro. 'What am I going to do after football?' he asked, with characteristic earnestness. 'To be honest, that has worried me since I began in the game. I've thought every contract I signed was going to be my last. I'm learning the game from a player's perspective, and I'd like to give management a go at some stage in my life. If you can get your foot in the door, you can give yourself a chance.'

Frampton needed only to look to Scott Fitzgerald, Millwall's head of youth, for confirmation of the potholes that complicate a manager's career path. He played for him at Brentford, during a six-month spell that put Fitzgerald off first-team management for life. Fitzgerald was a generation removed from Frampton, in playing terms, but a similar character. Measured and self-aware, he had a holistic view of the game, shaped during a sixteen-year career at Wimbledon, Millwall, Colchester and Brentford. Football, to him, had to mean more than the extended panic attack that began when he was promoted from youth coach to succeed Leroy Rosenior, just before Christmas in 2006. He was a bright, persuasive tutor, and quickly oversaw Brentford's first win in 119 days, but couldn't prevent their relegation to League Two.

'When I took the job I told the directors they'd get relegated. Things were too far gone. The board said that would be alright, they understood the situation. The day after we went down I was sacked. It wasn't a good experience. It got to me. I was poor at delegation, and took too much on myself. Everything was so extreme. If we won I'd have a drink to celebrate. If we lost I'd have a drink to obliterate. It had a bad effect on my family life. I've got no desire to go through that again. Ken is different to most managers

I have seen. He delegates brilliantly and has the ability to shut all the nonsense out. He misses nothing.'

Fitzgerald was sustained by his sense of vocation, at ease with a different set of pressures. He still pushed himself hard, but had the reality check of an abiding memory. He vowed never to lose control in the way he did at Bradford City, when he found himself marching on to the pitch to scream abuse at Harris' admirer, Darren Deadman. The referee had bought a dive, awarded the penalty that denied Fitzgerald's ten-man Brentford team a win, but was protected from the consequences of his incompetence.

The FA charged Fitzgerald with insulting behaviour and relieved him of his pocket money. After such ragged-edge anger, it was soothing to do a full day at the training ground, eat a couple of ham rolls in the car, and spend the evening at Millwall's Centre of Excellence, which trained 120 boys aged nine to sixteen. He no longer frightened himself. He relished one of football's most onerous privileges, the power of dreams. The boys around him had less chance of survival than a salmon swimming upstream to spawn, but their enthusiasm was cleansing. That didn't mean he was immune to the vagaries of human nature.

His principal problem should have been his greatest pleasure. The regression of Kiernan Hughes-Mason, which had accelerated steadily since he turned professional, challenged the coach's *raison d'être*. His timekeeping was poor, his sense of entitlement puzzling. On £150 a week, he could afford only to shop at Primark, but borrowed his attitude from Armani. 'It's as if he's been replaced by his evil twin', Fitzgerald said. It was time for the nuclear option, a summons from the manager. He was called in to the office following a 3–1 FA Youth Cup win over Southend.

'How do you think you did the other night?' Jackett asked him.

'Pretty well', Hughes-Mason replied, moon-faced.

'You were the best player on the pitch, scored a great goal, and then you disappointed me. I think you could have done more, worked harder. You've lost a bit of reality. You want to look a good player, rather than be a good player. You have such potential, but you're blasé. You need to work on your fitness, your attitude. Get in the gym. You are fortunate that you have something, and I know it ain't like you don't want to do it. But I see 10, 20 per cent that you're not giving. Alright, pal?'

The subsequent glottal stop, a signal of apparent acknowledgement, will be familiar to all parents of adolescent boys. As Hughes-Mason filed out, Fitzgerald feared the issue reflected unflatteringly on his programme. Youth development involves the inherent frustration of trying to solve a Rubik's cube puzzle. Get sucked in by the intellectual challenge, and you begin to wonder whether it's worth the effort.

Institutionalised inequalities had dominated conversation when Jackett invited Southend manager Steve Tilson into the chairman's room at half time in the Youth Cup tie. Jackett cited his former club Manchester City, who had nearly 100 players on professional forms. Even before the Arab takeover, they had an annual youth budget of £2.5 million, 'with the proviso they ask for more if they want someone special'. Fitzgerald's programme cost £250,000. Tilson had more profound and immediate financial issues to consider. Southend were 24 hours away from being wound up over an unpaid £2.1 million tax bill, and his relationship with his chairman was understandably strained.

'The club is in bits. People are wondering what they're going to do with their lives. I swear to God I haven't got a clue what's going on. The players have been great, playing knowing they weren't being paid. But I've only got eleven of

them who are fit. Even if we avoid administration I've got a transfer embargo because we owe all sorts. We sold two kids last year but what does that leave me with? I never see that money. What chance have I got?'

'You've done fantastic, pal', said Jackett, who lightened the mood by offering him two ham baguettes for the journey home. 'Go on, you know you want to'.

Tilson, one of the unsung heroes of his profession, grimaced, but wrapped them in a serviette. 'Cheers. I'll take what's going these days.'

Even as an avowed free-marketeer, John Berylson, the Millwall chairman, regarded English football's business model as unsustainable. Southend survived, just, but he was unsurprised by their struggle in a League that tempted the likes of Leeds and Southampton to spend up to £9 million on players' wages. He favoured the introduction of a salary cap, involving minimum and maximum payrolls, but, while the authorities were ambivalent to financial anarchy, he trusted Jackett's acumen: 'Kenny is a businessman as much as he is a manager. He is very conscious of value. I was very lucky. He spends my money as if it's his own.'

That trust was reciprocated, despite the speculation junkies who demanded signings. Jackett began to work through a list of fifteen players who would be out of contract at the end of the season. Jack Smith, outstanding over the first fifteen games, was rewarded with an eighteen-month deal. Jimmy Abdou, whose industry in midfield had led to several enquiries from bigger clubs, signed on until July 2013. 'To get him on the wages we pay, I had to give him a long-term deal', the manager rationalised. 'The money isn't silly, and we've given him more security.'

A manager with an accountant's instincts doesn't sit easily alongside the *Spitting Image* puppets of the Premier League, who tend to regard prudence as a particularly silly

name for a cat. The one exception, Arsène Wenger, left an enduring impression on Jackett when he spoke at a managers' seminar: 'In essence he was saying you have to be the manager you want to be. If you run around trying to please every other fucker, it won't work.

'My chairman is telling me that clubs like Leeds and Charlton are looking at financial meltdown. Football clubs live on the edge, don't they? This one has been shit or bust in the past, but I want to be known for doing a sensible job for my people. I pride myself in running a club properly, and well. I'm not one of those who comes in, blitzes a club and takes it into financial oblivion because he's going to be long gone before the consequences of his actions become apparent. Managers are short-term people, but I will not go over the top and leave this club in shit street.'

Management will remain a fashion parade, despite such worthy sentiments. Aidy Boothroyd had been the poster boy for the FA coaching department, and was spoken of as a future England manager when he took Watford into the Premier League. The media loved his thirst for knowledge, the military analogies and motivational stunts. Yet he was out of work for ten months until he replaced Paul Lambert at Colchester. He still knew what made a news story, encouraging his players to walk over hot coals during a team bonding exercise, but was ruthlessly pragmatic. He sought promotion as a poor man's Stoke City, and had fashioned a team of Frankenstein monsters who were relentlessly physical, and by-passed midfield.

Colchester were leading at half time in a pivotal fixture at The Den on 31 October, through an Anthony Wordsworth free kick, deflected by Marc Laird past an unsighted David Forde. Jackett abandoned his usual reasoned approach and let rip. His ability to switch instantly between rational analysis and rage is not used often, but it demands attention.

The key message – 'No team comes to Millwall and bullies us' – was delivered at maximum volume, with maximum effect. It was a form of anger management they don't teach at Harvard Business School. Jackett's players flew out of the dressing room with a controlled fury that matched the punters' mood.

Substitute James Henry, whose loan spell had been complicated by a hamstring injury, had been on for only six minutes when his deep corner was cleared to Alan Dunne, who equalised with a brilliantly struck drive from the edge of the box. Then, three minutes into added time, Henry hit a low free kick under Ben Williams, the diving goalkeeper. Cue pandemonium. Colchester had lost for the first time in ten games, Millwall were in the play-off places for the first time, and all was well with the world.

'Sometimes, at half time, you dig in and can get a response', Jackett reflected, with a hint of self-consciousness, when he was back in his small, spare office at the training ground. 'It's not generally my way, and the rage is usually feigned. You have to be careful – it's easy to listen to someone shouting, and not hear what he's saying – but you can influence the tempo of a performance. Anger is a management tool with which you can get a reaction.' A knock on the door signalled the arrival of press officer Deano Standing with the embargoed news that he had been named League One Manager of the Month.

'Is that right?' said Jackett, bashfully. 'Been a good month, eh? It's been a nice month.'

Marching on Together, Part One

It was like watching a Salvation Army officer prepare for war. Gary Alexander's aggression was out of context. He sounded serene, rather than intimidating, as he prowled around the staff kitchen adjoining the home dressing room at The Den. 'We've got to get into these guys, smash 'em around a bit', he said, to himself as much as anyone. 'They've never liked it here. They think they've got a right to time on the ball. They won't get it.' Alexander was unaware that he was the one living on borrowed time. He would be the hero of the hour, come off the bench to score the winning goal, before succumbing to the sort of injury that makes a footballer wake in a cold sweat.

Two floors up, in the boardroom, director Demos Kouvaris, an East Coast associate of chairman John Berylson, was hosting a group of friends who had crossed the Atlantic for a weekend of adventure tourism. Four of them had cried off and taken the option of visiting Stonehenge. The remaining sixteen, taken on to the pitch during the warm-up, were expecting something similarly prehistoric, the Flintstones in football boots. The tribal rite of Millwall playing Leeds United would be a culture shock for men weaned on the relative tranquillity of baseball's most bitter rivalry, between the Boston Red Sox and New York Yankees.

The hanging judges of the football establishment were watching, waiting. Nothing was left to chance. Millwall asked the Football League to ensure that the game began

and ended in daylight. The first planning meeting was convened on 16 June, the day the fixture was confirmed. The clubs had been in constant contact, at chief executive level, for a month. Ken Chapman, Millwall's head of security, coordinated Transport Police, railway operators, local councils, businesses, and community groups. He and his deputy Simon Clayton, a former football intelligence officer, toured local estates at 6.00am to check building sites had been cleared of potential missiles. A leaflet had been placed on each seat, warning of the potential damage to the club caused by FA sanctions.

Chapman and stadium manager Colin Sayer briefed FA observer Andy Smith as 500 police officers fanned out from the ground. A hundred ticketless Leeds fans, drinking from early morning in Surrey Quays, were rounded up and deposited on northbound trains. Supporters of six clubs passed, without incident, through a potentially dangerous bottleneck at London Bridge station. In the narrow control room at the top of the main stand, Superintendent Steve Deehan, the match commander, took stock. His team monitored Millwall's biggest crowd for five years on 41 pan-and-tilt cameras. Radio operators, sitting before a bank of screens, linked three police evidence-gathering units, St John's ambulance staff, and the Fire Brigade. A fatal accident involving a lorry and a motorcycle convulsed traffic around the ground, but a convoy of 21 buses, carrying the majority of away fans, was safely escorted from a rendezvous point on Blackheath Common.

Berylson should have felt a stranger in a strange land. He was from Viking stock and wore a family heirloom, the Royal Order of Vasa, a Swedish chivalric honour, around his neck. His pioneering instincts matched those of his forebears who arrived in Boston in 1820, before pushing west through St Louis and Missouri, and north into South Dakota

and Minnesota. His father, who helped build the Hoover Dam to fund his education through the Depression, was a senior aide to General George S. Patton during the Second World War. His role in the liberation of Dachau gave his son a moral imperative: 'When we had problems, my father used to say: "Just embrace the horror, embrace it. Put your knife into it, before it puts its knife into you."'

Spectres circulated in the discreet comfort of his usual suite at a boutique hotel in central London. Tonic water cascaded over cracked ice and a miniature of gin in his crystal glass, but Berylson was subdued. He had been transported back to a churchyard in New England, a military funeral, and a poignant meeting with the parish priest. Three members of his family were killed in active service in Vietnam, and there were few body parts to bury. Berylson, who joined the Marines just before the withdrawal from Saigon, had been in uniform as a pall-bearer. The memory led him to catch his breath, go back to basics, seek emotional symmetry with his new surroundings.

'I kinda like what Millwall represents, backbone English. I have the same values. I was brought up to work hard, do as well as I can. Not to be fearless, but to fight evil. An astounding number of people in my family have been killed doing the right thing. I am a Massachusetts Democrat. I believe in taking care of people, because there but for the grace of God go you. People deserve good education, healthcare, a roof over their head. I've no problem with making lots of money. Money doesn't make the man, you make yourself. None of us in my family are impressed with wealth. Self-respect comes from what you have done, not what you possess.'

A shrewd, multi-faceted businessman, he was sufficiently assertive to have attracted death threats when he attempted to refinance banks in Rhode Island in the late nineties.

His loans to Millwall, through family investment vehicle Chestnut Hill Ventures, were at hedge fund rates, between 10 and 17 per cent interest. His family's business portfolio spanned Harcourt General, one of the world's largest publishing houses, the Neiman Marcus retail group, and General Cinema. Their holdings also involved the transportation, energy, transaction processing and insurance industries. His cousin Jeffrey Lurie, a billionaire former Hollywood producer, owned the Philadelphia Eagles NFL franchise. His father-in-law, Richard Smith, was one of the biggest benefactors in the United States.

Berylson's investment in Millwall, £14 million and rising, was loose change, given that 'to an extent, our business is giving money away'. The family foundation exceeds £200 million, and invests an additional £100 million in cancer and diabetes research. It funds education programmes, university scholarships and a range of anti-racism initiatives, including Facing History, a global project that uses the Holocaust as a template for lessons in civil responsibility. Berylson, lean, tanned and looking a decade younger than 57, was one of the most generous alumni of Brown University and Harvard, where he earned his MBA. He was trustee of several hospitals, and chairman of the Boston Police Activities League.

He became intrigued by the emotional intensity of English football while setting up the Vision Express group in the UK. He considered buying Liverpool in conjunction with close friend Robert Kraft, owner of the New England Patriots NFL franchise, and rejected the opportunity to buy Leeds United. 'It was fool's gold', he concluded, with rare prescience. 'A lot of these clubs are driving at a metal wall, at 100mph, hoping that the wall is somehow going to disappear. They're spending themselves into oblivion. Payrolls are out of control. Your banks went crazy. They won't

withdraw loans, because they know they won't get paid any-
way, but they will not extend. When there's no lunch for
anyone, clubs will die.'

He was approached by a source in the London finan-
cial market, and presented with a 'mishmash' of regenera-
tion plans involving Millwall. He lent them £1 million in
November 2006 – 'If I lost it, fine' – and pressed on, in hom-
age to a Republican folk hero: 'It was one of those Ronald
Reagan moments: "If there's manure around, there must
be a pony some place." The radical racist nonsense is at the
edge of the football club, as opposed to its heart. You can
peel it off, like an orange. Eradicating such an evil doesn't
happen overnight, but look how far we have gone in so
short a time. Millwall is not Chelsea, but the problems have
dissipated.'

Berylson had an abiding respect for Kenny Jackett, even
if he did bemuse him by discoursing on the social fabric of
Roman Britain during a walk before Sunday lunch at the
manager's home in St Albans. 'I bathe in history', admit-
ted the chairman, who proceeded to draw an unlikely par-
allel between League One skirmishes and the battles of
Agincourt, Gettysburg and Midway. He was on safer ground
with military legend than the offside rule, which remained
impenetrable.

Leeds, the only unbeaten team in the country, were
formidable but Jackett, addressing his team, preferred to
remain in the here and now. 'It's a great game to play in,
lads. We have to be brave enough to go after the ball. Don't
be frightened. Enjoy the challenge. They ain't anything to
be afraid of. They grind out results – it's why they are where
they are – but there's nothing we can't handle. We defend
as a unit. We don't get done on set-pieces. That's us. All of
your thoughts should be positive. I don't like people who
respond negatively to mistakes. I'm looking at your fucking

reaction if you make them. If you are positive you will have a good game.'

The intensity of the pre-match stream of consciousness is a reliable indicator of readiness to put bodies on the line. On this day, illuminated by shafts of weak sunlight and shards of cruel wit that challenged the conscience, the alchemy was irresistible. Tony Craig, as ever, chanted his commitment: 'Ain't got legs on us. We overpower teams.'

Paul Robinson was on his feet: 'High tempo, lads.'

David Forde lurked in the corner: 'Don't get fucking beat.'

Joe Gallen circulated, urgently: '95 minutes to work.'

Jackett chimed in: 'We all want the fucking ball.'

Craig's eyes were wide: 'Fucking us. Lot of talk about us.'

Jackett moved to the door: 'Win the first ball, first header. Fucking go for them.'

Neil Harris advanced as it opened: 'We can be winners today.'

Craig demanded the final word: 'No fucking goals. Clean sheet. Got to be nasty, eh? Fuck these cunts, eh?'

Forde's sixth sense kicked in as they lined up in the tunnel. 'I'm in the best position to see their body language', he explained later. 'They were saying, "Oh no, not this mob again". We were flying at them and they didn't want to be there.' Within three minutes, Harris had used his quick brain, and quick feet, to get into position to head his tenth goal of the season, from Chris Hackett's free kick. Leeds equalised eight minutes later, Patrick Kisnorbo's close-range volley punishing Millwall's failure to clear Bradley Johnson's corner.

The atmosphere was sulphuric. Fast and unremittingly physical, a game for consenting adults was in the balance at half time. Jack Smith lay on the floor, an ice pack on his right knee, as Jackett went to work: 'I'm telling you the last

half hour will be the most important. We've got more deter-
mination than them, better fitness, organisation and fuck-
ing heart. We can't get tired. We can't become depleted.
We've got to keep closing 'em down, making them bang
it long. Let's have a bit more belief in the final third, bet-
ter second ball defending. Don't drop your levels of com-
mitment. We've got to grind them into the ground.' Steve
Morison was ordered to pull on to Kisnorbo in the right-
hand channel. Harris was urged to work the line, win free
kicks in good areas. Gallen sensed there was an error in
goalkeeper Casper Ankergren. 'You've got more time on
the ball than you think, chaps', said Richard Shaw, as the
buzzer sounded. 'Talk to each other, help each other out.'

Morison was mortified to be substituted by Alexander
fifteen minutes into the second half, but the hard call was
justified. Eight minutes remained when Smith kept the ball
in play on the left and set up Danny Schofield, whose cross,
pulled back from the by-line, was met by a firm header.
Alexander screamed at the heavens, slid on his knees, and
surfed on a riptide of noise. The pain of the heel injury that
was to wreck his season was a small price. Like a credit card
bill, it would be paid, with exorbitant interest, later. Jackett,
out of character, leaped into the air and danced a *pas de
deux* with Gallen.

The stadium shook with a primitive pride, rang with
malicious chants of 'Istanbul', a sick reference to the death
of two Leeds fans in the city before a UEFA Cup semi-final
in April 2000. Despite such malice aforethought, only four
fans were ejected. One was a schoolboy, apparently high
on hallucinogens, who needed to be restrained by a dozen
officers after being caught trying to smuggle a Turkish flag
into the ground. A plastic bottle was thrown onto the pitch
in bizarre celebration of the winner, and an alert freelance
photographer captured a goon in the upper tier, wearing

a Galatasaray shirt and making slashing motions across his throat. The Leeds fans threw a seat at Forde, and unveiled a Hungarian flag in mute contempt for two Millwall fans stabbed at a UEFA Cup tie in Budapest five years earlier. Little wonder Andy Ambler, the man at the eye of the hurricane, opened two bottles of red when he got home, and was in a deep sleep by 11.00pm.

The emotion was sucked out of the dressing room like oxygen out of a burning building. There was no triumphalism. Handshakes, a throwback to the days of brilliantine and dubbined boots, sufficed. 'The first half was even, but in the second half we battered them', summarised Jackett. 'The goal was coming. You deserved this. It's a fantastic win. Well done.' His players gave him, and themselves, a round of applause before bowing to the inevitability of Craig completing formalities: 'We showed today we're coming together. It's our time. Fucking get in there.'

And they did. A council of war was convened the following evening at the NFL game between the New England Patriots and Tampa Bay Buccaneers at Wembley Stadium. Berylson, the host, wore an apple-coloured rollneck under his Patriots jersey. It was emblazoned with number 51, that of inside linebacker Jerod Mayo, a defensive behemoth with attitude. His guests included Jim Sturman QC, who had led three unsuccessful attempts to get the FA to drop charges following the West Ham riot. A Tottenham season ticketholder and a Philadelphia Eagles fan, he loved the strategies and synchronised aggression of gridiron. As advocates go, he was unafraid to lead with his helmet, unconcerned by the occasional accusation of unnecessary roughness.

Sturman was a post-punk silk whose greatest musical memory challenged the conventions of his profession. He had warmed up for a Sex Pistols reunion gig at Finsbury Park by bungee jumping from a crane to the sledgehammer

riffs of Iggy Pop's 'Lust for Life'. He had 'followed football before it was fashionable' in the late seventies, supporting Spurs, from The Shelf at White Hart Lane, in the old Second Division. His all-time hero was Glenn Hoddle: 'I couldn't get over the number of times he was left out of the England team', he reflected, ferrying beers along the row of seats that overlooked the halfway line. 'What was it Ron Greenwood said, when he dropped him after he'd scored against Spain on his debut? "I didn't want him to become big-headed." I couldn't believe that. It should have been the beginning of the longest run in midfield for any England player.'

His first football case, ten years earlier, involved successfully defending Graeme Le Saux, who punched Robbie Fowler after the Liverpool striker indulged in the casual homophobia for which the game is notorious. Sturman was the nuclear option of choice for a growing list of clubs. He represented Chelsea in a succession of high-profile cases, acting for the 'cerebral' Didier Drogba in his serial appearances before UEFA's disciplinary committee, and for José Mourinho in the Ashley Cole 'tapping up' case. At the other end of the football food chain, he successfully defended Sam Bethell, the Stamford Bridge groundsman involved in the 'Mowergate' fracas with Manchester United's Patrice Evra. 'Fair dos to Chelsea, they defended that groundsman as if he was Frank Lampard. If he had used racist abuse he'd have been sacked like a shot. But they satisfied themselves he had not, and backed him to the hilt.'

To Sturman's enduring bemusement, he was named one of West Ham's three Players of the Year in 2007, for successfully arguing, at a Premier League hearing, that they should not be docked points in the Carlos Tevez case. His work for Newcastle involved championing the cause of Emre, acquitted of racially abusing Everton players, and

the inimitable Joe Kinnear. The portly, potty-mouthed manager allegedly called a linesman 'a fucking cheat' in a game against Stoke, but Sturman successfully argued that he had merely informed the official he had been 'fucking cheated'. Sturman understood the comic potential of the moment: 'If you're defending Joe F'ing Kinnear, he won't deny using the F-word', he said with a wolfish grin that, with his dark eyes and hair, emphasised his resemblance to a lived-in version of David Essex.

Sturman roamed on both sides of the fence, prosecuting the 'absolutely charming' Roy Keane on behalf of the FA. He had previously advised them that the secrecy of their disciplinary process was a strategic weakness. He worried that, in Millwall's case, the FA disciplinary panel would ignore the defence of due diligence. The stakes were high, and shaped by the legal reality that 'if they go and get a heavy hitter, you have to go and get one'. West Ham's defence would be led by Ken Macdonald, a former Director of Public Prosecutions. The FA's case would be made by Jonathan Laidlaw QC, who last confronted Sturman in court when Sturman was acting for Bilal Abdullah, the surviving Glasgow airport bomber.

'As a barrister you certainly don't associate with all your clients', he explained, deadpan. 'You want to be independent. You can't get too drawn in and lose your ability to objectively assess the evidence. But I like underdogs, and I genuinely identify with Millwall. It's amazing how you get an affection for clubs you represent. Millwall really have done more than anyone else to combat hooliganism and attendant racism. What they have done is quite phenomenal. I don't think the FA, and by that I mean the amorphous FA rather than the individuals within it who have some sympathy for the club, understands the real and particular pressures on Millwall, because of where they are located. They can't afford to take this lightly, but they're genuinely

bemused at being charged when they had done everything they reasonably could. It's become a case of us against the world.'

The price of principle was high, nearly £100,000, but Berylson was determined to make the most of his invest-ment in Sturman's services: 'I like to think my word is my bond. If your word isn't worth anything, you're not worth anything. Seconds after the FA charges came in I said we'd fight them to the death. We are innocent. There is a princi-ple involved and I am going to find a way to win. If you can't find a way, make a way. If you're walled in, kick it down. But don't get blocked. That applies to business, and to football. Nothing is easy.'

Jackett understood the sentiments. He had arrived with his sons, and shuffled along the row to chat to his chair-man as the hapless Buccaneers, victims of the Glazers' parsimony, subsided to a predictable defeat. He was pre-paring the ground for a strategic review of the squad, in December, that would assess which players would be offered contract extensions. The need for a more imposing central midfield player and additional striking options was acute. Alexander's recurring heel injury, the result of twelve years' wear and tear, would eventually require surgery. 'I'm get-ting pissed off, to be honest', Jackett admitted. 'I could see the Leeds players looking at Gary come on against them, and thinking, "That's the last fucking thing we need".' Yet he would not panic. He hoped to 'save my money for the second half of the season'.

Such pragmatism appealed to Berylson the business-man: 'What I like about Kenny is his brutal honesty. He's decisive, and questions himself as rigorously as he questions those around him. I am patient enough to let the soup get to the right temperature. I understand what Kenny is doing. I have watched him build a team. I don't ever have to criti-

cise him, because he criticises himself. He also doesn't take credit for very much. When we win the big games he will tell me his staff, and the players, were wonderful. One of the reasons I wanted him was his reputation as a tactician. If you're just a great guy, an attaboy, slap-on-the-back sort of manager, you will lose. You have got to know how to isolate a problem and fix it. That's true in sports, everything.'

The culture shock of the first-round FA Cup tie against AFC Wimbledon was off the scale. Sturman, a guest in the front row of the directors' box, was startled by Bethell, the Chelsea groundsman. Sam and his father Chris, Millwall's historian, were season ticket-holders at The Den. They shouted at the barrister, bowed low and made 'we're not worthy' gestures. Alexander, a huge boxing fan, gleefully blagged the autograph of world heavyweight champion David Haye, who arrived midway through the first half. He had flown in from Germany after winning the WBA title by beating Nikolai Valuev. A Bermondsey boy, his allegiance was reaffirmed by a Millwall scarf and bobble hat. He filled the narrow corridor, beaming as Jackett's team filed past him into the dressing room at the interval. Captain Robinson dipped his head in acknowledgement of the unspoken bonds between professional sportsmen.

Respect.

There was an air of irritation after a goalless first half, but the manager accentuated the positive: 'We're not play-ing a pub team, or a bunch of part-timers, but there have been a lot of teams who can't live with you in the second half of matches. We can be quicker, faster. Keep moving the ball. Keep discipline about your game. Don't change the game plan and start taking chances in the wrong area. It will happen.' Sure enough, within three minutes of the restart, Morison took advantage of defensive confusion and set up Harris for the opening goal. Substitute Jason Price shadow-

boxed in celebration of his two late goals, but the best strike, in a 4–1 win, came from Schofield, who was emerging as a key player.

Sturman had done pro bono work for AFC Wimbledon, following their parent club's annexation by the concrete cattlemen of Milton Keynes. Their 3,339 fans occupied both tiers of the North Stand, and radiated innocence. 'Womble till I die', they sang, ignorant of the incongruity of the message. They might as well have been reciting children's fables on death row. The home fans didn't know what to make of them – 'balloon-toting weirdos' was the most polite chat room comment – but they had a reputation to defend. When they set up a rolling chant of 'Who's the slapper in the white?', a big-boned lady in the third row of the upper tier was not amused. She splayed her hips, spread her arms, and gave her suitors the finger, with both hands. It was love at first sight.

The jolly japes continued the following Saturday, 14 November, when 300 Millwall fans, dressed in pirate gear, enjoyed a liquid breakfast on a Thames riverboat. They disembarked at 10.30am, and proceeded to take advantage of Brentford's status as the only League club with a pub at each corner. It was a filthy day. Horizontal rain, driven by storm-force winds, stung the eyes and chilled the soul. The beautiful game took one look outside, and snuggled back beneath the duvet. Binge drinking in a warm, fusty bar with Jeff Stelling doing his party tricks on Sky TV in the corner, had its attractions.

The 2–2 draw featured a cameo performance from a chosen one. At seventeen, Brentford's new loanee, midfield player John Bostock, had the strut of a trophy teenager. The hard word was that he was physically imposing but emotionally immature. Pursued by Chelsea and Barcelona as a schoolboy, he was nurtured by the Crystal Palace Academy

before being spirited away by Spurs in 2008. By common consent, the £700,000 fee, levied by five faceless worthies on the Professional Football Compensation Committee, was a steal. When Jackett considered loaning him, he sought the advice of Tony Burns, who had seen him blossom at Palace. 'A bit flash, but I like him, gaffer', reported the goalkeeping coach. 'He's a player.'

The words had an awful resonance within nine minutes of Bostock's Brentford debut when he eased his way to the edge of the penalty area and struck a sumptuous left-foot shot past Forde. Robinson equalised with a stooping header, but Bostock, using the elements, scored direct from a corner to give the home team a lead that lasted until the final minute. James Henry, once again, rescued Millwall, with an outrageous wind-assisted 40-yard free kick. The unbeaten run, begun by that dispiriting goalless draw against Yeovil, stretched to eight matches. It ended ignominiously a week later.

Wycombe are a small club, promoted beyond the natural limits of economics. They arrived at The Den as candidates for victimhood, yet the portents for Millwall were ominous. Harris had further reduced Jackett's options by pulling up in training with back problems, and Gareth Ainsworth, twelve minutes into his Wycombe debut, recklessly kicked Craig full in the face. The defender was unconscious in mid-air, but revived before he was taken to hospital. He had suffered a depressed fracture of the cheekbone and eye socket. As if unnerved, Millwall played without bite or fluency, and lost to second-half goals by Chris Westwood and Kevin Betsy.

Stevo and his mate Dave offered a degree of perspective. Veterans grievously wounded in Afghanistan, they helped Millwall launch the League's Help for Heroes campaign at the match. Stevo – 'My full name's not important' – walked around the pitch on a prosthetic leg that had been

fitted the previous day. Dave, similarly reluctant to offer name, rank or serial number, had survived despite his life-support machine being switched off. The home fans threw £12,548.90 in loose change into the collecting buckets, and treated the squaddies reverentially.

Although surgeons decided against inserting a metal plate in his face, Craig had a titanium version inserted during a second operation. Bad blood congealed, and would not be forgotten. Berylson, who had brought his wife Amy over from New England, was tormented by what he called 'a weekend from hell'. Yet, unlike many in his position, he refused to search for scapegoats. 'I have seen Kenny at low points', he reasoned. 'It's like sand coming through your fingers. You just can't save it. It happens in business too. I'm not worried. Look at great teams in the US: a great coach, backed long-term by a quarterback owner. Kenny is the strong man I end up measuring other people by.'

Chapter 12
From Scapegoat to Saviour

Steve Morison nearly got away with it. On another day, viewed through the veil of a comfortable win, his exchange of pleasantries with Wycombe's Tommy Doherty would have been overlooked. But, brooding over the worst home performance of the season, Kenny Jackett scanned the DVD with the merciless clarity of a hawk seeking an easy meal in the hedgerows. Morison, his pet project, needed a reality check. He was losing respect within the dressing room, and provoking supporters who had turned impatience into performance art.

'What type of centre forward are you going to be?' he asked the striker he had rescued from the purgatory of Conference football. 'What are you going to bring to this club? What can you guarantee us? You can't stand up there at 6′2″ and not win headers. You can't not close down, you can't not chase. You've got to go out there and have a tear-up. What were you saying to that defender?' Morison explained that he had turned sharply, and accidentally run into Doherty before the ball went for a throw. His reflex action was to apologise, laugh it off. 'Sorry?' exclaimed Jackett. 'Sorry? You should have been saying to him, "You come near me again you cunt and I'll snap you in two". That is how it has got to be.'

The manager quickly drew the dividing line between street-corner theatre and unprofessional spite. 'It's all an act', he told him, citing Bolton's Kevin Davies as a striker

158

who scored intermittently, yet justified his selection by contributing to the cause. 'If the goals aren't coming, what can you give the team? That's your biggest issue. Funnily enough, if you start putting yourself about, being a handful for the team, the lads will go with you, because that's what they want up there. The supporters will go with you, and the pressure for goals will be off. Then, suddenly the goals will go in. You will be thinking less about it, instead of over-analysing. You can think yourself worse, instead of better.'

Jackett allowed himself a contemplative period each morning, before the training ground came to life and the mobile began to ring. Two goals in Morison's first eighteen appearances represented a significant test of faith in his ability to turn non-League water into wine. 'Steve will start scoring goals', he said, swirling tepid tea around a ceramic mug. 'But he has to define what sort of player he wants to be. He's built like a brick shithouse. He's quick, he's strong and he's fit, yet in too many games he doesn't play his weight. They won't have that here, especially from someone like him, who looks like a Millwall player. He's got to use his physical attributes.'

Morison's penance began at Exeter, a road trip beyond the imagination of the elite. He braved rush-hour traffic on the M25, and was among the group scavenging coffee at a hotel in Slough at 9.00am. He squeezed on to the bus beside Jason Price, who had brought his own pillow. Price didn't care that, the moment he fell asleep, coffee stirrers, straws, and assorted packaging would be inserted into the wiry candy floss that passed as a hairstyle. The scouting reports suggested rich pickings. Exeter tried to smother teams, but were poor defending as a unit. They lacked height and guile at set-pieces. Morison would play as a lone striker, with Danny Schofield operating off him.

'Thank fuck there's a game', exclaimed Joe Gallen, as the team prepared in a setting familiar to any park footballer. There wasn't room to swing a centipede, let alone a cat. A Dr Dre dirge on the communal iPod prompted Richard Shaw to plead, in vain, for Luther Vandross. A sign on a scarred, whitewashed wall read: 'No chewing gum, cigarette ends, or any other objects to be put in these toilets or urinals.' Players stretched on the skips, or in a shower area with the dimensions of a B&Q bath. The bell was on the blink, so they were summoned by what sounded like a toy machine gun. They braved torrential rain, driven right to left by a gale-force wind towards 487 Millwall fans, corralled in an uncovered end. It was a night to define devotion, and disaffection.

Millwall took a 21st-minute lead. Dave Martin, tripped by Bertie Cozak, picked himself up to bludgeon a successful penalty. A shoulder injury forced the substitution of Jack Smith at half time, but seven minutes after the restart, Exeter defender Steve Tully was sent off for a studs-up challenge on Andy Frampton. That should have been game over. Morison contrived to put a free header wide from five yards out and hit the post, before the haphazard decision-making skills that characterise lower-Division players proved decisive.

Two minutes remained when Price, a 72nd-minute substitute for Martin, had the chance to clear. His natural out ball, to Chris Hackett on the right wing, was not on, because Hackett had wandered aimlessly into a congested centre circle. He opted for a witless back-heel in the vague direction of Frampton, which allowed Exeter to win an illegitimate throw-in from the swamp beside the dugouts. The ball had not crossed the line, but was hurled in quickly towards Adam Stansfield. His cross from the byeline, turned into a torpedo by the tempest, somehow evaded David Forde and

went in off the inside of the far post. A comfortable win had been transformed into a debilitating draw.

'We're fucking up time and again', screamed Forde, who punched the dressing room door for effect. 'Fucking bollocks, Pricey – get rid. Two or three minutes to go – put it out. We're better than this. We keep getting caught for fucking mistakes.' Price sagged like a child's helium balloon caught on a barbed wire fence. 'It's down to me', he said quietly without lifting his head. Darren Ward seized the initiative, shifted the mood: 'Time out, time out.' The sudden silence was filled by a ghost. Laura Branigan, who had died five years earlier of a brain aneurysm, was singing 'Gloria', her signature hit, over the tannoy:

Gloria, you're always on the run now
Running after somebody, you gotta get him somehow
I think you've got to slow down before you start to blow it
I think you're headed for a breakdown, so be careful
 not to show it

Jackett hid his feelings behind flickering eyes. He read the distress in Morison's pale, boyish face: 'Steve, that was more like it', he said. 'You whacked a few, challenged like you meant it. You will score, and the players will go with you. Lads, when they're down to ten men and it's a poxy pitch, get it wide. But, as much as we are disappointed, I saw some Millwall, some spirit, tonight. I feel gutted for you. I was angry with you on Saturday but this is different. The next couple of months are going to be no time for faint-hearted people, for people who are not physically and mentally strong. This is where we go again, get on another roll. Make sure we are ready, inside the group, for what is to come.'

It was a sombre journey home. Dominos had delivered a dozen pizzas, but no one was particularly hungry. Ward

shared blueberries and bitter chocolate without shifting his eyes from the screens replaying the DVD of the game. It was just after midnight, on the M4 just north of Bristol, when Exeter's equaliser was replayed. Jackett ordered it to be repeated, four times. He confirmed Hackett's error, and hissed: 'How many fucking times have we told him to stay wide?' He then asked the players, politely but firmly, to move towards the back of the bus. It was 12.31am. A staff meeting was convened on the front four seats. They ignored the irony of the first track on the driver's CD, Wilson Pickett's 'In the Midnight Hour'.

Less than 40 hours remained until the loan deadline. Leeds would get three players in, including Hogan Ephraim, a long-term Millwall target. Paul Ince would sign Nigel Quashie, who was somehow earning £1 million a year at West Ham. Jackett and his coaches revisited a prioritised list of six players. At 1.10am Gallen called Karl Robinson, Ince's assistant at MK Dons, who was brooding over a 4–3 home defeat to Carlisle. Gallen confirmed their interest in midfield player Peter Leven. 'Will your manager let him come to us?' he asked. Ince was willing, but overruled by chairman Pete Winkleman, who didn't want to do business with a rival. 'It's the difference in dynamics', rationalised Gallen. 'If results were better, the coaches would have more sway over the chairman.'

Tellingly, the five other players on Millwall's wish list were strikers. At 1.40am, at the first drop-off point, Jackett walked with Andy Ambler towards the chief executive's BMW. 'I'll try to get one in, and one out', he confirmed. Ashley Grimes, wanted by Conference club Crawley Town, was earmarked as the sacrificial lamb, but survived. Liverpool rejected an approach for Nathan Eccleston. Reading preferred to keep Hal Robson Kanu. Plymouth agreed to release Ashley Barnes, but reneged at the last moment, citing an injury

in training. Patrick Ageymang refused to move from QPR and, despite being Gallen's neighbour in west London, D.J. Campbell preferred to remain in the Championship, by moving from Leicester to Derby and on to Blackpool.

Jackett's mood was not improved by a 1–1 draw at Staines Town in the FA Cup the following Saturday, 28 November. It was a surreal occasion, a carnival of clichés. The Conference South club claimed Bobby Davro as its solitary celebrity fan. Ali Chaaban, scorer of the equaliser, morphed into Ali C in homage to Ali G, the comic character adopted as the town's cultural icon. Even Chaaban's conviction for intent to supply cannabis fitted the script. The fans – the Staines Massive, natch – dressed accordingly. Residents of Wheatsheaf Lane, adjoining the ground, hid their cars and barricaded their homes. They had been spooked by some creative journalism from the local paper, which all but promised that Millwall fans would eat their young. A poster on the paper's website, one Gary Cheesefinger, had not quite extracted tongue from cheek when he warned: 'Be very careful, residents of Staines. As you know, we have history. We will see it as a major defeat if some old girl hasn't called the Old Bill from her bungalow while 40,000 Millwall fans are urinating on her petunias.'

Rape and pillage was a poor alternative to watching endless reruns of The Miss. Morison was, inevitably, the culprit. It traumatised even a hardened pro like Jackett, who steeled himself to watch it again on his PC in his office on Monday morning. 'Christ, the header at Exeter was a bad one, but Saturday's one was far, far worse', he said, almost apologetically. 'Unbelievable. He's two yards out, open goal, and gone with his wrong foot. Missed it altogether.' The tone of the manager's day had been set. Marcus Bignot arrived early with PFA executive Nick Cusack in tow, to air his grievances.

The sound of raised voices carried through a thin wall and into the staff room, where Gallen was studying a video

compilation of MK Dons' goals in preparation for the following night's League game. 'It's not the morning to take on the manager', he said, eyebrows arched. 'He's on edge.' Morison's problems could not be viewed in isolation. The Guvnors, primarily defenders, were beginning to grumble about his profligacy. It put too much pressure on them to keep clean sheets. Jackett, already concerned by the danger of Martin being marginalised, met them head on:

'It does become a collective issue, and I've had to talk to them about it. As a player my instincts were basically defensive, so I can associate with them. But for defenders, it's relatively simple. You've got to get tight, get stuck in, get to the ball first. If on top of that, you can find a pass, then great. You feel pretty secure. For Steve Morison, Dave Martin and Chris Hackett, a different type of bravery is required. They need the bravery to go past someone, to accept the ball, to score a goal. Look at the top level – does Ronaldo track back, tackle, close down? No. He's brave in going past people, going in where it hurts. He takes the responsibility to put the cross in, to hit the target on a free kick. You won't always get people who accept that type of responsibility, who can also tackle and head it.

'When Framps had that go at Dave earlier in the season I understood what he was saying. It was within the ethos of the club. But Dave's bravery is different to Framps' bravery. Graham Taylor used to say that the bravest thing is to knock a ball past someone and run the other side. If you don't quite get there, the tackle on your standing leg, as you're trying to cross the ball, can finish your career. Your cruciates go. Although you think that wingers are scared, they're the bravest people. It's easy just to run up and clatter some fucker because it's all on your terms.

'What our lads have to understand is if someone doesn't work hard, isn't fit, and isn't committed to the cause because

they don't prepare themselves properly, that's different. That's opting out. I talk to them about Neil Harris. Does he tackle? No, he growls a little bit, but he can't actually tackle. Is he good at heading on the halfway line? No. He actually backs in, and wins free kicks there. He scores with his headers in the box. Has he got fantastic pace? Does he put himself about? No. He's got an attitude of mind. Neil's strengths are his touch, vision, movement and his finishing. They are technical, footballing qualities, rather than physical qualities. He has got a 100 per cent personality. The lads have to realise you can't pick a Tony Craig in every position. There has to be a bit of give and take. What I'm saying to Framps is: 'You pin Dave Martin if he doesn't prepare himself, doesn't train well, if he's like a fucking bag of shit. You pin him if he ain't physically fit, if his body fat is high, if he's opting out in terms of commitment to the club. But also recognise what his strengths are, and what he brings to the team. There might be a time when we need a better player of that type but he will still be a similar beast. It's the same with Steve. He's in a lonely place. He needs to score, ultimately, but if he's going to throw his weight around, people will give him more time, more of a chance.

'It's a pressure game, a pressure situation. It's good to find a couple of scapegoats who you can hammer. We're good at it in this game. It's easy to say, "Oh, the centre forwards – they're shit". What they are doing, in saying that, is letting themselves off the hook. That's wrong. A percentage of the problem does involve Steve, but a percentage of it is the performance of the whole team. We haven't had a clean sheet for a long while. People think it's black and white, but there are shades of grey. They need to think for themselves a little bit. Everybody has decided it's the fault of Steve and Pricey. We've only lost one in ten, by the way. We've drawn three out of the last four, and given the lead up

in two of them. Let's keep some perspective. I don't think
Fordie could have done anything about the Exeter goal, but
at Brentford, the week before, he let one in straight from
a corner. So hang on Fordie, do you know what I'm say-
ing? You've been fantastic for me, and if you have made
the occasional mistake you have generally been a very good
goalkeeper for me. Have a look at yourself. You have let
your frustration come out on two poor souls.'

Morison was listening. He was in the process of proving
things to himself. If that entailed subjugating his personality
in the interests of his profession, so be it. That morning, in
training, Omar Beckles was an unwitting extra in Morison's
passion play. The youth team defender got tight to him,
pushed him, and was hit by a retaliatory arm as the pair
jumped together. 'Fuck off', he yelled, in pain and surprise
rather than admonition. The youngster cupped his head in
his hands, while Morison distanced himself from his plight
and jogged away to keep warm in a bitter crosswind.

Jackett, aware of the significance of the incident, was
quietly delighted. 'Basics', he announced to the group.
'That's how goals come. Kick from the keeper, a challenge,
bits and pieces, then some good football and the ball in
the box. Do you believe? Your body language has to say to
me, "Yeah, I'm a good player. Give me the ball. I can make
it happen."' He challenged personal standards, valued col-
lective discipline. Paul Robinson collected used plastic cups
that were blowing across the pitch, and deposited them in
a black bin bag. It was a revealingly small, humble gesture.
Detail, detail, detail.

Pain is an occupational hazard for footballers. Gary
Alexander shuffled around the dressing room on crutches
the following evening. He ached to be involved, but a scan
delivered bad news. 'The doctor told me that in a normal
job this would mean being off my feet for 100 days', he said,

with a clumsy gesture towards the offending heel spur that would have to be shaved down in an operation. 'I told him I don't have a normal job.' When the team went out to warm up, Craig pleaded with Jackett to sanction his return, within a week, from his facial injuries. He had been christened the Phantom by his team-mates, because of the white carbon-fibre mask he was obliged to wear. The manager's duty was to protect him from himself. 'I can tell when someone is ready to play football', he told him, 'and you're not, yet.'

Millwall rapidly asserted themselves over their pro-motion rivals. Frampton gave them an early lead with a near-post header, and a quick Morison free kick resulted in Hackett adding a second, twenty minutes in. Midway through the half, Morison callously left a foot in on MK Dons captain Dean Lewington. He got away without a book-ing, and walked away without a backward glance. Jackett does not condone arbitrary intimidation, but he under-stood Morison was undergoing a rite of passage. The atmos-phere at half time was quiet, purposeful.

Morison asked Adrian Wisson for a banana, only to be told they'd run out. He turned down a chocolate bar in favour of an isotonic drink. 'Steve, for me, that's exactly what I fucking want', Jackett said, hunching his shoulders slightly and stooping as he made his point. 'The keeper's made a great save from you, but you're being a right hand-ful. You're helping to get us up the pitch.'

Gallen, a ball of compressed energy in the corner of the room, interjected: 'This suits our mentality. Stamp on them, press the life out of them.'

Jackett moved to the door as his players filed out: 'Do not step off them. Work your fucking bollocks off. Run, run, and run.'

So much for earnest entreaties. Within 30 seconds of the restart, Ward had backed off and allowed Jermaine Easter

to curl a shot into the top corner. When Easter equalised with a quarter of an hour remaining, Craig, sitting next to me, made eye contact and muttered: 'If I was out there now I'd be screaming.' The faithless were restless. Morison nearly scored with an instinctive volley, but was skewered for a momentary lapse in control. His principal tormentor was a sour-faced spectator in spectacles. He had become a familiar figure, sitting behind the home dugout spewing baseless criticism. 'Get that cunt off, Jackett!', he screamed, safe in his insignificance. The manager duly ignored him.

The game had entered the second minute of added time when the ball was played through the defence on the left. Morison burst on to it, waited for goalkeeper Willy Gueret to commit, and, from an acute angle, scored with a lofted shot, struck with the outside of his right boot, into the far corner of the net. Morison hesitated for a split second, as if celebration was an alien concept. But then, in an explosion of exultation and relief, he ran towards the crowd to share his first goal in nine games. When the final whistle went, seconds after the restart, he punched the air. Robinson was the first to reach him, and swallowed him in a bear hug. The Guvnors sent their regards. 'That', said Frampton, 'was the biggest fucking lifeline ever.'

Jackett studiously underplayed Morison's impact when his players sat, flushed and strangely subdued, around him. Redemption comes a poor second to the next result. 'We've gone and done the Dons, and that's a fucking great win', he said. 'But lads, start looking forward right now. We need to be up for Hartlepool. We've been here before. When we've beaten top teams, we've followed up by losing to poxy Wycombe. Don't spoil this with a shite performance at Hartlepool.'

No prizes for guessing what happened next. Millwall were three goals down within 29 minutes, and succumbed

without a murmur to their worst defeat of the season. Inaction had consequences. Ward was dropped, much to his chagrin. Adam Bolder, angry to be recalled and rejected at half time, never started a game for the club again. 'It's over', confided Gallen, signalling the start of a four-month spell in solitary, which ended with Bolder's loan move to Bradford City. Morison, booked at Hartlepool for the third time in four games since his pivotal conversation with Jackett, was at the other end of the emotional see-saw.

'I took what the gaffer said on board and it seems to have worked. My natural game will come. Maybe I was thinking about it too much. I'm just concentrating on the basics of the game: working hard, using my size. Even though I'm quite big I don't feel big, but I'm starting to feel I'm a presence. You almost have to become someone you're not. I have started going on the pitch, thinking, "If I get hurt, I get hurt. That doesn't matter as long as I hurt them as well." My missus says, "When I watch you it's not you out there". Yeah. That's what it's like. As soon as you step over that white line you are different. It's not me at all. Battering people is not in my mentality.

'But everyone is a little like that, you know? Robbo's angry. Tone's angry. Frammo's angry. I might have gained a little respect. It's all calm. I feel comfortable now. I can hold my own. I will score goals. I will beat players. Maybe this is me, getting down to basics. I've never felt the fans were against me. It's a weird one. They gave me stick for the miss at Staines, but the worst piece of abuse I got was against Huddersfield, at home when we were 2–0 up. I was playing on the right of a three, so I could hear this guy giving it plenty. I just looked at him and thought, "Are you sure?" It's just as strange when you meet fans who tell you how brilliant you are. Am I? Am I that great?'

No, but he was growing into himself. The youth whose life caved in, for the umpteenth time, when he was released

by Northampton Town was beginning to make good judges doubt premature conclusions. Morison began to hold himself differently. He was easy to engage, and began to understand the mechanics of his trade. That occasionally involved shutting himself down emotionally. He began to speak for the group: 'The margins are so fine. The gaffer knows we need a player, maybe a couple more players. As a team we will work our nuts off. We won't stop. We feed off that never-say-die spirit.'

Jackett was in bed, stricken by a bad bout of flu, when Morison scored the first of Millwall's goals in a 4–0 replay win over Staines Town. The manager couldn't help himself, and watched live streaming of the game on the FA website on his laptop. Morison's two goals, which retrieved a half-time deficit in the following home match against Walsall on 12 December, maintained momentum. The finishes were crisp; the second, struck on the run into the top left-hand corner, was the product of a quick, cold brain.

Complete acceptance came six days before Christmas, when the snow had been cleared from the pitch at The Valley. The south London derby, like many, is dictated by pride, prejudice and presumptions of superiority. Charlton were chided for their condescension, their assumption that promotion, distance from the hoi-polloi of League One, was their birthright. But they were not reviled like West Ham. They were pitied for their emotional anaemia. The nicknames reveal all: to Millwall fans, West Ham are, simply, the Vermin. Charlton are derided as the Anoraks or the Trainspotters. It took a breathless match, shaped by a poor refereeing performance, to stimulate the bile ducts.

Morison was at its heart. He gave Millwall a two-goal lead within 24 minutes, beating two men on an icy surface for his first, converting the rebound from Frampton's shot, which had struck the crossbar, for the second. Welcome

Mike Jones, the referee relegated from the Premier League as punishment for his complicity in Sunderland's notorious 'beachball' goal against Liverpool. Jones appeared to be intimidated by the atmosphere, influenced by its inevitable stresses. His decisions alienated both teams.

Frampton felt he had won the ball, yet his challenge on David Mooney resulted in Charlton's first penalty. That was a hair-trigger decision, exposed as an error by TV replays. Jones' next big call, which led to the home team equalising through Deon Burton's second successful penalty, was crass. There was daylight between Jimmy Abdou's extended legs and Lloyd Sam, when Sam fell extravagantly. Abdou clutched his head in disbelief when he was sent off, and left the field in tears. The mistake was rectified, and the red card rescinded, on appeal, but too late to change the dynamics of a match that marched to the tune of Jones' Acme Thunderer.

Confusion between Smith and Martin, a minute into the second half, allowed Sam to set up Nicky Bailey, whose 25-yard drive put Charlton 3–2 up. Martin made amends by equalising in the 78th minute, but Morison's misplaced clearing header into his own net restored Charlton's lead. 4–3. Most teams would have buckled. Millwall fashioned another equaliser, two minutes into stoppage time, through Schofield's run and angled finish. Players, coaches and fans forgot the cold, and felt the love. Even Lewis Grabban decided he was not too sexy for the shirt. He celebrated his chance to share Morison's journey from scapegoat to saviour.

'All of a sudden he's looking', said Jackett, who had played the odds by giving Grabban his first League start of the season. 'Lewis is an athlete. He's got some power, but hasn't got the nous he needs in a wide position. Running free, up the middle, might work for him. I just don't know

what I'm going to get out of him from one game to the next. He's immature, but there are loads out there worse than him. When they are out of the team, and can't see the light, you see the worst of people. They down fucking tools. They don't do enough to earn another opportunity. Lewis is thinking, "It looks like we need a quick one up front, I'm quick". He fits the profile, the mobile type we need. Since we've not brought anyone in, he thinks he has a chance. It will be interesting to see what he'll do over the next couple of weeks.'

The doors to the Last Chance Saloon had swung open. The barmaid had daubed on a fresh layer of rouge, and the landlord was battering a hopeful tune on the piano.

Darkness on the Edge of Town

Christmas is the worst time. There's always an empty place at the table, a thoughtful gesture that emphasises the depth of loss. This year's emotional tipping point involved the present of a signed Millwall shirt, featuring personalised messages from the first-team squad. Margaret Mizen caught her breath when it was given to her by club sponsor Nicky Hayes, to pass on to Harry, one of her six surviving sons. 'That's fantastic – bless your heart', she said, her face scoured by suppressed grief. 'Our Harry was part of the attack. He witnessed his brother get murdered. Football has helped keep him sane.'

Life, for Margaret and Barry Mizen, is a search for sense in a senseless situation. They are good people, with the burden of a great cause. They find solace in the respect of strangers, promote good amid overwhelming evil, preach understanding and reconciliation rather than anger and vindictiveness. Nothing will bring back Jimmy, a son born half an hour before the FA Cup final kicked off on 9 May 1992. He weighed 10lbs 4oz that afternoon, grew tall and strong. He played rugby, served at the altar at the local Roman Catholic church, Our Lady of Lourdes, and helped Barry in his shop, mending shoes and cutting keys. He completed his GCSEs – he was to pass eight, post-humously – and was offered an apprenticeship by Leathermarket JMB, which runs social housing in Bermondsey and Borough.

The day after his sixteenth birthday he went out to buy his first lottery ticket. He bled to death, in Harry's arms, on the floor of the Three Cooks bakery, where they had stopped for something to eat. His jugular vein had been severed by a 1½-inch sliver from a glass dish, hurled at point blank range by Jake Fahri, a would-be rapper and school dropout who had bullied Harry for several years. Margaret Mizen rushed to the scene and fainted at the nightmare image that confronted her. Her only consolation was that Jimmy was not alone as his life ebbed away. Barry Mizen was haunted by the fear in his son's eyes.

He was murdered a fortnight before Rob Knox, a Charlton fan, was knifed to death protecting his brother. The south London derby was dedicated to their memories. Their teams played in shirts emblazoned with the message Street Violence Ruins Lives. Their parents, who wore their names on the back of their shirts, endured a poignant but painful occasion in the hope that it would be a catalyst for change. 'You wonder if people at the highest level in football realise the influence they have, to be a positive force for good', said Barry, with the quiet urgency of those empowered by tragedy. 'Most victims and their families have an allegiance towards a football club, however tentative. Imagine the power that could be harnessed if we speak with a single voice, and get the message across that we all have to change.'

Millwall and Charlton are close-knit clubs. Each offered practical support to the bereaved families within 24 hours of their son's murder. The charitable trusts, created in memory of Jimmy and Rob, don't seek football's money, although Neil Harris donated £1,000 from his testimonial fund to the Mizen Foundation. They want its authority, advocacy, and humanity. Sport is a reference point for a campaign that incorporates visits to schools, prisons, and

young offenders' institutions. 'I've got kids of my own', reflected Kenny Jackett. 'I feel humbled to be part of something like this.'

When a minute's applause was held at The Den to commemorate the murdered boy, the ground rang with the chant, 'There's only one Jimmy Mizen'. It was a uniquely powerful symbol of solidarity. 'There was such passion behind that chant', said Barry. 'This was one of their own. You get the salt of the earth at Millwall, ordinary, decent hard-working families. They are family-oriented people, coming from working traditions. I don't mean that in any patronising way, but there is a very strong community feel about the club. Look beyond the elements who would make you believe otherwise. There is such goodwill and respect towards us, as a family. It makes you feel the loss, so much more.'

A workshop at The Den, entitled 'It doesn't have to happen', was supported by the Mizens and Richard Taylor, father of Damilola, the ten-year-old who bled to death in the stairwell of a block of flats in Peckham, after being stabbed on the way home from school in 2000. It attracted 200 teenagers, who concentrated on the twin evils of gang violence and knife crime. The club's Community scheme was working alongside police in seven centres throughout the borough of Southwark. Football may exist on a diet of empty rhetoric, but it can command a mass audience.

'Something must grow from this', said Barry with affecting dignity. His wife instinctively followed his narrative: 'Don't you get the feeling the message is spreading out across the country? I do. People are saying, "We have had enough, we don't want to live like this any more". I need to know that when my children go out they are safe and well. We talk about knives and guns, but people will pick up any weapon. We share Jimmy's story, in the hope that

somewhere along the line young people will see there is a different way. We've met murderers, in prison. You look at some of them and they are lost young people.'

Football can often be found at the vortex of violence, which occasionally has a chilling symmetry. Fahri, sentenced to life with a minimum of fourteen years imprisonment, had been stabbed, reportedly with a pair of scissors, in Moorland prison, Doncaster, in November. His assailant, Sean Mercer, murdered eleven-year-old Everton fan Rhys Jones when he was walking home from football practice in 2007. The Mizens, organising a service for peace in Westminster Abbey, scheduled for early May, were plaintive voices in the wilderness. They met with Jermain Defoe, whose half-brother was murdered in similar circumstances to their son, but attempts to contact other members of the England squad failed 'because we got no further than their management'.

A sign above the desk of Ken Chapman, Millwall's security and operations advisor, reads: 'Football is the answer, not the problem.' He doesn't need a sociology degree to appreciate the scale of the problem. His background, as a senior police officer, involved dealing with the consequences of social dysfunction. Millwall's Community programme covers Lewisham and Southwark, where demographics are daunting.

Southwark has the highest teenage pregnancy rate in the UK, one in thirteen teenaged girls having children. It has one of the highest murder rates, eight per 100,000 according to 2008 figures. Unemployment rates, approaching 10 per cent, are the second-worst in London. Poor health and housing are endemic issues. Infant mortality rates are nearly double the capital's average.

More than 70 per cent of the population in some wards are black, or of ethnic origin. Father Owen Beament, the

club chaplain, has fifteen nationalities in his congregation. No fewer than 46 languages are spoken at the junior school nearest to The Den. English is the first language of 59 per cent of pupils in the borough. The next most widely used language is Yoruba, a West African dialect used by 6 per cent. Nearly 32 per cent of pupils in the borough qualify for free school meals. Almost 52 per cent of households do not own a car.

There is a significant Muslim population, around 8 per cent, but, for the football club, the Christian tradition holds sway. Father Beament is a bluff, cheerful man blessed with instant recall of Millwall teams, which punctuate 40 years as a fan. Installed as Canon of Southwark Cathedral in 1997, he was awarded the MBE four years later. He played a pivotal role in the creation of a Garden of Remembrance at The Den, so he had an alternative to scattering supporters' ashes on the pitch. As he said: 'It damages the grass, and the players don't like it much.' He insisted Bermondsey, the club's heartland, 'is like Wagner's music. Sounds worse than it is.'

Millwall's Anti Racism Trust had been renamed Millwall For All. It organised an international League featuring African, Bangladeshi, Portuguese and Brazilian teams, which it affiliated to the London FA. It piloted a SCARF (Schools, Citizenship, Anti Racism and Football) project to schools at either end of the social spectrum. Pupils aged between seven and sixteen addressed the recurring issue of racial tension, leavening discussions with an analysis of contrasting football cultures. 'We teach them about racism, what it is, and why it isn't good', said organiser Marc Elliott. 'We explain different parts of their heritage, increase understanding of other cultures in order to break down barriers. If there is no mixing of backgrounds there is no understanding. People are scared of what they don't know, so we show them what they have in common. They appreciate the

differences aren't all that big. All the work in the classroom is reinforced on the pitch.'

Elliott's efforts led to Millwall becoming the first Football League club to achieve the intermediate level of the Racial Equality Standard. The award assisted a subtle rebranding process, which beguiled the football authorities but alienated a vocal element of the club's traditional support. A 'no tolerance' approach to racism might work within The Den, but it cannot win cold hearts and closed minds. The launch of a club brochure, featuring suitably uplifting multi-racial images, was consumed by a mushroom cloud of cynicism.

The prevailing mood in the chat rooms was captured by the complaint: 'Anything the club seems to produce at the moment doesn't represent the people that go every week.' Before the chaps got too serious, someone shot back: 'Do you really want a catalogue full of balding, overweight, menacing looking blokes with a pint in one hand, traces of powder around their hooters and a Millwall tattoo on their calf modelling the latest home shirt and tracksuits?'

Harsh, but fair.

Political correctness was another indignity for men stranded on shifting sands. When Millwall staged a women's international, one sage suggested it 'was like watching a man with a feather duster strenuously cleaning. Wrong and shouldn't be happening.' Their traditional pubs around The Den, where Osama Bin Laden stickers were taped to urinals for freeform social comment, were closing, renovated as flats for City workers. The legends of such institutions as the Duke of Albany, of Skylark, Tall Tel, and early orders that began at 6.00am when there was a home game, had a sepia-tinged feel. They seemed as distant, yet as definitive, as the tales of Scotsmen from Morton's Jam Factory, in the summer of 1885, forming Millwall Rovers in the Islanders pub on the Isle of Dogs.

Allegiance was still passed down from father to son. First matches were afforded the reverence more usually associated with a child's first Communion. Yet the majority of Millwall's fans had moved away from the area, to Kent and the Greater London borders. Matches were acts of pilgrimage, unfashionable diversions in a sport that, at Premier League level, slavered over cash-rich, time-poor suburbanites. Tectonic plates were bumping and boring. The self-styled lovely, lovely geezers of the seventies and eighties were irritated by the antics of teenaged chavs in the East Upper Stand, pwoper nawty boyz who threw plastic bottles and issued threats in pidgin gangsta.

One question, which recurred with increasing intensity, was thrown over the generation gap like a rope bridge over a gorge: who, or what, was Real Wall? It was a key test of ideological purity whose answers lay in the eye of the beholder.

Real Wall never sat in assigned seats.

Real Wall were world-class pessimists.

Real Wall were old enough to have been there when the petrol bombs were flying, and life was lived in machine-gun bursts of exhilaration, fear, and manic humour.

Real Wall embodied a strange mixture of defiance and compassion.

Real Wall were the 487 who stood, soaked to the skin, at Exeter, the 200 who turned up on a freezing Tuesday evening at Carlisle later in the season.

Real Wall were the twenty or so who trekked to Torquay, eight days before Christmas, to see the kids win 3–1 in the third round of the Youth Cup, with goals by Kiernan Hughes-Mason, Grant Ludford, and John Marquis.

You pay your money, join the membership scheme introduced in the aftermath of the umpteenth riot, and take your choice.

As an outsider, I don't qualify. But, begging Real Wall's indulgence, for me, three men stood out. Frank Whipple, Bill Smedley and Pete Garston speak for themselves, across the generations.

Frank was 102, Millwall's oldest fan. He stole in to see his first game just after the First World War, when his father, a political refugee from the 1916 Easter Rising in Ireland, eked out a living as a gardener and gravedigger who earned an additional crust by laying out the dead. His mother was in service. The family lived in a single room, and existed on soup at a penny a bowl from the soup kitchen. Frank worked on steam wagons when he was fourteen, and eventually became a presser at a Jewish tailor.

He married Lily Kosky, a banjo player, tap dancer and singer who was one of Jean Murray's Merry Maidens, a popular variety act. His activism, a family trait, was rooted in the 1926 General Strike, and grew through the thirties, when he was involved in anti-fascist fighting in Cable Street. He devoured political and economic debate at the Jewish Friendly Society in the East End, and became a shop steward for the National Union of Tailors and Garment Workers. It didn't enhance his employment prospects.

When Lily died suddenly, a year after he retired, aged 68, he took over the care of his daughter Peggy, who had been born with severe special needs. She was 31, and had been kept hidden from the world. Frank took her to Millwall, to boxing matches and greyhound meetings. In 1984, they collected food from their council estate and drove to Shirebrook, in Nottinghamshire, to distribute it to families of striking miners. When he became wheelchair-bound, his son Harry, a 69-year-old cab driver, assumed the responsibility of getting him to The Den. Frank's definition of Real Wall? 'I'm an optimist – you have to be if you support Millwall.'

Bill Smedley was a mere stripling of 75. He oversaw the tunnel on match days, and had worked, free of charge, as a training ground aide for twenty years. He was Real Wall's version of the player liaison officers who rescue Premier League imports when they're lost on the London Underground, or fretting that their goldfish are swimming in the wrong direction. His litany of kindness ranged from running errands for players to ensuring that shirts were signed for grieving relatives of deceased supporters. They were worn in coffins, as a last act of devotion. The smaller the shirt, the more poignant the gesture.

He watched his first game in 1947, when he acquired the enduring habit of discretion, ducking and diving. Millwall players would congregate at the Southwark Park club after matches, get the taste, and adjourn to his Uncle Bill's house for a proper session. Sunday mornings, for the starstruck Bermondsey boy, involved stepping over the prone bodies of players, who slept where they fell. Smedley's hero, full back Len Tyler, was a sleek figure in a Crombie overcoat who flirted with a film career. 'They were working men in those days', he remembered. 'This club still means every-thing to people, in life or death.'

Pete Garston, at 45, faced the fight of his life. He had walked the wild side in his youth, built a substantial career in the telecoms industry, and had been the fans' representative on the board since 2006. He advised on ban-ning orders, used his knowledge of the terrace culture to ensure he wasn't a token presence at the high table. He distributed monthly reports, posting as Gordon Hill on one message board, in homage to the former Millwall winger, and as Yasser on another. His sign-off – 'English by Birth, Millwall by the Grace of God, Palestinian because I know what it's like to be homeless' – hinted at his own rite of passage.

When he was diagnosed with oesophageal cancer in July, Millwall's extended family rallied round his wife Linda, and sons Harry and Alfie, who had been named after club legends Harry Cripps and Alfie Woods. He underwent a thirteen-hour operation on 20 November, when the tumour was removed after surgeons broke his back ribs, collapsed a lung, and removed part of his stomach. He underwent a tracheotomy to assist his breathing following a chest infection, and spent six days in a coma. 'Real Wall, or what?' he wrote, as he recuperated. 'It was very touch and go and I was very frightened. Luckily, I had so much support. Without the family I wouldn't have coped.'

Boxes were being ticked in the boardroom, but lives were being influenced on the ground. Millwall delivered programmes in special needs schools and adult day care centres. Their coaches provided respite care for the parents of autistic children. Prison officers in Peterborough, Millwall fans, involved the club in a programme designed to improve reoffending rates. A Street League targeted unemployed youths, and pre-school children, as young as three, were drafted into the Cubz Kickers. More than 60 part-time coaches from the club fanned out to the estates that spawned them, role models in the fight against gang violence. Loo Brackpool, who became regional manager for the Football League Trust after spending six years heading Millwall's Community programme, set the parameters of influence with a simple statement: 'We have the power to change kids.'

She had only to look inside the head of Zampa, the Millwall mascot, for evidence of football's redemptive potential. Eighteen months earlier, Adam Scanlan was, at fourteen, a victim of the system. Pigeon-holed by his dyslexia, alienated by his struggle to read and write, he retreated within himself. He became sullen, uncommunicative, and

finally refused to get out of bed. He lay there for days on end, surrounded by posters of Millwall players like Paul Robinson and Alan Dunne, and withdrew into his computer games. He lived across the road from The Den, could hear the muffled chants of the crowd on match days, but inhabited a different planet.

His mother arrived in a state of desperation on Millwall's doorstep. Brackpool recognised that formal education was out of the question, and, in effect, adopted him on behalf of the club. In return she demanded a full working day in the Community offices. Adam passed his GCSE Physical Education examination. He qualified as a Level One coach, passed his Junior Football Organisers' course. He became a team leader, a role model for the disaffected. 'I used to think no one cared, no one understood me', he said. 'My job now is to find kids like me, and make sure they don't make my mistakes.' The transformation of an introspective adolescent into a confident young man was hidden only by his fake fur uniform. It softened even Brackpool, a strong-willed, strident woman. 'Adam has moved on', she said. 'His mum isn't the only one in tears when they see the difference in him.'

Dave King, who assumed Brackpool's responsibilities, understood the intensity of emotion. His son George was, to use the official euphemism, 'given extended study leave' by his school. To all intents and purposes, he had been dismissed as human landfill. For Dave, who oversaw Millwall's social inclusion projects, the danger signs were bathed in a halo of neon light: 'George had no confidence, no energy, no sense of self-worth. He spent the days attached to his bed. He was overwhelmed by the feeling life had given up on him.'

George enrolled on the Kickz programme, earned his coaching badges, and gained an NVQ Level Two in Activity

Leadership. He volunteered to work twelve hours each week on Millwall's disability programme. Again, a monosyllabic adolescent had become an eager, empathetic professional. He won a national award for outstanding personal achievement. He belonged. 'Football has given him his chance', said Dave. 'Young men are too conditioned to negativity. Give them an opportunity, and they will feel positive, about themselves and other people.'

For the players, the season of goodwill ended at the dressing room door. They trained as normal on Christmas Day, and travelled to Norwich in the afternoon. Family life was on hold – scout Steve Jones had organised his Christmas lunch for the first weekend in June, after the season had ended. A deceptive 2–0 defeat at Carrow Road, after an early kick-off that showed traditional contempt for the travelling fans, didn't stimulate the festive spirit. Wes Hoolahan justified Jackett's praise as League One's most effective player with the opening goal, but Millwall were in the game until a Lewis Grabban error allowed Grant Holt to add a second.

Boxing Day marked the halfway point of the season. Millwall were ninth, twenty points behind leaders Leeds, who had a game in hand. 'Not bad at all', reasoned Jackett. 'We're quite compact, close-knit. Not much wastage. It's a hard working group in a very competitive division. It's there for us in the second half of the season, should we make the right decisions. At my level the dividing lines are very thin. You have to bear that in mind. When you actually watch the DVDs and analyse the facts, not the shit that people talk about, it's close.'

There could be no seasonal sentiment in the decision-making process. Danny Senda sat outside Jackett's office before the final match of 2009, a home game against Bristol Rovers. Even his Christmas present from his girlfriend, a Lamborghini testing day, highlighted his predicament.

She was supporting him financially, as he sought to save his career. 'At 28, this is my last go', he acknowledged. 'I've been with the lads, during my rehab, but I have not been one of them. All I can do is try to prove myself to the gaffer, all over again.'

He was joined by Ashley Grimes, whose pallor was as grey as his chain-store, thin-lapelled suit. He had come from the dressing room, where he learned of his exclusion from the eighteen-man match day squad. 'Not on the bench', he confirmed, exhaling deeply. 'Funny old game ...'

'Chin up, son', said Senda, who had previous in that area.

They were disturbed by Adrian Wisson, who gave youth team striker John Marquis a sheaf of brown envelopes, containing the monthly wage slips, to distribute.

'When do we get paid this month?' Grimes asked, casually.

'Dunno. I've not been paid for five months', Senda replied with revealing haste.

'Oh, sorry mate', said Grimes, concentrating so hard on the screen of his mobile he had become saucer-eyed.

Jackett gave Senda dispensation to return to training with his first-team squad, who marked the occasion with a round of applause. He was a popular figure, admired for his persistence, but the group had evolved without him. He left, after a couple of reserve games, with everyone's best wishes.

Senda would have recognised the half-time tableau against Bristol Rovers. David Forde was typecast as an angry young man. 'Get your fingers out!', he yelled. 'You're fucking embarrassing us!' Forde had kept the game goalless with a brilliant reflex save that pushed a Chris Lines free kick onto the crossbar, and Jo Kuffour had struck the base of his left-hand post. Jackett sensed familiar failings

in central midfield and up front, where he replaced Jason Price with Grabban. The substitute was approached by Andy Frampton, who had evidently reconsidered the relative merits of carrot and stick: 'You've got a great strike, Grabs – use it.'

Frampton began the pivotal move of the match in the 62nd minute with a percussive clearing header, picked up by Dave Martin. The winger looked up and arrowed a 60-yard crossfield pass into the path of Steve Morison. He controlled it on his chest, lobbed it over Danny Coles, an advancing defender, and scored his seventh goal in as many games with a rasping, rising shot. The fluidity of the movement, and the finality of the finish, added to his burgeoning reputation. The game was in added time when goalkeeper Mikkel Andersen could only palm Morison's shot at retreating defender Pat Barrett. Under pressure from Grabban, he prodded the ball into his own net.

At last, something tangible under the tree.

As Neil Harris was acting as recruiting sergeant for a night out at the World Darts Championship, Scott Fitzgerald ushered a wide-eyed boy into the dressing room. It was another case of respite care, a moment of wonder away from a traumatised household. His sister was in the final stages of terminal cancer. No one batted an eyelid, but the fleeting satisfaction of victory, and subsequent study of the League One table, lapsed into irrelevance. It was a time to count blessings.

Price joined the fans scurrying to South Bermondsey station at the start of a journey that included two changes of train and a 70-minute flight from Gatwick to Leeds-Bradford. He paid for being conspicuous. 'I was getting hammered by some dickhead all the way to the station', he reported when he returned to training on New Year's Eve. 'The gaffer was good letting me go home. I had to fly because that

M1, man, is never-ending. We'd won 2–0, and they were giving me grief. I didn't see my son at Christmas, and I won't see him for another month. I tell you, if I was 22, 23, I'd be crumbling. All you hear is, "Price, you're shit."'

Yo, ho, ho.

Chapter 14
They Fought the Law

And the law lost.

Andy Ambler didn't need the caffeine hit, but he needed time to gather his thoughts. The transit passengers in Costa Coffee, on the northbound side of Toddington Services, just before junction 12 on the M1, didn't spare a second glance at a small, smooth-headed man, self-consciously cupping his hands around the mouthpiece of his mobile. He returned to his black BMW Z4, phoned his wife with the good news, and was soon accelerating in the fast lane, past the frozen tundra of a trout farm in the mid-Bedfordshire village of Tingrith.

I was in the passenger seat, oblivious to the schoolboy error of forgetting to register my car in the service station car park. Thanks to the highwaymen of CP Plus, who operated out of a post box address in Borehamwood, that cost me £50, or, to put it into context, the price of a couple of well-crafted sentences from Jim Sturman QC. Ambler made sure he was hands-free, and hit the speed dial. It was just after 9.00am in Wellesley Hills, thirteen miles west of Boston. He was quickly put through to John Berylson.

'This is embargoed until noon tomorrow, so we can't share', Ambler teased. 'But the FA find Millwall not guilty of all charges. West Ham guilty on two.'

A smile played on the chief executive's lips as he savoured his chairman's silence, which seemed to span aeons, rather than a couple of seconds.

'I'm tickled pink', said Berylson, proving that, subliminally at least, he was an Englishman abroad. 'That is absolutely fantastic. You were our point guard, Andy. Congratulations to you. I will have to speak to Jim, and to Ken too. Wow. This is a great day, something we must build on.'

Ken Chapman was understandably emotional when he heard of the success of Millwall's case. His son had begun chemotherapy, to combat testicular cancer, that day. Neil Harris was counselling the family, quietly yet effectively. Chapman is a measured individual, but vindication reached the deepest recesses of his soul. The confluence of personal and professional life justified his belief in human nature, and the wider value of his cause. He went as far as his character allowed, in condemning the jobsworths who had compromised The Job, to which he had devoted 33 years.

'Nobody pretends these matches are easy', he said. 'I am really conscious the decisions you make on the day will influence the next fixture. Not only from the view of policing, stewarding and security, but how it influences the hooligans. Can you imagine the next Millwall–West Ham match? The press, for a start, will throw what happened at Upton Park back in our face. It will be hyped up. It might be next season or in five seasons' time. But some people are going to have to face up to the consequences of what happened on that night. The sad thing is the hooligans think they won. They got publicity, and feel they had a victory against the police. Look at the websites. You have to get to grips with it. Young officers demand positive and professional leadership. I'll leave it to others to decide whether they got it that night.'

The FA panel, chaired by Richard Smith QC, accepted Millwall's Rule E22 defence, that they had used due diligence in the planning process. West Ham were found guilty of two of the four charges levied against them, and fined

£115,000, to be paid by 15 April. The alleged racist abuse of Carlton Cole and Jason Price was 'not proven'.

It was not the Met's finest hour. Scotland Yard had already been obliged to issue a public apology when six of 66 images issued, of individuals apparently involved in violence at Upton Park, were revealed as stills of actors from the hooligan-themed film *The Firm*. The most germane comment came in paragraph 16 of the FA's summary, which concluded: 'The Commission find it astonishing that any fixture, and certainly *this* fixture, continued without immediate and effective lines of communication between the two persons principally concerned with the order and safety of the entire crowd.'

Smith, the Rugby Football Union's in-house lawyer, had been joined, in a fourth-floor executive box at Wembley Stadium, by Paul Elliot, the former Chelsea defender, and Peter Hough, FA Council member for Dorset since 1988. Together, over three days, they recognised that the FA had not laid a glove on Sturman, who instantly put the verdict into a broader context: 'The FA have, in the past, proposed the abolition of the due diligence defence. That proposal has not gone away. Had abolition been accepted, Millwall would have been found vicariously liable, on a strict liability basis, for the misbehaviour of fans over whom they had no control. Many of those fans were in the ground illegally. That is a nightmare scenario for any club.'

Chapman was praised for being 'fair and informative'. The Commission accepted that 'both clubs, and perhaps especially Millwall, have exemplary histories in challenging the scourge of racism'. Ambler had lobbied assiduously, sharing a coffee with Sir Dave Richards, whose influence at the FA and Premier League gave the gesture the significance of a gentle kiss on a Papal ring. Millwall were supported by the Football League, and, most pertinently, Lord

Herman Ouseley, chairman of Kick it Out. He grew up in Peckham, began to follow Millwall as a boy in the sixties. As a young black man in the seventies, he was driven away from the game by violence and naked prejudice. His testimony was concise, compelling:

'Millwall Football Club have made enormous progress in making football a safer and more enjoyable spectator experience. The Den is no longer a no-go area for decent football fans. Instead Millwall FC have made it a no-go area for louts, yobs, bigots, racists, homophobes, and others who are hateful. Football fans do not learn their racism through football; they take it to football. As much as clubs have been doing to tackle effectively the worst excesses of anti-social behaviour associated with a minority of their fans, the problem has not gone away.

'It is well managed, better controlled, sensitively suppressed. There is an awareness of what is acceptable behaviour, and what will not be tolerated. The present social and economic climate, coupled with the rise of BNP activities, pose huge challenges, including a resurgence of unacceptable behaviour from so-called football fans. I know that Millwall have done as much as anyone, and more than most, to get rid of the louts and, while we must encourage them to do more, we must not penalise them for not doing what was not possible to do.'

Berylson demanded, through Sturman, an ex-gratia payment from the FA, to cover their costs. The price of innocence was, according to the barrister, 'a nonsense'. Yet Millwall had as much chance of redress as they had of signing Lionel Messi. Ian Watmore, the FA chief executive, recognised the inherent injustice of the system, but resigned before the conflicting factions on the FA Council could vote on his proposal that the process be 'de-lawyerised', to save money.

Chapman understood, the moment he was called to give evidence in that executive box: 'I just looked around and saw how much money was being spent on lawyers on something that could have been avoided by cooperation. I knew how much good that money could have done had it been used in the community. I actually believe in this football club and this community. It's a challenge but I have stuck by it. Most policemen become senior officers and clear off. I have never lived in the borough, but I have committed twenty years of my life here because I think it's a great place that doesn't get its fair share of the breaks. I want to make sure that this club, which means so much to so many people, gets a fair hearing.

'I was speaking to a senior military man recently, about soldiers from our part of south-east London. He told me: "They do cause you problems, but when push comes to shove they're the ones who win VCs." There is a certain amount of logic in that. Cornered, we all fight together. For all the chants of "No One Likes Us", we do care. There is a siege mentality. I have never had any pretensions, even when I was of senior rank. You can have any corporate philosophy you like, but at the end of the day an organisation is made by its people. Senior officers who sit behind fucking desks never get anywhere. You have got to get out there, be amongst it, take a bit of stick.'

The minority of Millwall fans who reviled Chapman for his vigilance ignored the chances he spurned to move to Premier League clubs, because of his emotional attachment to the club. He took his sons and grandchildren to The Den, just as he had been taken to Preston North End by his father, who had been taken to Sunderland by his father. Football squared the circle of life, whether you were a senior policeman or a former F Troop foot soldier with a nostalgic attachment to the set-piece battles of your youth.

Chapman acknowledged hooliganism's warped attractions, accepted that it had never really gone away.

'They have a terrific pride in their clubs and feel supporting through aggravation makes them more loyal. They are almost prepared to die for the cause. A lot of them grow out of it. A lot of them, old and valued clients in the past, have turned their lives around. They're really good supporters, who bring their families here. They have moved on. There are others who when they say, "Good Morning, Mr Chapman" I look at my watch to check it's morning, and to see I still have a watch. They seem to want to live in the past. They seem to want to reminisce.'

Sturman, addressing the issue in a book-lined meeting room at his chambers, had case histories to hand. One ringleader had embraced legitimacy in his early twenties and developed a successful business, which he sold in late middle age. Bored by material wealth and personal security, he embraced his old ways. 'He simply had time on his hands', Sturman said. 'In his late teens and early twenties he didn't have a particularly good job and no responsibilities. He settled down, raised a family, worked hard and ran a business. Every police officer in London knows him and he's well at it again. Extraordinary.

'You see them at every ground. I go to Spurs every week. I first got my season tickets the year before we lost to Blackburn in the Worthless Cup, as it then was. We ended up at Cardiff with my godson, who was aged about seven or eight, in amongst four or five people who were, ugh, coming up with a constant stream of bad language. After a couple of minutes my mate and I said, "Look, we've got a kid with us, can you tone it down? Even every other word would do." There was a blazing row. The stewards actually moved them, amazingly. I still see them at games. They're always stood just away from the action, on their mobile phones, sending texts, organising it.'

Sturman is rather proud of comparisons to Chelsea's fabled enforcer, Chopper Harris, and the links to football are not as specious as they sound. A successful barrister, like a prominent player, is a perfectionist, driven by private doubt and public image. The inquisitorial process involves the application of intellectual power, rather than tactical, technical or temperamental acumen, but the little things matter most. The game plan was a product of instinct and experience.

'I don't get a kick out of power. I want to win. The comparisons with football are valid, in that you have to prepare and prepare and prepare and prepare. I won't say you are driven by a fear of failure, but I have always thought the minute you lose that insecurity you become arrogant. With arrogance comes complacency. With complacency comes lack of preparation. If you don't prepare you are not going to win. I know the facts backwards, so that when a witness comes out with something brand-new, you can nail them. You need to have total recall. My guiding rule is that you are only as good as your next case, not as good as your last one. I have seen many people in my profession who rest on their laurels, and it's downhill from there. When you are doing a really big criminal trial there is often a feeling of loss, when it's all over. What am I going to do next? You have to draw breath and move on to your next challenge. I'll probably keep working until I keel over in court. I am very driven. It's very peripheral success, isn't it?'

Berylson already had another target in his sights. Graham Ferguson Lacey was blocking his attempts to raise a share issue to deal with the club's annual losses, in excess of £5 million. A former wallpaper salesman based on the Isle of Man, Ferguson Lacey had acquired a distinctive reputation as a corporate raider. He melted away from London in the seventies, when Birmingham and Midland Counties Trust,

his private holding company, collapsed. He subsequently found God, and, according to legend, adopted 'Graham' as a Christian name in homage to evangelist Billy Graham. He popped up in the popular prints, buying the world's largest Tyrannosaurus Rex skull, and operating on the margins of negotiations to free Beirut hostage Terry Waite. The Millwall connection was provided by former Charterhouse schoolmate Peter de Savary, a previous club chairman, from whom he purchased Land's End and John O' Groats.

Ambler had arranged a directors' box pass for him for that evening's FA Cup replay at Derby County. 'Look after him', Berylson ordered over the transatlantic mobile as we sped north. 'Despite our differences, I am not small minded.' The chairman's patrician façade was, however, being eroded. The balance between benefactor and businessman had lost its equilibrium. Berylson was reluctant to give Ferguson Lacey and Canadian Bill Shenkman, another dissident shareholder, the satisfaction of buying them out. The doomsday scenario, of forcing the club into administration, had been ruled out, but it remained in everyone's peripheral vision, as vaguely disturbing as a discarded Halloween mask.

'We are all in the same boat', Berylson reasoned. 'If the boat leaks we are all wet. If I want to take it private, there is a real simple answer. Take it into administration, wash them out. I'm secured on everything, they're gone. They sue me, they don't sue. Whatever. I have a perfected secured loan. There is nothing they can do. Frankly, they put the knife in my hands. They forced me to have these secured loans. That action has been open to me since the first day I lent the company money it has not had the capacity to repay. I don't take it personally, it's business, but the relationship is not great. He just won't tell me what he wants.'

The mental image of Ferguson Lacey as a swivel-eyed Gordon Gekko clone did not survive his arrival in the Brian

Clough suite at Pride Park. He was a ruddy-cheeked, bulbous man, a Dickensian throwback adept at social inanities. 'Cool, isn't it?' he said, as Ambler gave him a Millwall scarf and bobble hat to keep him warm on an evening when temperatures plunged to minus seven. Trevor Keyse, another director, was politeness personified. He enquired after Ferguson Lacey's sons, who had opted for the vicarious thrills of a place on the away end.

As ever, Millwall fans were preceded by their reputation. Police had earmarked the third-round replay as a Category C match, which enforced the closure of the Starbucks franchise at the stadium. The good folk of Derby stayed indoors, safe in the knowledge that they wouldn't be menaced by hooligans brandishing cold cups of skinny latte and Fairtrade tuna mayonnaise baguettes. The crowd, 7,183, was the lowest ever at Pride Park for a competitive first-team match. Derby were hit by a double whammy of Arctic weather and anxiety generated by a team mired in mediocrity towards the bottom of the Championship. The first prize in the half-time raffle was precisely £14.

Millwall should have won the initial tie, but conceded an equaliser within 110 seconds of Lewis Grabban's headed goal, from a Chris Hackett cross, four minutes into the second half. Derby manager Nigel Clough, feeling the weight of his father's legend, was edgy, compulsively confrontational. The unspoken assumption, that he would struggle to survive a defeat against lower League opposition, became increasingly insistent as Millwall dictated the pace and intensity of play. Ferguson Lacey retreated inside, twenty minutes from the end of normal time, which finished goalless. His grasp on events was tenuous. 'What is it, fifteen minutes each way?' he asked, when we dived in for a warming cup of coffee as the teams prepared for extra time. 'Do they stop if someone scores a goal?'

If they had, Steve Morison would have been a hero. Millwall had already hit the bar, through a 25-yard drive by substitute Scott Barron, when he gave them a 108th-minute lead. Goalkeeper Steven Bywater touched Morison's header, from a Hackett corner, on to the post, but the striker reacted fastest and lashed a follow-up shot in from close range. The travelling fans, a raucous contrast to home supporters, who resembled an ice sculpture, were in their element. They capered along rows of empty seats, reminding Clough: 'You're gonna get sacked in the morning.'

The Job Centre was denied another client six minutes later, due to a poor decision by Hackett. He forfeited possession, deep in his own half, with an illogically extravagant backheel. The ball was worked to the right wing, from where Steven Davies cut in to loft a shot over the advancing David Forde, who failed to make a single save in the ensuing penalty shoot-out. Bywater made one, diving to his right to beat away Danny Schofield's effort, which was well struck but at a comfortable height. Millwall were out, taunted by fresh injuries and their inability to hold a lead.

Morison deserved better. Phil Brown, who had come to watch him with his coaching staff, was on the M180, heading towards Hull, when the League One team were confronted with the consequences of failing to find him an adequate partner. The frustration ate away at Kenny Jackett as he sat, taut and silent, on the bus on the way home. He insisted that the screens, showing the Sky Sports News round-up, be turned off, and chewed ruminatively on cold pizza. Such was his mood, a culinary feast organised by Heston Blumenthal would have tasted similarly septic.

It was a sombre journey. Adrian Wisson spoke with a sense of almost paternal concern about Paul Wilson, his young assistant. He had attended two friends' funerals in as many days. The second was of Rifleman James Brown, eighteen.

He had been in Afghanistan only two weeks when, on 15 December, he was killed alongside Lance Corporal David Kirkness by a suicide bomber who had targeted a crowded marketplace near Sangin, in Helmand Province.

The incident, all too familiar, touched a raw nerve. Rupert Hamer, my newspaper's defence correspondent, had been killed three days earlier while he was embedded with the US Marines. He was the first British reporter to die in a war zone since another friend, ITN's Terry Lloyd, in Iraq in 2003. The vehicle in which Rupert was travelling hit an improvised explosive device near the town of Nawa. He was 39, with three young children. Phil Coburn, his photographer, had been repatriated earlier that day, and would lose his legs. Their tragedies stripped away the patina of cynicism that is attached to every news desk.

A pall hung over the *Sunday Mirror* office. Journalism is a desperately competitive business, with its fair share of mavericks and malcontents. But when there's a death in the family, we recalibrate. Reporters like me, from the toy department, are in awe of the resilience and sheer professionalism of men like Rupert and Phil. Rupert would never be so presumptuous, but the motto from Rifleman Brown's platoon – 'We lead, you follow' – was made for him, and his oppo. I did my best to share the impact of his loss, explain the nuances of what is occasionally a rough trade. 'Christ', said Jackett, as we discussed the moral and military logic of the Afghan conflict, 'what are we doing there?'

Not before time, the result of a game of football seemed obscenely irrelevant.

Chapter 15
Scouting for Boys

Scouting heaven is a night in Scunthorpe. There's a Travelodge, a KFC, Frankie & Benny's and a football ground, Glanford Park, within a minute's walk. The combination gladdens the heart, even if it hardens the arteries. Avoiding the alternative, falling asleep at the wheel in the early hours on a dark, endless motorway, is worth £29, the cost of a room booked a week in advance. Both Jamie Johnson and Steve Jones have snapped awake and struggled to control a momentarily weightless car, edging across the carriageway. Little things remain in the mind, like the eerie sense of calm which enveloped them, and the sudden clarity of the CD player. It's the price of 60,000 miles on the road each year, watching up to 200 matches.

They have different roles, but are members of a distinctive tribe. Jones scouts impending opposition, Johnson surveys potential recruits. Each is denied the luxury of ambivalence. Their judgements must be measured, informed, accurate. They must justify the trust placed in their ability to assess talent, temperament and tactical dexterity. For Johnson, in particular, the January transfer window was Showtime. As chief scout, he was under pressure by proxy. 'Got us a striker yet?' asked Neil Harris, as he bumped into him in the corridor leading to the training ground dressing room.

'Yeah. He's young, quick, scores goals, all for £150 a week', Johnson replied through a rictus grin. 'I get the feeling everyone is looking at me', he admitted, quietly. He

worried he was in danger of becoming one-dimensional, a slave to his mobile, his database, his DVD collection, and his network of contacts. His vow to join a table tennis club to broaden his range of interests, and tackle the burger bulge, was wildly optimistic. He ate on the run, learned to live with disrupted sleep patterns, and flirted with boxercise classes. When he did stay overnight in a hotel, he ensured he covered four matches, within 24 hours, to make it cost-effective.

Johnson knew, everyone knew, that the missing pieces in Millwall's jigsaw were an assertive central midfield player and a quick, dextrous forward. His targets had been defined and refined over the previous three months. The probability was that they would be young, on loan from the fringes of a Championship squad. Plan B, which ran concurrently, was confirmed at 8.00am on New Year's Eve in Kenny Jackett's office. The pair pored over the squad list of every Football League club, and assessed reserves at each Premier League club. Done poorly, it was a trawl through the legion of the lost. Approached intelligently, it was a search for the undercooked, under-rated bargain.

Jackett was looking for 'a good nick'. That was his description of Danny Schofield, bought from Yeovil for £25,000 after he had initially been asked £300,000. Some suggestions were buried alive – 'He's got a new agent? Needs a new fucking heart, more like' – others were resuscitated by their reputations. Bournemouth striker Brett Pittman was coveted, but would cost 'top dollar'. The hint that Theo Robinson was surplus to Huddersfield's requirements grabbed their attention. A long-standing interest in Southend's Lee Barnard was ended by the scorn of a supercilious agent, who told Jackett to 'move on, you can't afford him'.

Southampton were distorting the market. They spent £1.2 million on Crystal Palace defender José Fonte,

recruited three other loan players, and then agreed to treble Barnard's wages. While Southampton enjoyed a week's warm weather training in preparation for their visit to The Den, Millwall's brains trust got busy. Johnson crammed six games into four days, while Jackett worked the phones. They had known each other for ten years, and dovetailed well. Each had his own range of contacts. Mutual respect was natural, unforced, despite the manager's authority.

Jackett decided against returning to Tottenham for John Bostock, or Jake Livermore, who had regressed during his loan spell at Derby. 'He looked sluggish in their reserves', Johnson reported. 'They don't bother, do they?'

Jackett grimaced: 'They can come to us and play. Something's missing in reserve team football. Young players lack the focus they would have in the first team. They have all the talent in the world, but it's sometimes hard to judge.'

Their attempt to sign Carl Baker, a goal-scoring midfield player stranded at Stockport, ended when he joined Coventry on a 2½-year deal.

The sight of Zak Whitbread, training with the youth team following successful rehabilitation from his hip operation, signalled the inevitability of his departure. Zac Efron, the tweenybopper's delight, had more chance of making the USA's World Cup squad. Whitbread's proposed move to Huddersfield broke down when they wanted to take him on what amounted to a month's trial. Norwich were £23 million in debt, but quickly agreed to pay £125,000 for the defensive cover he represented. A penny more and Millwall would have been obliged to pay half the fee to Liverpool, his original club. 'A good one for everyone', said Jackett. 'A great move for Zak, and for us there's a big wage off the budget for the second half of the season.'

That gave him leeway in contract negotiations, and cleared a small corner of his brain. 'Ipswich isn't a bad

club to watch', he mused. 'Everything's up in the air there.' Liam Trotter, discarded by Roy Keane after the first twelve games of the season, was a live one. He had already coped with the unique challenge of playing for Millwall, in a short loan spell soon after he turned professional with Ipswich, in 2007. He impressed against them, for Scunthorpe, in the 2009 play-off final.

At 21, he had filled out what was once a spare frame. Broad-shouldered and physically imposing, he had the strength to break up play, and the intelligence to use the ball wisely. He was a mature, settled character who still lived in the family home. He didn't enter the Academy system until he was sixteen, and lacked the pretensions of those who have been hot-housed from the age of eight. Johnson instinctively liked what he saw when Trotter scored in a 3–1 reserve team win at Luton Town on 17 November. It was all he had to go on, because he hadn't played since. 'Most of the scouts there were slagging him off', he recalled. 'That's when you need to back your own judgement. You are putting your reputation on the line every time you say yes or no and you learn, early on, to trust yourself. It's not rocket science. You've got to get in better than what you've got. If you get it wrong, they sit there, and take up your budget. Sometimes you will see something others don't see, good and bad. Football is about decision-making. No one makes the right decision every time, but they need to do so more often than not.'

His judgement calls were informed by his weaknesses as well as his strengths. Johnson was once a talented young footballer with an attitude problem. He was a prized prospect at Oxford United 'when they were good', but went through the motions and saw his career peter out at Torquay, following a spell at Norwich. 'I had all the ability in the world, but I was lazy. I just drifted away from the game.

If I'm honest, I hated football. I wouldn't even watch it on telly. I felt I'd been put under massive pressure from an early age. You have to let kids enjoy it. When you get older, and the pressure kicks in, you have to remember why you play the game. If you are just doing it for money, you end up coasting. That's why I didn't want any part of it. I never touched a ball for two years.'

He came back, literally, for beer money. He earned £70 a week playing for Egham Town in the Isthmian League, and would 'spend most of it in the bar before going home'. He worked in the family greetings card business with his father Mel, who scouted for Jackett when he was at Watford, but was rudderless before a stranger had the foresight to gamble on his bloodlines. Geoff Lee was Huddersfield's chief scout, knew of his father, and offered Jamie a job, for mileage expenses only. 'My body was giving up on me', Jamie recalled. 'I was always injured, and so I thought, "Let's give it a go".'

He spent three years at Huddersfield, learning his trade, before moving to Sunderland, where he spent another three years scouting the south of England. He rejected the chance to join Jackett at Swansea because he couldn't afford to go full-time, but re-evaluated his career options when Damien Comoli, who had taken him to Spurs, was sacked. At 37, he had spent a decade exorcising his demons. When Jackett called, 24 hours after he had become a victim of the purge at White Hart Lane, Johnson had spoken to his wife, and was ready to restructure his life.

Self-awareness was essential in an enclosed world: 'I understand the kids' mentality. So many think they are better than they are. Society's blame culture is even more apparent in footballers. First-teamers in the reserves should be absolutely pissing it, but they haven't the character to cope. I know it's difficult. We've all been in games where

we feel 'I shouldn't be here', but that failure to deal with reality is why I'm sat here, behind this desk, instead of being behind the wheel of my Aston Martin. It's because I didn't pull my finger out.

'Scouting is like any business: someone burns you at the beginning. When you're new you tell someone something, a snippet of information. It goes around and you think "shit". It's such a cut-throat business, because there aren't a million fantastic players around. We've all got budgets and the job is results-based. I'm not going to tell people who I'm watching. If you do, then you're an idiot. You tell people what you want to get out. As you get older, you learn to stand back and listen. People love to gossip, and tell you things they don't mean to.

'There are a lot of chief scouts, the old school, who don't really want to go to games. You've got to commit to the job, work all hours God sends. If you've played, it certainly helps, but it's not essential. It's what your eyes see. You have to process that information, relate it to what your club wants at that particular time. Football is changing. You have to look for an athlete, as well as a footballer. You then have to ensure the player fits into your club culture and system. I'm looking for a Millwall-type, with the right attitude. Someone with ability, who can't be bothered, wouldn't work.'

Trotter signed on a month's loan, with a view to staying for the rest of the season, in time for Southampton's visit on 16 January. It was an educational experience, a revealing reintroduction to Millwall's siege mentality. Southampton's sense of entitlement stirred tribal passions, and The Den reserved a traditional welcome for their manager Alan Pardew. Courageously in the circumstances, he was dressed for the TV studio rather than the dugout. His sin, of self-satisfaction, was compounded by his association with Charlton and West Ham.

Southampton had the gaucheness of the nouveau riche. They couldn't be bothered to hide their impatience to flee the mudflats of League One. The self-imposed handicap of a ten-point penalty was seen as a minor inconvenience by chairman Nicola Cortese, who, six months earlier, had been managing the finances of billionaires at the Banque Heritage in Geneva. He had previously overseen the sports business desk at Credit Suisse, where clients included Silvio Berlusconi, but had no practical experience of football.

Ominously for Pardew, Cortese had become preoccupied by an online match predictor. When he projected Southampton's results until the end of the season, they always made the play-offs. The virus of unfeasible ambition and ignorance had claimed another unsuspecting victim. As he told an interviewer: 'On Saturdays I can't sleep. I get very nervous. I wake up at 5.00am and can't eat before the match. My hands feel icy cold – it's the only time. Normally they are warm. It's terrible.'

Millwall should have chilled him to the marrow. Lewis Grabban missed four good chances before he was substituted by Harris midway through the second half, and Kelvin Davis made a world-class save to defy Schofield. Jackett, an increasingly urgent figure on the edge of his technical area, had a sixth sense that Southampton would score. One statistic, gleaned from his diaries, screamed in his subconscious as the match entered added time: Rickie Lambert had an average of six shots per game against his teams.

This time it took him 93 minutes to fashion his first shot, following Paul Robinson's concession of a free kick, 30 yards out. The three-man wall did as it was ordered, shuffling within eight yards and jumping when the ball left Lambert's right boot. It flicked off the top of Liam Trotter's head, and sped in a parabola into the far corner of the net. Game over.

Or so Southampton thought.

From the restart the ball was worked to Trotter, on the right side of the Southampton defence, twenty yards inside their half. He brushed aside one challenge, then another, and had the composure to look up and adjust his body shape before striking a low-angled drive past the diving Davis.

When he returned to earth, Joe Gallen caught a glimpse of Lucie, his partner, in the crowd. She had turned to the away end and was flashing V signs with both hands. 'I tell you, it gets to you, this Millwall lark', he laughed, when he recalled her defiance at Monday morning's debrief. Tony Burns summoned another image, that of Southampton defender Ben Harding ordering the kit man to cut a stray piece of lace from his boot. 'If he was my player I'd have smacked him', he said. 'I'm not having that.'

Johnson had done his work well. Trotter obviated the need to spend £300,000 on another long-term target, Southend's Alan McCormack. 'I thought he was going to die but he came on strong', said Jackett. 'We are not going to buy the finished article, but I can see some development there. There's something to work with, over the next couple of years. Southampton would have been too much, physically, for Lairdy. Trotter will contribute in both boxes.' Burns agreed: 'I'd sign him, gaffer, and tell him to win that tackle in midfield.' Richard Shaw added: 'There's more to come. He adds steeliness to the group. The togetherness and spirit is fantastic – most teams would have gone under.'

Jackett estimates that an effective central midfield player can add 5 per cent to a team's potency. The sort of striker he sought could improve his side by 10 per cent. Joe Garner fitted the bill, but Nottingham Forest wanted to recoup a decent proportion of the £1,140,000 they had paid Carlisle eighteen months earlier. He was, literally, out of Millwall's League. So was Lee Hughes, who had dropped down to

League Two in return for £7,000 a week and emblematic occupation of Notts County's hall of mirrors.

Jackett appreciated his qualities as a footballer, but Hughes was compromised by his past. He had rehabilitated himself after being sentenced to six years' imprisonment for causing death by dangerous driving and leaving the scene of an accident, but Millwall fans were not noted for their libertarian leanings. They also made use of an effective intelligence network. When rumours spread of an approach, the challenge to the club's culture was spray-painted across the chatrooms:

'I go with my boys, aged 15 and 13, but I might have to chuck it if we sign this slag.'

'He can fuck right off. If this is our big signing I feel like jacking it in. After going to Millwall 41 years I'm deadly serious. I'm really hoping we are not stooping so low.'

'I would never go to a game, even after he left.'

The counter-arguments were hardly pearls of philosophical wisdom, delivered from the moral high ground:

'I would sign Peter Sutcliffe if he scored 20 goals a season for us.'

'He knows where the goal is. This is football. It is about business and pound notes.'

'Millwall fans having morals, and getting in a fluster about signing someone like that? Fucking Hell, something's changed.'

Realpolitik ensured that Jackett's notional signing never got beyond a brief conversation with his chairman and chief executive. As Gallen reflected: 'Imagine him playing for us at The Den, with chants of "Murderer" ringing around the ground …' But the vacancy needed to be filled. Grabban's psychodrama took another twist during a fortunate 1–0 win at Oldham, where he was taken off fifteen minutes after coming on as a 58th-minute substitute for Harris, who had converted a bizarre penalty. The ball was upfield, 50 yards away, when linesman David Storrie spotted an off-the-ball scuffle between Oldham captain Sean Gregan and Morison. The Millwall bench shared the general sense of bemusement. It was only when the coaches replayed the DVD of the game, which captured Gregan throwing Morison to the floor, rubbing his face in the mud and seizing him by the throat, that they understood.

Grabban was not to be appeased. He had suffered the ultimate humiliation, and sought an explanation before training on Monday morning. 'Ooh, that's an angry knock', said Jackett, who heard Grabban at his office door while he was overseeing a staff meeting in the coaches' room. 'I think I've got quite a few angry knocks in me today.' He sent word that he would see Grabban later, and turned his attention to Jones' analysis of Southend, the following day's opponents.

The scout dispensed information in bite-sized chunks: 'Cuts inside, technically poor … quick, comes in on right foot … isolated, but can bring others into the game … possession-based, and no long throws.' He built a picture of a club in stasis, and a team in transition. 'They've given up on the season a bit', he said, summarising a state of mind that would end in Southend's relegation to League Two. The consequences of a sustained struggle to survive were all too apparent.

Jones empathised, because he's another Everyman. Released by Southampton as a trainee, his career effectively ended two weeks after Harry Redknapp signed him for Bournemouth. He landed awkwardly after going up for a header in pre-season training, wrecked his cruciate ligaments, and, at nineteen, was consumed by his sudden insignificance: 'I knocked about in non-League, where I could cheat a bit. Ability gets you through against lesser players. I'm not proud of that, especially because of my role as a coach later in life.'

He 'ducked and dived', worked on building sites, and eventually ran Gillingham's Centre of Excellence, where he was a slave to the club's dysfunctional nature. He began scouting, looked after age group teams and the reserves. He drove the minibus, swept dressing rooms, and even cleaned players' boots. When Gary Penrice offered him the chance to become Plymouth's European scout, he left without a backward glance. Penrice recommended Jones to Jackett when he moved on to Leicester.

'If I get it wrong and we lose, my reputation suffers', Jones admitted. 'My job is different to Jamie's in that I'm asked to assess a team's strengths and weaknesses, rather than a specific individual's. I try to look at things tactically, and psychologically. I look for a player's reaction when he's subbed, or when he does something wrong. I look for the group's reaction to things they have no control over, like the weather, crowd, or referee's performance. A working knowledge of the Division is paramount. In League One a lot of players have still got that bit of quality, but they're falling away. The lower you come down the harder it is, the more physical you have to be. For a lot of people, football is a social event. This is our job, our livelihoods.' It was a dark, cold morning. Rain sluiced from a stormy sky, and Jackett mirrored the mood. He quickly dispensed with Grabban

and Ali Fuseini, whose immaturity was highlighted by his peripheral presence in the dressing room. 'At the end of the day, they've got a contract', he said. 'It's my choice who I pick, and who I don't. Anybody who comes up my stairs has to accept that as part of football.' He was similarly blunt about Marcus Bignot, who was finalising his compromise agreement with Andy Ambler, and would sign for Kidderminster Harriers: 'He had a lot to say for himself, but in the end even the lads stopped listening.'

Barry Fry, however, was all ears. By noon, Jackett had persuaded him to change his mind and release Shaun Batt from Peterborough, on loan, for the rest of the season. He put Millwall's money, a modest sum, where Johnson's mouth was. The chief scout had watched Batt in three reserve matches before confirming his recommendation. The striker was excellent against Norwich in September, where he scored twice and harried the experienced Gary Doherty, and against Southend in October, where he scored and won a penalty. Against Luton, in Johnson's final check call, on 20 January, he was 'woeful'.

Johnson trusted his instincts, and closed his ears. Other scouts at Kenilworth Road saw Batt as uncoordinated, ineffective. They were polite, but privately peddled conventional wisdom that Johnson had bought a pup. 'I could tell what they were really thinking', he said. 'Normally, when you sign a player, everyone queues up to say, "Nice one". Here they were saying, "So you've taken him then?" I just had to blot Luton out of my mind, and concentrate on the good things I had seen.'

Batt folded his 6'4" frame into his Peugeot 307, and introduced himself to his new team-mates as they were finishing their afternoon strength and conditioning session. The only tracksuit they could find for him was a size too small. His arms were too long for the standard sweatshirt,

but he exuded enthusiasm when Jackett called him into his office the following evening, to confirm whether he felt ready for a rushed debut. 'I know you've been in the car for a couple of days', he said. 'It's up to you.' Batt's eyes widened: 'I've come to play', he insisted earnestly.

Every dressing room has a player who rarely deletes the expletive. Millwall's version, Tony Craig, was on the prowl. 'Expect the fucking best out of each other', he yelled. 'Football isn't about being nice to each other. Fuck that. If someone is not doing the job, fucking tell them.' The coaches smiled instinctively. 'I'm a fan', said Burns. 'I love people who stand up in front of others and shout about how much they want it.' Jackett understood: 'Sometimes you don't see enough heart, or hunger. Attitude is important, and I like them roaring.'

There was not, in truth, much to shout about. The game was edgy, fractured. Southend did their best to fragment play, and enraged the crowd with exaggerated responses to Millwall's aggression. They were disorientated by Batt's pace, but he pursued the ball with the desperation of a commuter chasing the last bus home. 'Fuck me, we've got a music hall act', said a disembodied voice, sending a shiver of laughter through the lower tier of the East Stand.

Millwall took the lead, four minutes into added time at the end of the first half. Batt could have been penalised for a foul, and there were understandable claims for offside when Schofield applied the finishing touch to Jack Smith's scuffed shot. Jackett's love affair with McCormack was over – 'He's throwing himself about, and lying on the floor, moaning' – but the essence of his half-time team talk was directed at Batt and Morison: 'You're frightening the shit out of them. Let's put them away. We go for them. The chances will come. They don't like coming here. We have to use that. Drive on.'

The sour-faced season ticket-holder, who sat three rows behind the overspill area for the dugout, had made his mind up halfway through the second half. 'Get that Batt off, Jackett!', he screamed during a lull in play. 'He's going to cost us the game. He's fucking useless.' At that precise moment, Trotter was threading a pass to Batt, midway in the Southend half. He advanced with the ball, arms swinging like a tightrope-walker, as he cut inside a covering defender and scored with a deliberate shot, angled across the goalkeeper. His critic was, of course, one of the first on his feet, doing the dervish 'Eio, Eio, Eio' dance. Scott Fitzgerald flicked a thumb in his direction and said: 'That sums Millwall up. This is the best place in the world to play when you're winning, and the worst when you're losing.'

Jackett was in reflective mood as he analysed the night's results in his office. Millwall had returned to the play-off places, but he was looking long-term, at the potential of his new recruits: 'They are two good kids. They're not the edgy, chippy sort. They want to improve. They are where we are. I can't go out and buy a Barnard. I've seen something I can work with, bring on. I like Batt's attitude. He's got that urgency Grabban lacks. We can make something out of him.'

Relief offered Johnson momentary distraction. He worked meticulously through fifteen circulars, sent by clubs or agents, peddling players. The right-hand drawer of his desk contained piles of CVs, which ranged from one-page semi-literate scrawls to 30-page professionally presented pleas for a trial. All were given the courtesy of a reply, and the privilege of being denied false hope. Johnson also pored over a DVD of a friendly between Brazil and Estonia, whose players were being offered, on short-term deals, for £1,500 a week. He was unimpressed:

'It's about building up knowledge, forming stories in your head. Ninety nine out of 100 things you are sent are

a waste of time. Every agent has got the best player. I've never had anyone phone me up and say, "He's not quite good enough for you". The Estonian project will be a no. They're not better than what we've got. Hard work is number one. I know it's a cliché, but you don't always get that from a foreign player. They come from a culture where no one is allowed to tackle them. They come over here, see people coming at them studs up, and say, "No thank you very much".'

With that, we were off to Frankie & Benny's in Northampton. Representatives of Championship clubs were given a place in the official car park. Millwall were expected to pay £3 to park with the punters on wasteland at the edge of the Sixfields Stadium complex. Johnson wolfed down his over-cooked pasta and considered the night's main course, a sallow-faced Accrington Stanley midfield player named Robert Grant. He had been identified as 'one to monitor' by Millwall's northern scout.

Johnson exchanged small talk with his namesake Peter, Bristol City's chief scout, and Lil Fuccillo, who was not to survive the season in a similar role at Swansea City. He quickly ascertained that their priority was Accrington's Michael Symes, an unremarkable centre forward in what was an unremarkable team. For a match between play-off contenders, the standard was poor. Northampton won 4–0, thanks largely to Adebayo Akinfenwa, a striker with the girth of a pub landlord and the speed of a steamroller. The Accrington Ultras, who chanted 'We came in a taxi', had cause to rue their loyalty.

Grant lacked physical presence, made the occasional intelligent run in to out, but touched the ball only five times in the first half. He changed positions three times as Accrington shifted between 4-4-2 and 4-3-3, but lost focus, with the rest of the team, as the game ebbed away. The

other scouts, predominantly middle-aged men in quilted coats, were more interested in picking up gossip about Steve Morison. 'I'm starting to get people asking me what he's like', admitted Johnson. 'That's dangerous. The last thing we need at the moment is to lose him.'

Peter Johnson and Fuccillo left with half an hour to go. We headed for the exits with eleven minutes remaining. It was just another night on the road. When Jackett called about Grant on the way home, he was told: 'Decent brain, but not a night to judge him.' Johnson was already attuning himself to another run of matches, starting with Manchester United reserves, and ending with Nuneaton Borough.

'It's good when you have a manager who understands scouting. Ken gets out there, sees the games. The best ones are when you go to watch your man, find he's crap, and someone unexpected catches your eye. In my business, the noes are easier than the yeses. But I'd much prefer one of my noes to be a yes, than one of my yeses to be a no. That costs you.'

Simple, really.

Chapter 16
Show me the Money

This is how it works.

The manager counts the pennies with the chief executive and the chairman. They consider cash flow forecasts, income streams, resale potential, and the intrinsic value of the player to the club. The agent stalks the player, who, if he's a sentient being, takes the agent's sales pitch to his family or a trusted friend. A word is dropped in the ear of a compliant reporter, on condition of anonymity, in the hope of kick-starting an auction. Rival clubs whisper sweet nothings, which occasionally approximate to the truth. Fans take the bait, chunter on about a lack of loyalty or the club's lack of ambition. The player's wife, or significant other, worries about the children, who cry when they're forced to find yet another set of friends. She tries to avoid screaming at the estate agent, who calculates repeat commission behind a painted smile. It all comes together during two annual transfer windows, in football's version of the Hadron Collider, the particle accelerator that boffins promise will reveal the secret of the universe.

At Millwall the conversation goes something like this:

Player X arrives in the manager's office. His agent carries a metaphorical pooper scooper, but prays Kenny Jackett will provide the kitty litter, in the form of legal tender, to soak up life's little misunderstandings.

Deep breath. Deceptively casual, world-weary, or see-you-Jimmy aggressive, according to taste: 'There's more money elsewhere in the Division.'

The manager sucks his teeth, studies his notes as if they're hieroglyphics written on priceless papyrus. 'It ain't here. Pound notes are going to be difficult. We've got a ceiling, and we're not going to go above it.'

It's not the sort of negotiation you can prepare for by playing internet poker, or studying Sun Zhu and *The Art of War*. It's eyeball-to-eyeball, mano-a-mano, mud wrestling. It's enough to make TV's cartoon survivalists, like Bear Grylls, consider the alternative delights of basket-weaving.

On this bare midwinter morning, David Forde was first in. He smeared honey on two slices of brown toast and tried to digest his situation. His contract talks were proving difficult. The challenge of finding the right balance, between being a breadwinner and a good pro, had ambushed him in the wee small hours. He was a key player, the squad's only ever-present. He worked hard, and listened when his coach Tony Burns transmitted the lessons of a lifetime in the game. Yet, even inside the forcefield of his dominant personality, he felt exposed, alone: 'I was lying there in bed this morning, thinking there are no friends in football. It's true. There's no one to whom you can really say, "C'mon, I'm in a hole here, help me out". People use words like honesty and integrity, but you don't see a lot of it about. This has been going on for four months. I've played nearly 100 games on the spin and I deserve a bit of respect. I feel like battering the walls. You have your agent, and the gaffer, talking and you feel out of it. It's a distraction. My game is about having that edge and it does get jeopardised. I try not to let that happen, because if you are 5 per cent off it has an impact. This is why I'm looking at that business degree on the Open University. As a pro, you obsess about things. Life can close in on you. Everything can seem too important. You need something else to think about.'

Millwall's contract strategy had been mapped out before Christmas. It would be a three-month game of cat and mouse. Chairman John Berylson addressed the dynamics of the duel from a businessman's perspective: 'I like David Forde a lot, but things have gotten quite sticky. I understand individuals have to make as much as they possibly can, but the economics have changed. I have to worry about the long-term welfare of the club. Everyone is a seller, no one a buyer. The success of the team has a lot to do with its character. We know who the heart and soul is, and would like to keep that core together. There are a number of individuals who have played beyond their apparent ability and should be rewarded for that. In truth it may not be until February or March that they hear about it, but we already know who we want, and who we don't want.'

Chief executive Andy Ambler was rationalising costs across the club. He was talking to Jackett about withdrawing the reserve team from its League, instead staging training-ground friendlies for fringe players and emerging youngsters. The idea made sense on a number of levels. A 3–1 defeat at Brentford, on a gluepot surface, was the reserves' first game in three months. There was no continuity of competition for anyone outside the first team, which, with the return of Darren Ward and Tony Craig in defence, was beginning to acquire the solidity that signals stability. A 1–0 win on a frozen pitch at Brighton, courtesy of Steve Morison's eleventh goal of the season, suggested Millwall were shifting up the gears.

Ambler had an accountant's eye for the bottom line, but was not blind to the game's social dimensions. He gave up his free time to the Bobby Moore Foundation, volunteering to help build a community school in the remote Brazilian village of Bandeira, where illiteracy rates were 38 per cent. It gave him perspective, a break from simple yet daunting

mathematics. Give a senior player at The Den another £300 a week and five others will demand parity. That adds up to £90,000 extra on the wage bill, the equivalent of an additional squad member.

'Players sometimes get their heads filled with agents' nonsense', Ambler reflected. 'There's no problem with a modest increase – someone like Robbo, for instance, has been a good servant of the club and has the responsibility of captaincy. But players have got to get real. The money is not there. There will be a correction in the summer. Players have to take into account that agents are feeding off scraps. Some of them won't have earned a penny in this window. They're advising players to do nothing now, and are telling them they'll get them a good deal when they're out on a free in the summer. They're being naive. It's amazing how much faith players put in these people.'

Paul Robinson's personality has been sculpted by circumstance. He was released from the Watford Academy because coaches feared that his knees wouldn't be strong enough to survive the percussive punishment of his trade. Now, thirteen years later, he was a diligent professional, a level-headed leader. His life was dedicated to the game. He listened to his body, ate organically, took power naps in the afternoon and maintained a personalised stretching programme. At 28, this was a key contract. He had already begun looking to the future and a possible secondary career in the media, or in sports science. His perspective had been changed by the arrival of children, Ella and Isabel. They were three and one, 'a great age. You have no time to be grumpy and mope around the house after a bad day. But, at times like this, you do dwell on things.'

He signed a new contract, taking him to the summer of 2013, with a palpable sense of relief. As he said: 'I have grown up here as a footballer, and as a person. This is a club

like no other.' On the same day Neil Harris, symbol of that oneness, agreed an extension of his contract to the summer of 2012. His sparring session involved interest from North Queensland Fury, in Australia's A League. 'There is pressure, all round, when it's contract time', he acknowledged. 'It kicks in when you go home and deal with the questions: "Has the manager had a word yet? Are we going to have to take the kids out of school? Will we have to move?" The whole family is subjected to uncertainty. I can handle it, because I know I'll find a club, but it's good to know where we are.'

Jackett's respect for Harris had grown as he began to understand the man. They spoke of a transitional role as player-coach, but he sensed the striker's career would progress naturally. There was no need for him to rush, to set false timescales. 'Neil is an iconic figure at this club', Jackett said. 'As a manager, you are continually looking at the balance of the squad, the profile of player you need. Neil has brain and experience, which gives us something else. He thinks he can play until he's 36, 37. He missed a little bit of his career because of the cancer, and I get the impression he wants to make up for lost time.'

The situation called for a mixture of steel and sensitivity. As a family man, Jackett understood the issues: 'Players do get distracted, without a doubt. Wives are very important in this process. A lot are strong characters. She wants the money. She knows he's only got so much time in the game. She's got children. It's: "You've got to earn the money. What are you going to do after your career? I like this house. I like this school." It's all massive, massive pressure. I'm dealing with decent people, and you just can't leave it without rewarding them, because they will get pissed off.

'It's a tough one. Do the deal too early and they can go into a bit of a comfort zone. There's an old saying in football

that a man needs a mortgage. You need to keep the lower-Division footballer hungry, if you can. Having people whose contracts are up is as much a positive as it is a negative. The club doesn't get tied in financially. When the time comes to change things around, you need people out of contract. The transfer market isn't really there now. You're trying to be one step ahead in your planning and your thinking. You have to be constantly assessing.

'You're looking at the long term, but players get paid this month, this week. They have to put a shift in today, tomorrow and next week. I'm not the greatest fan of agents, but the player has to understand the agent is their representative. That means he must take responsibility for everything he says and does. It helps no one if the agent pisses my chairman or chief executive off. I accept we're in a business, a hard business, but it's about dealing with people on a human level.'

Chris Hackett's contract talks had been put on hold because of the illness of his mother, Linda. She passed away on 22 January, after a long battle against breast cancer. The senior players made a 150-mile round trip to attend her funeral on transfer deadline day, and collected for a cancer charity in her memory. They felt it was the least they could do, because a mother's devotion was one with which they could all identify. Linda, and his father Andy, had been with their son every step of the way, from Garsington Under Sixes in Oxford, to Wembley, via Edinburgh. They took Poppy, the family's Old English sheepdog, in the back of the car, whenever Chris played for Hearts. To put the RSPCA's mind at rest, Poppy tended to mark his territory in three service stations to break up a seven-hour journey.

'My Mum was a massive influence', reflected Hackett, on a morning when his emotions were still raw. 'She travelled all over the place with my Dad, watching me, taking me to

training. They're inspirations in my career, my life. Without them I would not have been able to break through. They supported me, through all the ups and downs. Mum was eventually in a hospice. The people there were fantastic. She was not 100 per cent conscious of what was going on at the end, but I know she wanted me to do well. She was my biggest fan.'

The last time she watched her son, at Hartlepool, Linda was too ill to manage the whole game. Her final full match was at home against MK Dons, where Chris scored Millwall's second goal: 'That's why I celebrated in the way I did. I just feel it was almost meant to be. She had just been told she was terminally ill. She was able to get around, but kinda went downhill from then on. She usually sits in the top tier, but my Nan, who is disabled, came with her. They sat right at the front. I went over to her. I was right there. I could see her. She said that meant a lot to her. It was quite a moment.'

He caught his breath, and stared, moist-eyed, into the void. The banter and bedlam of dressing-room ritual went on around him. His team-mates instinctively gave him space, paid him respect. 'This club, and the group, is such a close-knit environment', he said, when he had recovered his composure. 'The amount of help I have had personally, from staff and players, is amazing. Everyone pulls together. We want to do the best for each other. To see so many of the lads at her funeral was brilliant.

'I agree when people say that, at the highest level, football has lost its humanity. At this level it's all about team spirit. It's great. We have struck it right. There are no big-time characters, no real egos. The boys who have played at a higher level are grounded, and want to help out. They've known, for the last three months, I have been driving up and down the motorway as soon as I have finished training, just to see Mum. Football has been a kinda weird release.

'Sometimes you can't get up for training. Maybe it's a shitty day, or you've had a bad game. Weeks can drag out, and you ask yourself, "What am I doing this for?" Through all of this, football has given me an escape, a place to get away to. Chopper told me: "Make sure you come in and do your training." On a couple of days, I've got up at 6.00am to come in and do a session, and then gone on to the hospice. The manager said I didn't have to, but I wanted to. You realise what football can do for you, even if it's only an hour. A blast with the boys and a training session gives you that mental break.'

Jackett's release from negotiations came on the training ground, in a cold wind and fine rain. He was preparing for the visit of Norwich, unbeaten in sixteen matches, and the threat of Wes Hoolahan. He paid Harris a backhanded compliment, trusting in his intelligence to play Hoolahan's role in a shadow side that operated Norwich's 4-3-3 system. Jimmy Abdou was deputed to man mark him, to duplicate an assignment that required concentration and anticipation. 'If we can get ten v. ten, I'm telling you I'm having that', Jackett told his players. 'He murdered us in transition at their place, getting past Jimmy and between the full back. Lads, these are different. We have to respect that. We have to be on it, all the time. Switch off, and we'll get beat. Unlucky doesn't do it. We'll be 2–0 down before we know it.'

Millwall were a goal down within three minutes, when Chris Martin struck a low free kick, from just outside the area, into the bottom corner. But, with Abdou neutralising Hoolahan, they seized the initiative and equalised through Tony Craig, who volleyed in a hesitant clearance from a Hackett corner. The Den was on heat. The Monk's chant, a verbal version of a death stare, was at full volume. Enter, stage left, Neil Harris. He had been on the field only five

minutes, following his replacement of Lewis Grabban at half time, when he headed the 130th goal of his Millwall career, from a deep Hackett cross. Hoolahan was substituted by Zak Whitbread, who endured thirteen minutes of bitter-sweet abuse.

Harris gleefully recalled a pre-match telephone conversation with Norwich's leading scorer Grant Holt, who manfully concealed his grief at missing the trip to The Den through suspension. 'Why do I want to play there for?' Holt asked. 'No thanks. It's horrible.' Forde sensed the opponents' discomfort in the tunnel beforehand: 'They gave themselves away with little sideways glances as we lined up to go out. They hated it, and know we're coming. It's not even out of the realms of possibility that we can finish second in this League.'

The goalkeeper was Mr Congeniality. He had signed his new contract, which offered security until the summer of 2013. 'It's made a massive difference', said Burns. 'I won't tell him this, but his concentration levels have gone up 10 per cent. He's happy now. Still wants to kill people, mind.' Jackett also knew the animal with which he was dealing: 'You will never completely control a dressing room. Fordie was frustrated, and when that happens some fucker gets it. The geezer I inherited in goal was double laidback and he'd fuck about. I'd rather have an aggressive one all day, even if it is occasionally disruptive. Fordie gets over it pretty quick, fair play. He's a fucking good goalkeeper, a good signing. Sometimes I start laughing, at his honesty. I do like him. I like his enthusiasm. You have to put in context what he's saying.'

Hackett had kept an eye out for his father, in the stands for Norwich's visit. He winced when a low moan greeted an over-hit left-footed cross, but was stunned when the crowd began to chant his name. He had earned the right

to respect, by playing through his grief. 'If you're doing your business, they're going to give you everything', he explained, with a self-conscious sense of wonder. 'If you're not, you will get some stick. They're honest fans. You know where you are. I really enjoy playing for them. 15,000 feels like 30,000, and when they're jumping, it intimidates the bigger teams. It's unique. They're wired. In the last half an hour of games, when they set the rhythm, you can see other teams crumble. You rise.'

Harris duly rolled away the stone the following week, at home against Exeter. He had made the schoolboy error of ridiculing the pink kit of goalkeeper Andy Marriott in the tunnel. The veteran responded with a string of improbably elastic saves and, with seven minutes to go, was preparing to laugh last. A free kick was conceded on the left-hand edge of the area. Harris, conscious of the symmetry of being the match-winner on his 300th start for Millwall, hit it with perfect weight. The ball, aimed towards the wall-side of the goal, fell beyond the scrambling Marriott. A fifth successive win was in the bag. Suddenly, the statistics became compelling. Millwall had taken twelve points out of leaders Leeds, in the blink of an eye. The defence, which now featured a resurgent Alan Dunne, had last conceded a goal in open play at Carrow Road, on Boxing Day. At the same stage the previous season, they had the same number of points, 52. Nine of the remaining sixteen games were away from home.

Hackett's overdue agreement, on a contract covering the next two seasons, had been ratified. It was balanced by the departure of Dave Martin, loaned to Derby County in a byzantine loan deal worth £200,000, because his transfer had stalled on deadline day. 'He doesn't come cheap, does he?' said Derby manager Nigel Clough, who had more than trebled the winger's weekly wage, to £4,000. Martin

represented a significant success story. 'I'm satisfied I've played my part in developing him', said Jackett. 'Dave has got an amazing deal. He's come some way. Just think, three years ago he was a scaffolder.'

Jason Price was sent out on loan, to sustain his career at Oldham Athletic. Jon Obika turned up with Kiernan Hughes-Mason, who didn't think to inform the group that his new friend had been signed, on loan from Spurs, for the rest of the season. Obika sat on his own in the dining room, away from the only occupied table where I shared a cup of tea with Forde and Gary Alexander. Once they realised the significance of the stranger, they were mortified. 'He must think we're right ignorant bastards', said Alexander, who went off to find the striker who had been brought in to cover for his absence.

Alexander's heel injury, a result of the stress caused by over-use during a combative career, pitted his natural optimism against the professional caution of Bobby Bacic. The physiotherapist considered it one of the most severe, of its type, he had seen. Surgery had been the last resort. Bacic had tried manual therapy, high-intensity shockwave treatment, injections under ultrasound, and intrinsic stretching exercises. Alexander was a hugely popular figure, who had a puppy's eagerness to please. He was the first to report to the treatment room, a prisoner of a netherworld that knew his name, but not his needs.

He had a contract until the summer of 2011, was doing his coaching badges, but steeling himself to take The Knowledge if his worst fears were realised. There was something ominous about the pain, beyond the set price of being kicked on the ankle, for a dozen or so years, by desperate defenders caught on the turn. 'I want to play for as long as I can', he insisted. 'That might involve jogging on in non-League. If that's the case, I'll be out there on my moped.

Knowledge will come in handy, even if one of my mates gets a job and offers me some coaching. I want to stay in football because it's part and parcel of my life.

'It's not like being a normal 30-year-old. You are mixing with kids from 16 to 35, who all fuck about. It keeps you young and fresh and you don't want to leave that environment. I know I need options. I'll push myself as hard as I can to get back as soon as I can, but I needed the operation. I have been playing with the injury, carrying it. It gets to the point where you say, "Hang on. I'm letting myself down and letting the lads down." You are never 100 per cent fit, but I was playing 80 per cent fit. I want to be able to play, train and be with the lads all the time. The alternative, breaking down again at the start of next season, will mean I'm fucked.'

Not for the first time, the words of Jackett filtered through the fug of my brain: 'You have to bring enough to the party to justify yourself.'

We were dealing with an altered state. Millwall was different, according to its manager: 'At this club they won't let you take a short corner. We tried one the other day and they all went fucking mental. That's OK. You go to MK Dons, there's a different type of crowd. You can throw the ball out from the back. It's quiet and settled, like being in the cinema. It's new and it's modern. Millwall has a fantastic old-fashioned feel about it. It's a strength, a good thing. The nature of the people they like is different. People like Tony Craig are in the ascendancy here.'

Craig had given the left side of the defence stability. He was learning to play again without the white mask that protected facial damage but interfered with his vision, especially in training. His eagerness to risk pain for normality ensured he got more than he bargained for, in barely credible circumstances, at Adams Park on 20 February.

The reunion with Gareth Ainsworth, the man held responsible for his broken cheekbone, did not go well.

Wycombe, without a home win for ten weeks, were winning, through a Julian Kelly goal scored on his debut in first-half stoppage time. Harris had a penalty saved, and both Shaun Batt and Dunne had hit the crossbar. Frustration mutated into blind fury in the 77th minute when Ainsworth, who had been on the pitch for four minutes, jumped with Craig and appeared to elbow him in the face. Danny Schofield was the first to reach him, shoving him to the floor as a twenty-man brawl broke out. He was fortunate to be given a yellow card, instead of the red that was flourished at Ainsworth.

Craig, tended to by Bacic in the midst of the mayhem, continued with a fat lip, but all bets were off. Defeat was damaging, and his team-mates were seething that a line had been crossed. Another mass confrontation, involving the Wycombe coaching staff and featuring Darren Ward, took place in the narrow corridor leading to the dressing rooms. Ainsworth's protests that the incident was accidental were ignored. He had forfeited the usual protection of professional convention. Robinson branded him 'a thug' and 'a coward'. He insisted: 'I've lost all respect for him as a footballer and a person.'

The FA charged both clubs under rule E20 (a), for failing to control their players. Millwall, whose case was presented by Jackett and Ambler, were fined £2,500, Wycombe £3,500. The chief executive fretted about the long-term impact of even such a minor slap on the wrist: 'We have to respect that Millwall is a unique club. The concern is the crowd dynamic if we were to play Wycombe, and Ainsworth, again. We don't need to give some of our lot an excuse. I know Paul is captain. The strength of feeling in the dressing room was very high, but …'

The sentence trailed off into silence. Ambler knew, deep down, that he was wasting his breath. When push came to shove, a team-mate, a friend, needed help. He got it. The chaps fronted up, without exception. At Millwall, belonging to a band of brothers is a birthright, a badge of honour money cannot buy.

Marching on Together, Part Two

Darren Ward, proprietor of the Silverhill Cattery, settled down to lunch, a grey mush of liquidised fruit and vegetables scooped from a drinks container. 'Muck' he called it, with an exaggerated grimace. Ward had risen early that morning to attend to his feline clients, fed organic morsels as part of the Purrfect Pussy programme. He then liaised with Chinese suppliers for his trophy and memorabilia company, Pro Team Sport. The afternoon was set aside for New Incentive, his financial planning and lifestyle management initiative. Life, like the wine investment market in which he dabbled, was good.

'Eh, Wardie, you got any of them dodgy DVDs?'

Richard Shaw had a smile as wide as a slice of melon. Discussing business strategy, in a dining room full of footballers, invited intervention. Over the next half an hour, Ward dealt with the mock innocence of his team-mates. They took turns to interrupt, asking him about illicit car boot sales, murky middle men named Pinkie, and the lorry that was about to shed a consignment of consumer goods. According to them, their centre half was a fusion of Fagin, Arthur Daley, and Fred the Shred. 'Love it', said Ward, even when the jokes were wearing thin. 'Can't live life straight-faced, can you? Football is business, work, serious stuff. But this is what they all miss when it's over.' He was in Millwall mode. From 10.30am to 2.00pm, nothing else mattered. When the manager spoke, Ward was a straight-backed study

in concentration. He was habitually one of the last to leave the training pitch. He stayed on to practise defensive headers. He improved his mobility by shuttle-running between cones he had placed deliberately along the touchline. He was invariably the last to get changed after games, because of his insistence on a structured warm-down programme. The smart ones watched, learned, and made their move quietly. They asked him about nutrition, the standards set in the Elysian fields of the Premier League.

At 31, Ward had the respect accorded any player who was financially secure. He had formally rejoined the club, on a free transfer following an initial loan, at the turn of the year, when Wolves paid up the remaining six months of a weighty contract. His alter ego, the Peckham Beckham, had been a key contributor to Millwall's 2004 FA Cup final team. He joined Crystal Palace in an ultimately unfulfilling £1.1 million transfer that taught him the value of self-reliance and an active brain. At heart, he remained the schoolboy who had a milk round, a paper round, and walked 40 minutes to school, to save money.

Kenny Jackett worked with him, and his three brothers, at the Watford Academy from the age of fourteen. Lee, the eldest, became a jobbing goalkeeper in the lower tiers of non-League football. Elliott, the youngest, joined West Ham, who sold him to Coventry for £1 million. Scott, another goalkeeper, suffered a career-ending injury, and trained in taxation strategy. All four inherited their parents' work ethic. Father John worked for the Post Office until his knees gave way. Mother Lesley was a part-time child minder.

'Top people, a strong family', Jackett said, softened by the memory. 'They had fuck all, and you should have seen the size of the four boys. I wouldn't have liked to have had to fill their fridge.' It was difficult. Darren remembered: 'The food bill was more than the mortgage. We were no poverty

case, but Dad worked all hours for us. I'm no different to most sons. I try to model myself on my Dad. He's my hero. You have got to make things happen in life. That is what I am doing. I know a lot of people in the lower Leagues, and it's tough. It's a different game. This is 110 miles an hour, and you don't get a lot of football, unless you're winning.'

Experience had taught him hard, sharp lessons. He was a second-year YTS apprentice when he was called up by the England youth team. Wales and the Republic of Ireland offered an alternative, but he lost two years of his career to a naive tackle in a reserve game against Norwich, rearranged to suit the rehabilitation programme of former Liverpool striker Ronnie Rosenthal: 'Bang, that was it. I snapped my leg – double fracture of the right tibia. It was my fault. It was a ridiculous tackle, impulsive, and it set me back. I was fortunate, in a way. It could have been horrific. I used my time to improve myself in other areas.'

Millwall eventually signed him for £500,000. When the club discovered that the bank manager didn't consider FA Cup final memories convertible currency, he was a cost base they couldn't afford: 'I got asked to leave, basically. It wasn't that they wanted me to go, but they needed me to go. The money seemed to disappear. I discovered the grass wasn't greener elsewhere. You realise, eventually, that you are suited to playing for a certain type of club. I fit in here. At Millwall you have to have a bit of fire in you.

'I structure my day, but I don't want the manager to feel business has taken over from my football. I will never do that. If you are not on it, not organised, you will fall by the wayside. I am strong mentally. My work ethic is never going to be questioned. At my age, some players find it hard; I don't. I won't waste this opportunity. There's no time to start moaning and mumbling, that everyone's crap, or everything's shit. I learn from other people. I observe.

It might seem that I'm not doing a lot, but I assure you, I'm taking it all in.'

So was Jackett. He recognised the importance of the strength of character that saw Ward through an initial struggle to readjust. He would be a pivotal figure as the season entered a decisive stage. 'I'm a Darren Ward fan', he explained. 'You look at him, over two or three weeks, and you might not be sure about him. But if you have him in the building for two years I guarantee he will be a resounding success. Dropping down a level is harder than stepping up. Football surprises you. But he's a top pro, a top bloke. Having him around in this day and age, when there are too many with a questionable attitude, is good for everyone. He does things right.'

That's why Ward reported to a soulless hotel on the southern fringes of Milton Keynes with his pre-match meal, a macrobiotic creation in a plastic tub, in his kit bag. He was an eager disciple of Paul Chek, an American expert in holistic health and corrective high-performance exercise. Ward followed his mantra that commercial farming denudes the soil, and creates unhealthy plants and animals. He ate only organic food, studied metabolic typing, and was conscious of the cumulative effect of stress on his body. Some of Chek's conclusions, that 90 per cent of us have fungal or parasitic infections, zoomed in from left field, but Ward exuded serenity. To borrow one of his guru's recycled Chinese proverbs: 'When the student is ready, the master appears.'

The dressing rooms at Stadium: MK, reached through a darkened hotel storage room from the players' entrance, are unfeasibly large and airy. It was a cold night on which snow flurries gave way to rain. A hard, closely-cropped pitch would place a premium on anticipation, confidence and control. Jackett had tweaked training, following the

Wycombe debacle. He set up a series of eight-a-side games to encourage mobility and instant assessment of options on the ball. The sub-plot was simple: 'Lads, I'm always trying to make you better players. I'm trying to make us a better side. Undoubtedly this is a massive game, one we are capable of winning.'

Ward sat sipping extra-filtered Penta water, at room temperature to aid rapid hydration, as Chris Hackett contorted himself on a small red towel, laid on the floor in the centre of the room. Scott Barron and Ali Fuseini passed a ball over and around him. Bobby Bacic was still chuckling over an approach to become Iron Maiden's physiotherapist – he was more of a Primal Scream man – but the general air of purpose was summed up by Alan Dunne, hunched over Shaw's scouting report. David Forde, alongside him, closed his eyes and envisaged another clean sheet.

Chairman John Berylson was intrigued by the bravery of the MK Dons business model, which challenged football's tribal conventions. They were building a new club, a new culture, a new fanbase, in a new city. The stadium was a leap of faith. Overwhelming civic support had helped win host city status in England's 2018 World Cup bid. Economic logic told Berylson that English football would evolve, and even encompass mergers between clubs. The atmosphere on the evening suggested otherwise. The good folk of Milton Keynes were polite hosts. Millwall's 1,400 fans, whose journey had been complicated by chaos on the M1, celebrated their infiltration of both ends with a defiant chorus of 'No One Likes Us'.

No contest. Millwall matched fluency with urgency, and, at half time, should have been ahead by more than Danny Schofield's sweetly-driven goal, created by the touch and vision of Morison. 'The next goal is ours, and they will go', said Jackett. He was wrong, and saw the danger a

split-second before everyone else, seven minutes into the second half. 'No!' he screamed, from the edge of his technical area, as he read the flight of an innocuous Aaron Wilbrahim shot, which took a double deflection and looped over Forde.

Joe Gallen, standing on a concrete step beside the dugout, absent-mindedly kicked a wooden advertising board as the tension settled. It was lifted when Neil Harris restored the lead with a scrambled goal on the hour, and returned when Bacic noticed Hackett in distress. 'It's his heart thing', he shouted at Jackett, who collared the fourth official. 'I want him off, now', he said with revealing urgency. Masseur Chris Harvey, who suffered from the same condition, the haphazard acceleration of heart rate, rushed into the dressing room to prepare an ice bath. Bacic summoned the MK Dons doctor.

Hackett, who endured a similar trauma at Norwich on Boxing Day, quickly stabilised. He walked to the bench just before Harris sealed Millwall's sixth win in seven games with an 85th-minute goal, after an initial header from a Barron corner had been blocked. Morison was incandescent, following an exchange with the MK Dons bench in injury time, when he was accused of throwing an elbow. The impact of defeat soured Paul Ince, who stared blankly as he leaned against a wall at the mouth of the tunnel.

'That's Millwall', said Jackett. 'That's how it is. We will have that all day. I want them to think bad things about us. We got under their skins, beat them with brains and control. It was at least a 5–1 game. As a performance that is as good as you have given. You created some chances. Defensively, you were solid. As a unit, you worked your bollocks off. You looked different class, a fucking good team. Excellent. Well done.' Somewhat abashed, the players gave themselves a round of applause.

Harris was in his element. He awarded the prize for worst underpants of the evening to Morison, who wore a green and grey lateral stripe number that could only have been a gift from a colour-blind mother-in-law. 'This is why we do it', he said. 'Do you feel that buzz? We can't wait to get back into training on Thursday. Their keeper Willy used to play with us. But I looked into his eyes and saw he was scared.'

Jackett and Gallen sat together, emotionally spent. The manager turned to his assistant and said quietly: 'We are going to have to wrap Neil in cotton wool and bring him out on Saturday mornings.' Gallen nodded slowly, and summarised the significance of an evening that left Millwall six points clear in seventh place, but reeling in the leading pack. 'That's killed them off', he said, sensing correctly that it was the beginning of the end for Ince's regime. Kill or be killed. It's the nature of the game.

Harris, as ever, did not require a reminder of the value of perspective. When he returned to training there was a replica shirt to sign, to commemorate yet another cancer victim. 'RIP Mr Millwall', he wrote, in a silver highlighter pen supplied by Bill Smedley. He was accustomed to being a conduit of emotion and, on the following Saturday, responded to a growing sense of expectation. His conversion of a ninth-minute free kick, won when he drew a foul 25 yards out, was sufficient to see off Hartlepool at The Den. It was enough to guarantee him another award, as League One player of the month for February.

Automatic promotion, though, would be decided away from home. Millwall could ill afford the listlessness that led to them trailing by two goals inside 26 minutes at Walsall. Morison pulled one back quickly, chasing an apparent lost cause and creating confusion between goalkeeper and defender. Hackett was tormenting full back Matt Richards, who was booked for kicking him in the head before he

received a red card for another crude lunge at the winger, midway through the second half.

The equaliser didn't come until the 93rd minute when Dunne, 25 yards out, struck a bouncing ball on the sweet spot. His technique was as perfect as his timing, and it flew, arrow-straight, into the top corner. It was, with good reason, voted Millwall's goal of the season.

Harris needed more cotton wool. He had sustained knee damage, and was being quietly prepared for a comeback against Charlton on 13 March. It meant he missed the idiosyncratic delights of a Tuesday night trip to Carlisle United. 'These are quite lively at home, lads', warned Jackett. 'Every player has a yard more.' He knew what was coming: opposition that threw up two banks of four, hit long balls into channels, and tried to mask their vulnerability when teams had the courage to attack them.

Carlisle defender Ian Harte, veteran of Leeds' suicide leap to the Champions League semi-final, had scored fourteen goals. 'He's had too many "well dones", too many pats on the back', said Jackett, ejecting the words with the vigour of a car driver spitting chewing gum through an open window. 'Sort him.' Mildew scarred the walls of a high-ceilinged dressing room. A stencilled sign read, bizarrely: 'José Mourinho, Inter Milan: what he looks for: 1 Ambition 2 Passion 3 Desire.' Mascot Ewan Polak was ushered in with his father. The players were attentive, at ease, and at pains not to swear. Jackett added his autograph to the hieroglyphic mix, and ruffled the boy's hair. He told him, tenderly: 'Here's hoping you bring us luck.'

When he had gone, the mood changed. Jackett announced: 'You have to rip the fuck out of this back four. You are capable of it. Talk all the time and be aware of where they are, and who is floating.' Up in the boardroom Demos Kouvaris was operating on two hours' sleep after an

overnight transatlantic flight, followed by a 90-minute car shuttle and a 3½-hour train journey. Pints of John Smith's bitter warded off jet lag. He saw, in Jackett, the single-mindedness he admired in successful basketball coaches like Bobby Knight and John Wooden. 'We've got so much faith in Kenny', he said. 'He's got full strategic control.'

Brunton Park is an architectural oddity. Millwall's 200 fans were cloistered in the corner of the incomplete East Stand, which ran twenty yards past the end of the pitch, which could not be moved to compensate. They bounced around to keep warm, and struck up a chant of 'It's just like watching Milan' when Morison scored with a sumptuous eighteen-yard chip, after Shaun Batt had headed on Forde's clearance. His second goal, a header after goalkeeper Adam Collin had over-committed on a Hackett cross, came twelve minutes from the end.

Forde could have got himself sent off in added time for squaring up to Richard Offiong, but escaped with a booking. The squabble punctuated further goals by Carlisle captain Danny Livesey and Schofield. The locals were disgruntled as they shuffled off old-fashioned terracing into an eerie sodium-lit gloom. One yelled: 'This is football, not boxing, Jackett', but should have saved his breath. The manager kept marching across the pitch to pay heartfelt respect to the travelling fans. The Carlisle directors, who had earlier fawned over Charlton manager Phil Parkinson, smiled through gritted teeth. 'Your goalkeeper was a touch fortunate to stay on', said one, with icy courtesy.

Jackett couldn't have cared less: 'It's a good sign they're bitching and moaning. If they're standing there telling you what a good side you are, it's because they've just beaten you.' Business was business, however. Despite the lukewarm welcome and defensive body language, Andy Ambler stayed on to thrash out an outline loan deal. Jason Price, who had

not done enough to extend his spell at Oldham, would spend the rest of the season at Carlisle.

The team bus pulled into The Den at 4.20am. The majority of the players spent their day off in bed. Adrian Wisson went straight to the laundry room to get their kit ready for Saturday's derby against Charlton, and didn't bother with sleep. As a fan, he knew what was at stake, why The Den would have a rare capacity crowd. Charlton's sense of superiority grated. It even led to one supporter posting a poem popularly attributed to Jesse Owens, which, coincidentally, I have on my study wall as I type these words:

> If you think you are beaten, you are.
> If you think you dare not, you don't.
> If you like to win but think you can't,
> It's almost a cinch you won't.
> If you think you'll lose, you're lost.
> For out in the world we find
> Success begins with a fellow's will,
> It's all in the state of mind.
> If you think you are outclassed, you are.
> You've got to think high to rise.
> You've got to be sure of yourself before
> You can ever win the prize.
> Life's battles don't always go
> To the stronger or faster man.
> But sooner or later, the man who wins
> Is the man who thinks he can.

Parkinson didn't look like that man. He had sat behind me in the directors' box at Carlisle, shuffling nervously and making copious notes. His skin had the colour and consistency of nicotine-stained linen. His eyes were deep-set, with a dark, tired undercarriage. The word from the boardroom

at The Valley was that promotion was vital to the club's welfare. Charlton's runaway start seemed so long ago it would have required an archaeologist to uncover the optimism it so rashly generated. Local pride made the pressure more difficult to bear.

Berylson gave a small speech to the squad before Jackett's main team talk. Such occasions are, by their nature, forced. The players listened respectfully, but their minds were elsewhere. 'This club has waited eight or nine years for a day like today', he told them. 'You guys have come a long way in a short time. I congratulate you on what you have done. I can't tell you how proud I am today. Make sure it's us going up, not them.' Jackett thanked him, and got to work.

He sensed weaknesses on the left side of the Charlton defence, and ordered senior players to counteract their captain Nicky Bailey, who was notorious for attempting to manage the game through constant carping at the referee. Millwall needed to use the emotion of the crowd as an auxiliary energy supply rather than a life-support system. Jackett moved to the whiteboard to illustrate Charlton's counter-attacking tactics, quoted statistics to underline his team's goal-scoring potential. 'Lads', he summed up, fists clenched and shoulders hunched as he unconsciously adopted a boxer's crouch. 'They will not match you in fitness, tempo, and heart.'

Gallen warned about the intelligence of Charlton's movement off long throws. Harris checked the referee's Christian name so he would have a false, yet easy familiarity when things got heated. That was inevitable, because when Millwall went out to warm up at 2.20, they were greeted by the howl of a rabid underdog. 'Christ', said Wisson. 'I haven't heard a roar like that, at this time, for years.' Bodies were running on football's equivalent of a tequila slammer, a cocktail of adrenaline, testosterone, and simmering gastric

juices. 'Rough 'em up. Get in their faces', screamed Tony Craig, munching Gaviscon antacid tablets like Smarties.

In the corner, Dunne cleared his head with smelling salts. He was emboldened by his growing stature within the group. 'Let's get into these cunts', he yelled, before Harris took centre stage: 'Let's give the punters some bragging rights. We can win this in five minutes. They won't fancy it. Remember, boys, this is what we play the game for.' For a few, eternal seconds, voices stilled. The scraping of studs, worn by prowling footballers, filled the silence. Jackett watched, hawk-like, and wordlessly opened the door.

The Charlton players were late coming out. Parkinson, tie loosened beneath a black V-necked pullover that sagged in the wash, made the gesture of emerging first. He shook each of his players by the hand as they entered the tunnel, addressed them by their Christian names, and wished them 'all the best'. He radiated the superficial serenity of a defendant awaiting the verdict from a jury foreman. It was a charade, exposed by his restlessness from the first whistle. He held his arms wide, in supplication, when decisions went against him. He bounced off the fourth official, and affected not to hear the Millwall fan behind his dugout who repeatedly intoned: 'Welcome to your worst fucking nightmare, Parkinson.'

Retaliatory chants of 'We pay your benefits', from the Charlton fans, had the effect of flies smashing into a windscreen. The home crowd generated a deep, constant hum, like an idling jet engine. It mutated into white noise two minutes before the interval, when Ward escaped his marker from a Hackett corner to head his first Millwall goal for exactly six years. 'Now is the time to throttle them', said Jackett at half time. 'We ain't dealing with mugs here. If there's time for constructive football, fine, but let's take the zero. There's no point in fannying about.' He turned to

Hackett: 'They've been quick on to you. But keep going for it, at the right time, in the right area. You have to be hard, mentally.'

Point taken. Sixteen minutes from time, he was set up on the right by good combination play between Morison and Harris. Hackett beat one man, nutmegged the covering defender, and delivered a hard, low cross, which Christian Dailly could not avoid diverting into his own goal. Charlton's spirit was broken. Two minutes later, Miguel Llera presented a suicidal square ball to Harris, whose neat pass received due reward: the crisp finish that was becoming a hallmark of Morison's progress. Morison's second goal, Millwall's third in seven minutes, was a consequence of Rob Elliott's failure to deal with a fierce Hackett drive. The police decided to showboat at the final whistle, staging a training exercise involving six mounted officers fanning out across the penalty area. They were supposed to be guarding the away end, which had already emptied.

Jackett, back in the dressing room, radiated a quiet pride: 'Fucking hell, lads. It's an undervalued thing, character.' His players exuded a post-coital glow. 'What about that for a feeling, eh?' said Craig. 'Quality', replied Harris. Liam Trotter laughed, and extended an arm around Hackett's shoulders. 'I knew what you were going to do the moment you got the ball for that goal, Hacks', he said. 'The only person in the ground who didn't know you were going to put it through his legs was the guy himself.'

Morison was allowed to steal Shaw's bath, but Forde changed quickly. He had been given compassionate leave to return to Ireland, where his uncle had been diagnosed with terminal cancer, and his aunt had been rushed to hospital with a brain aneurysm. Jackett and Gallen's families congregated in the manager's office, where Parkinson completed grim formalities. He offered a weak joke – 'Think I'll wait

until the traffic clears' – but was ashen-faced, glass-eyed. 4–0. Each goal a flashing blade. He sat on a table, drained a bottle of Becks, and offered monosyllabic answers to gentle questions until he had done his professional duty. 'Fair play to him for coming in', said Jackett. 'That must have been really hard for him. It's how it gets you, I'm afraid.'

Millwall were fourth, a point behind Charlton, six behind second-placed Leeds. Ten games remained, and Jackett had eight days to plan for a televised visit to Elland Road. His first act, when he arrived at the training ground on Monday morning, was to pin a statistical summary of the season on the notice board. It was an unspoken challenge to maintain momentum:

First Twelve Games: W3 D6 L3. Second Twelve Games: W6 D3 L3. Third Twelve Games: W9 D2 L1.

Back in his office, he explained: 'I like to think I understand the mentality of a promotion season. It's about knowing when and where to focus. You're on the front line, whether you're dealing with the press or taking training. People take their lead from you. There have been times this season where we've been hanging in there, but there's a nice pattern to things at the moment. There's a consistently picked team. Keeping that intact, keeping people fit, is massive. I pride myself on getting the right people around me, decisive characters with mental toughness. That gives you the chance to create a team ethos, within which individuals can over-achieve.'

In the coaches' room, Gallen was trying to make sense of a malfunctioning DVD of Leeds' season. It had the milky, fuzzy quality of film from the earliest moon landings.

Steve Jones, who had watched Leeds summon a single shot on target in a narrow loss at Southampton, had asked

Stuart Murdoch for a video of the game, only to be told he needed permission from Alan Pardew. 'You've asked them for a favour?' said Gallen, to laughter that suggested pigs would fly in formation along the south coast before it was forthcoming. 'I ain't worried', said Jackett.

Training would concentrate on neutralising Leeds' greatest strength, their set-pieces. He trusted the maturity of the group, and was encouraged by rumblings on the grapevine. Jermaine Beckford, Leeds' leading scorer, was a symbol of the disintegration of their team ethic in the aftermath of a fabled FA Cup win at Manchester United. Gossip suggested, correctly, that he had tacitly agreed a summer move to Everton. Jackett's key message, throughout the build-up and into his final team talk, was the confidence he derived from the strength of the human bond between his players:

'There are so many signs of a good team: understanding, collective spirit and individual strength. Football doesn't give you anything easily. You might have touch, technical ability and be easy on the eye, but to win up here you need mental strength. I wouldn't be standing here if I didn't think you had that. Be strong enough to respond to a bad pass, a bad decision, even a bad goal. Programme yourself to give everything you have, to be a proper player. I want you to be able to look back, at the end of your career, and know that you could have done no more to be successful. That means accepting the club comes first. The result on the day is everything.

'Leeds can out-power sides. They've got the ability to play around you. Win the first ball. If not, make sure you win the second. We get the knock-downs, we break, we play. Lads, they will definitely be wary of you. Tonight they will try to smash you. They will be on at the ref. They will want a kick-up, a moan-up. Don't shy away from anything physical. I know you won't. I know also that they're worried about

you. Don't let them force us into afters. We are strong, but calm. We've got clear heads. It's a big pitch, a good pitch. You have the ability to play. You will be composed on the ball. You wore Charlton down. You fucking murdered them. We can wear these fuckers down. They are thinking they are going to stop you. They won't.'

They didn't. Leeds made a late choice to omit Beckford, citing a hamstring injury. Within eight minutes they had lost Patrick Kisnorbo – who had sparked a melee by grabbing Harris by the throat – to a snapped achilles tendon. That was to cost the Australian defender a World Cup place, and Leeds an immediate goal. Millwall poured through the breach, Dunne and Trotter playing pivotal roles in a six-man move that ended with Morison converting at the far post. Leeds, anxious to the point of sterility, were fortunate not to concede another just before the interval, when Paul Robinson's header, from a Hackett corner, clipped the crossbar.

The players returned to the changing area, a horseshoe behind a narrow corridor, in which Jackett waited. While he structured his thoughts, Robinson maintained focus: 'We show them what we're about. We're horrible, hard to beat.' The manager was remorseless: 'I want even more from you. In there they'll be telling them to pass, pass pass. Our ambition is to challenge them, all over the pitch. The key is not dropping off them.' Gallen painted pictures: 'This is the scenario. You come out on top in all areas. You're composed. There's a counter-attacking mindset. Your possession kills the crowd, saps their spirit. You're on the front foot. You score a second goal and win the game.'

Eat your heart out, Mystic Meg. Leeds' desperation was embodied by veteran striker Paul Dickov, penalised for stamping on Forde's ankle at a corner. The goalkeeper was in Zen Master mode. 'Silly cunt', he hissed at him through

a condescending smile. Millwall controlled the tempo of the game and scored a second ten minutes from time. Batt, close to the corner flag, cut inside, slaloming past two defenders before beating Casper Ankergren with a low shot inside the near post.

'What the fuck is going on?' chanted the home fans, who quickly set up a counterpoint of 'Grayson out'. The 400 Millwall supporters, obliged to swap vouchers for match tickets at an M1 service area, extracted full value from such indignities. Uniquely in my experience, they had been joined on the terraces by three non-playing squad members, Gary Alexander, Adam Bolder and, to general astonishment, Lewis Grabban. All were required to sing a song. Grabban earned unaccustomed respect by leading a Monk's chant. Alexander burbled amiably. Bolder sounded like a poor man's Joe Pasquale as he declared: 'We are going up, say we are going up.'

The fans were kept back for 50 minutes after the game, as part of the security operation. Jackett agreed to a police request to provide a diversion by staging a full warm-down session in front of them. 'Millwall, Millwall, give us a song', they ordered. Harris, whose son Cameron, a mascot on his birthday, was safely out of earshot, obliged by leading a chant of 'Fuck 'em all'. Ward and Bacic did a 'We love you Millwall' duet for the tone-deaf. Even stern stewards, conditioned to suspicion, could not resist a smile. Jackett walked across, after finishing his media duties, bowed low and applauded, slowly.

The family had come together. Anything seemed possible.

Chapter 18
April Fools' Day Massacre

Kenny Jackett was deep undercover. He paid £10 to stand behind the goal, threw in a fiver to help a fighting fund for a new stand, and declined club membership, which carried the incentive of a 15 per cent discount at the local Pizza Hut. The Camrose, home of Basingstoke Town, had seen better days. On this cold late March evening, the day after Millwall's win at Leeds, it staged the biggest match in the young life of John Marquis. He was on work experience with Staines Town, blissfully ignorant of the fact he was playing for a professional contract.

The Conference (South) is where dreams go to die. It's populated by wannabes, never-will-bes and never-quite-weres. 'I know a lot of players at this level', explained Jackett. 'Many of them have been at League clubs. I can assess the standard. I can't be arsed to do the boardroom bit. They'll just make a fuss. I just want to see how John copes. It's a crucial one for him. I've been undecided. He seems a really good kid, but if he goes under, we won't bother. He's not eighteen yet, but there's a decision to be made.'

The striker's equitable temperament had impressed Jackett when he made his first-team debut, as an emergency 49th-minute substitute in the defeat at Bristol Rovers in early September. He had decent strength and touch, brought others into play, and had outgrown youth football, where he was the alpha male. Could he cope with men, centre halves whose scar tissue was a badge of honour? He began

well enough, putting his arm across the defender, and winning the first ball played up to him.

His marker's pride was dented. When the next ball came, his malicious intent was obvious. Marquis saw him coming, stiffened for the inevitable battering. He stopped, trapped the ball on his chest, and took the challenge. He had imposed himself, accelerated the process of earning the right to play. He scored the only goal of the game, seven minutes before half time, and allowed Jackett to melt away early from a crowd of 306.

Scott Fitzgerald and Jamie Johnson were in the small stand, oblivious to his presence. Jackett felt guilty about his subterfuge. He trusted their judgement, but wanted to make an independent assessment. He called them on the way home, with a simple question: 'Yes or no?' Each answered in the affirmative. They, too, saw development potential in a young man who carried himself well and wanted to learn. Marquis would be the sole survivor of the April Fools' Day Massacre.

It was the day Fitzgerald dreaded. It played on his conscience, cast a pall over the training ground. As masseur Chris Harvey observed: 'You can't help but be affected when you see people going through the worst day of their lives.' When it was over, a brutally concise statement was posted on the club's website. It read: 'Millwall have released eight second year scholars. The club would like to thank Wayne Drummond, Chris Hegarty, Omar Beckles, Danny Fitzsimons, Hassan Janneh, Ikenna Ofoche, Grant Ludford and Kamil Tevfik for their efforts during their time here, and wish them all the best for the future.'

Fitzgerald had commandeered Jackett's office for the day. They were called, one by one, up the fifteen stairs, to learn their fate. He gave them as long as they needed. Some wanted the ordeal to be over as quickly as possible. Others

sat and shared their secret fears, worked through their pain in staccato bursts of self-awareness. Two were particularly distraught, unable to turn a tide of bitter tears. Fitzgerald found himself welling up with them. He was a good man, a father, and an outstanding coach. He had welcomed these boys into his home. Now he was sending them, emotionally naked, out into an unforgiving world.

'I'm not stone cold', he said, with the sort of hollow laugh that acts as a defence mechanism in such circumstances. 'It's tough, very tough. I've done this for six years, and I'm constantly trying to find a better way. I've spoken to more experienced coaches than me, but no one's come up with a solution. You can see by their faces whether they are ready to go, but you can also see them fighting themselves, trying not to break down. They are treated very well here. They are respected members of staff, not bodies.'

Fitzgerald understood the parameters of the problem. He was long-sighted, in a short-sighted business. Jackett, like all managers, needed players who would merit an immediate first-team squad place. Even Marquis, the pick of the litter, was some way off that. He was, however, a symbol of success and solidarity. Home-grown players absorb a club's culture, represent its future. They are cherished. Jackett did not hide from the consequences of his decision – 'Days like these are bad days, very, very bad days' – but was conditioned to accentuating the positive:

'If you are in professional football, the odds are you have been released, retired or sacked a few times. It's part of the industry. You have to explain to the youngsters that, in football as in life, you have to use such experiences positively, and bounce back. You are trying to give them a life education. Sometimes the day you get your first free transfer is the day you get the kick up the arse you need. You see some of them cruise through to 21, on good contracts in good

facilities, and they never get that shock. Then they come up against someone with more hunger, who might have had a couple of years somewhere, and been released. The hungry one wins.

'You try to explain it's not an exact science. The system is to some degree flawed. A scholar's training is part-funded by the government, so most clubs take players to fill up youth and reserve sides when they haven't much chance of becoming professional footballers. But what else would those lads do for two years? They get excellent college opportunities. I wouldn't undervalue the experience, even if they don't make it. You are automatically a member of the PFA for life. That brings major benefits, funding for future training. You've acquired life skills, discipline, and a sense of what is needed when you have something to work towards. There is a broader picture, but I understand the difficulty. I have kids myself.'

The weeding-out process had begun in earnest on 22 October, the previous year. Jackett called an 8.00am meeting with Joe Gallen, Richard Shaw, Fitzgerald and Barry Dunn, head of youth recruitment. It was another yes/no interlude, which opened into a strategic discussion on the potential of younger age groups. Millwall were vulnerable to the collapse of the gentleman's agreement that clubs would not cross traditional borders. Chelsea caused offence by setting up a satellite centre in Southwark, Millwall's manor, but all Premier League clubs behaved with the disregard of robber barons. They sprinkled Skydust, stole the National Lottery slogan. It could be you.

The talent pool of south-east London shimmered invitingly. Yusuf Mersin, the schoolboy goalkeeper who relished Tony Burns' tough love, rejected Liverpool. However, Millwall's chances of signing Freddie Yeo, an improbably imposing twelve-year-old who worshipped Neil Harris,

receded when he began to be treated as a family heirloom. 'Every club in the country is chasing him', Fitzgerald sighed. 'It's dog eat dog out there. They're not shy about tapping people up.'

Most managers pay lip service to youth development. Why bother to plant bulbs when you will never enjoy the beauty of the flowers? But Jackett empathised with Fitzgerald. He missed nothing, and would often surprise the youth coach by complimenting him on the quality of his sessions. He had watched from afar, and knew what he was looking at. Fitzgerald had impressed after inheriting a self-regarding group who had been over-indulged. He signalled regime change by kicking open the dressing room door and throwing away such status symbols as carbohydrate gels and customised training kit. His message was clear: If you want to be treated like a first-team player, convince me of the credibility of your ambition. He slashed support staff, re-evaluated principles. The Road Closed signs had been posted across Easy Street.

Ludford had, by common consent, a sweet left foot. His downfall was a sweet tooth. He effectively sealed his fate by returning overweight from a break, despite warnings from Fitzgerald. 'He knew he was going to get tested. We've been on at him for eighteen months about the right things to eat. "What have you been eating?" I ask when he comes back. "Crisps and chocolate …" His epitaph would read: If only he could pass a kitchen, the way he passes a ball.'

Janneh was personable, but lacked impact. Ofoche lacked the clarity of thought to make the most of his physical gifts. He had the muscle definition of a middleweight boxer or an outside centre, but made too many wrong decisions under pressure. Tevfik lacked stature, although he read the game intelligently, worked incessantly and was a garlanded midfield player in Turkey's Under-19 team. If he

was three inches taller, and less injury-prone, he would have been a Premier League prospect. Beckles got caught under the ball too often to be a reliable central defender. He was, however, an outstanding individual. When he was released, he rose, made eye contact with Fitzgerald, and extended his hand. 'I want to thank you for everything you have done for me', he said.

The memory was too fresh to be comfortable, but there was a quiet pride in Fitzgerald's voice when he reflected: 'I expected nothing less. It was so typical of Omar's character, very adult, mature.' Beckles would make himself a life. He was academically able, one of the top twenty scholars in the country. The Football League wanted him to join an elite coaching course for young players released by their clubs. His tutors were impressed by his thoughtfulness, consideration for others, and analytical approach to problem-solving.

The fate of the others was shaped by two contrasting matches, on 12 February and 2 March. The former was a fifth-round FA Youth Cup tie at Villa Park, the latter a reserve match against Queens Park Rangers at Dartford. Each exposed flaws, physical and mental limitations. The Cup tie had the additional dimension of the spectre of hooliganism, which flickered back from beyond the grave of good intentions.

The youth team emerged to a first-team fanfare, which echoed eerily around three empty stands. The pitch looked bigger in isolation, the players smaller. A meagre crowd, swollen by one official coach party from The Den, made itself heard. Millwall held their own until they conceded three goals in a calamitous three-minute spell at the end of the first half. Ofoche pulled one back, but an unlikely recovery stalled when Kiernan Hughes-Mason hit the underside of the bar with a penalty. His response, a protracted mime of self-pity, was infinitely more disturbing than the retaliatory

goal that completed a 4–1 win for Aston Villa, who would be beaten by Chelsea in the final.

I wandered down to the dressing room area with Shaw, whose faith had been shaken. 'They've done themselves no favours', he said. 'On that evidence none of them will make pros. Kiernan was appalling, not interested. I hate it when he blames everyone but himself. All that shrugging of the shoulders, don't look at me stuff. Ugh.' Fitzgerald was seething, pushing the door open to reveal a glimpse of crestfallen boys staring at the floor in a wood-panelled changing area.

Hughes-Mason had driven him to distraction: 'He's late for training, even late for the bus coming here. He thinks it's all about being judged on what happens out there, on the pitch. He was atrocious. There was nothing, no commitment. I didn't say what I wanted to in there, but I'm going to ask the manager to take him out of my group.'

A dispiriting evening was about to take a turn for the worse. At just after 10.00pm, having steered the car through Spaghetti Junction, I took a call from Brian Doogan, a former journalistic colleague who had become Martin O'Neill's aide de camp. In his role as Villa's director of communications, he was seeking to speak to Andy Ambler. Initial police reports suggested that thirteen Millwall fans, among a group of twenty refused re-entry after half time, had been implicated in a stabbing. 'Unbelievable', Doogan said, a natural response given the occasion. As Ambler checked the names against the 49 Millwall members on the official coach, I briefed his press officer Deano Standing. 'Whaaat?' he exclaimed, alarm piercing the static on his hands-free. 'Of all the matches, why does it have to happen at this one?'

Ambler sounded world-weary, as midnight came and went. 'There I am coming back from a youth team match and you call, saying, "Sorry, but I'm going to complicate your

life". I pull into a service station and spend the next hour or so speaking to police, press, Villa and Ken Chapman. Just another day at this football club. People look at you as if you're on a different planet when you tell them what goes on. You just have to get over it, do these sorts of things. That's the way it is.'

The usual headlines were exhumed, restricted to regional outlets because the nationals focused on disturbances at Chelsea and Southampton. It was a 'drunken rampage'. Anonymous eye-witnesses fulminated. West Midlands Police appealed for information on what was described as a racially-aggravated assault. Reports of a stabbing were revised: a 42-year-old man had suffered a cut to the head after being struck by what was thought to be a bottle. The suspects, who had arrived in a minibus, were bailed, had their houses searched, and were served with banning orders. Three months later, charges were quietly dropped.

The damage to the reputation of Drummond and Hegarty endured. They had arrived as a pair from Northern Ireland, where they were mainstays of the Under-18 team. Drummond was pale-skinned, a brave, agile goalkeeper who lacked physical presence. Hegarty, darker and more obviously intense, was also deemed too small. Had he been born a fortnight earlier in 1992, he would have qualified as a first-year scholar. As a central defender, nudging past six feet in height, he needed all the growing room he could get.

They were endearing, earnest and unable to strike a pose. Their wide-eyed response to the UEFA Under-19 tournament in Bosnia revealed their innocence. They were awestruck by the cluttered civil war graveyards on either side of Sarajevo's Olympic stadium. Drummond spent his 20 euro pocket money on milk and yoghurt for the children of a street beggar, and wondered why he was shadowed on the

way to the shops by a local warlord, behind the tinted windows of a 4×4. Hegarty maintained contact with Shaw, whom he viewed as a surrogate father: 'He tells me so much, gives me so much encouragement.' Hegarty shared a birthday, 13 August, with Fitzgerald, whose advocacy failed to give him an additional year's grace: 'It's very difficult. Chris has been my best player this year. I feel my job is to make recommendations. The manager's job is to go with or against them. It would be coming out of his budget, and I understand I have to be realistic. From his point of view, Chris won't play in his first team next season. Look around. How many eighteen-year-olds are there in the League?'

Drummond represented a more subtle problem. Had he been retained he would have been third choice, a training-ground goalkeeper. Jackett viewed that as a luxury item, but made a deadline day move to sign Tony Warner, who had been released by Hull. He was promptly gazumped by Charlton, who, like Leeds and Colchester, were gambling on promotion with increasing recklessness. Millwall took the opposite tack, loaning Lewis Grabban to Brentford, and sending Hughes-Mason to sample the real world at Cheltenham Town, in panic mode towards the foot of League Two.

Jackett had some sympathy for Fitzsimons, who failed to survive another reserve team fiasco, a 2–0 home defeat against QPR. He was an identikit Millwall recruit, a raw-boned local boy weaned on the club's outlaw culture. He had come into form at the right time, but was exposed in a team that had too many senior professionals going through the motions. The exception was Andy Frampton, whose frustrations were honed by the twin extremes of anger and encouragement.

'Danny was borderline', Jackett admitted. 'He's a left-sided centre half or left back. I have Darren Ward, Tony Craig, Andy Frampton and Scott Barron under contract to

fill those spaces. In other years, Danny would have got an extra year, to be honest. A few people have asked me about him. I think he may train on. It might be that he'll be one of those who come back, at 21, and make it.'

Such fine words, given weight by QPR's immediate offer of a trial, made little impact. 'All I want to do is play for Millwall', Fitzsimons exclaimed, with a childlike sense of exasperation, when Gallen put his contacts at his disposal. 'It's my club.' Even I felt guilty, watching his plight. My conscience stirred by default. It was as if I had tossed away a charity circular without bothering to open the envelope.

Life went on. Jackett and Steve Morison, who had scored seven goals in five games, were named League One manager and player of the month respectively. Scratch beneath the surface, however, and austerity budgets were beginning to bite. Danny Spiller, still struggling to recover from the setback of his abrupt departure from The Den, was told his short-term contract at Dagenham and Redbridge would not be renewed. He posted a career highlights montage on YouTube in the hope that it would trigger interest from Scandinavia, Australia, or anywhere else he could earn a crust. 'You can usually spot a good player when you see one on TV', he reasoned, whispering into a whirlwind.

Stockport County, adrift at the bottom and without a goal in 587 minutes, arrived with relegation as the least of their worries. A club founded in 1883, as Heaton Norris Rovers, was being crushed by the Panzer divisions of so-called progress. They'd lost their only asset, their ground, and had been in administration for a year. Every day, each humiliation brought liquidation a little nearer. They duly succumbed 5–0. Jon Obika, a refreshingly humble presence, completed the rout with his first Millwall goal. Stockport's 178 fans sang incessantly, and received that most rare of accolades: a standing ovation from the Cold Blow Lane End.

In Jackett's office afterwards, Gallen was struck by the blind optimism of Stockport manager Gary Ablett. The privations he endured were an insult to his professionalism. He dug deep, into his own pocket, to buy recovery drinks and heart-rate monitors for his players. There was no landline or internet connection at the training ground, so all communication was channelled through his mobile. Most of the gym equipment had fallen into a state of disrepair, but the administrator refused to fund replacements. The oven in the canteen kitchen had a broken door. It remained closed only when a chair was wedged against it.

And they call it the Glory Game.

The value of such life lessons was not immediately apparent to the eight rejected scholars, ball boys for Brentford's visit on Good Friday. Jackett warned his players of the impending challenge, a physical form of flattery: 'Lads, you've set standards. These have an aspiration to do a Millwall, be a Millwall. People say you can't play against Millwall. You can't get on the ball. You can't work harder. All those things are why we are where we are.' He reckoned without Paul Taylor, at 50 the League's oldest referee, who had been in charge of the Upton Park Cup tie. His final visit to The Den accentuated the wisdom of impending retirement.

Strangely, for someone of a grandfather's vintage, Taylor adopted a gunslinger's strut. He blithely ignored Morison's complaint that he had taken a kick to the solar plexus, outraged the crowd with a series of petty decisions, and appeared to revel in his notoriety. An excusable indulgence, perhaps, until he was caught out of position by a Karleigh Osborne punt, and let down by his linesman, William Bull. Both officials failed to spot that Carl Cort was three yards offside when he took the ball down and went on to beat Forde with a low shot. Referees, like spin doctors, should never become the story.

Paul Robinson had to step in to soothe bickering between Neil Harris and Tony Craig at the interval, when Jackett pointedly ordered his troops to 'stick together'. The captain salvaged a point with a trademark header from one of fifteen corners that Millwall forced in a match they dominated. They were to spend the next nineteen hours in second place, but Jackett recognised the danger of disappointment. 'That might be a good point', he said, facing an audience whose blank faces suggested otherwise. 'They defended for their lives. A couple of them had the game of their lives. I've faith in you as professionals. Don't opt out, do what you have to do to prepare yourself for what is to come. Take responsibility.'

Pressure was building, but at least their challenge had clarity. Fitzgerald and the coaching staff hit the phones to try to lift the mist shrouding the lost boys.

Dignity in adversity received its due reward. Hegarty was offered trials at Derby, Preston and Hibernian. Shaw was sorting one out for him at St Johnstone. Then Fitzgerald took a call from Rangers, where the Northern Ireland connection had kicked in. He unhesitatingly recommended Drummond and Hegarty, who were given two weeks to prove themselves.

Fitzgerald arranged for Fitzsimons to fly to join them, if QPR did not pursue their interest. Ludford's skill on the ball alerted Barnet, who liked what they saw and asked him to return for an extended trial after the summer. The inference was obvious: he could no longer play on Ronald McDonald's team. Janneh hoped to lick his wounds with Welling United, in the Conference (South).

'In my position, you take all the help you can get', reflected Hegarty. 'I've been better, but you've got to get on and prove people wrong. This has been a good club for me, but if there's no development programme, it might be

best to move on. I know I was close.' Drummond, who had turned down a first-team place at Glentoran, one of Belfast's Big Two, was more upbeat: 'You hear people talking about one door opening as another closes, but it's not until it happens to you that you realise the truth of it. Rangers was the club I supported as a wee boy. This is a great chance for me.'

He took it, as did his friend. They were given one-year contracts, and returned to the training ground to say a proper farewell. Jackett sought them out, offered his congratulations. 'You will be successful in football because of the people you are', he told them. Fitzgerald, buoyed also by news that Fitzsimons had been given a six-month contract by QPR, was in the Portakabin that serves as his office when the pair knocked on the door. He sprang from his seat and attempted an awkward embrace. 'Listen guys, good to work with you', he said, taking two steps back to bathe in their smiles. 'Keep in touch, let me know how you're getting on. It's been an absolute pleasure. You will go on to better things – and they are not just words.'

A final handshake and they were off, to chase the same rainbow in a different nation. Fitzgerald was wistful, paternal. 'It's really hard, at eighteen, to get another pro club', he said. 'I like to think I'm whole-hearted in my job. I give it everything I've got, physically and emotionally. You put your heart and soul into this, and tell yourself you cannot do any more. They are brilliant kids, just brilliant ...'

Maybe, just maybe, Millwall had been cruel to be kind.

Love Story

Alan Dunne is not the happy, shiny role model the PR and social responsibility industries seek in football. He's a complex character who has made his mistakes, taken his lumps. He's been the butt of the crowd's cruel wit for too many years. If the system's victims required lessons in mental strength, intestinal fortitude and painfully acquired humility, he was their man. He waited in the car park before scaling those fifteen steps that led to Jackett's office, and the scaffold. When Dunne emerged 25 minutes later with a two-year contract extension, the weight of the world was lifted from his shoulders. He was singing a redemption song.

'There were so many pressures on me', he said, in a quiet, gruff drawl. 'My missus is six months pregnant. We're waiting for a letter to see if my little girl has been accepted for school. The way football is going now, in a recession, you don't know what's around the corner. I've been playing through big games, worrying where I was going to be after this season. I've realised a career is short, that what I have is special, important. I have a family. I'm starting to play some of the best football of my life.' It had taken time for Dunne to reveal the essence of himself.

He entered Millwall's youth system on his tenth birthday. He defiantly wore an Arsenal shirt, as befits a boy from a council estate in the shadow of Highbury. He was in the same secondary school class as Joe Cole, and turned down Arsenal to sign apprentice forms, at the age of fifteen, after

'a lot of scouting and touting'. He was raw, headstrong, and devastated by the death of his mother six months after he became a professional. His life, denied its cornerstone, crumbled.

'As young and naive as you are, you think you have made it when you become a pro. When I lost my Mum I went down a different road. I was up to mischief, things I shouldn't have been up to. Football wasn't really in my head. I was feeling sorry for myself. I was injured. I wasn't involved in the first team. There was nothing for me. I had too much time. I was earning a lot of money for someone of my age. I was living with someone ten years older than me. It was asking for trouble. For two and a half years I was numb, looking for something to make me feel better.' With his shaven head and wary nature, Dunne is the antithesis of an airbrushed Mills & Boon hero. Yet his is a love story. He met his wife Aimee and 'everything clicked'. They had a similar background, and each struggled to cope with the death of their mother. Aimee gave him stability. They set up home in Beckenham, close to the training ground. His new-found sense of serenity enabled him to overcome a succession of injuries: a broken metatarsal, fractured cheekbone and twice-broken wrist. He made his Championship debut against Sheffield United under Mark McGhee, and became the regular, in a midfield three, under Dennis Wise.

'I was happy again. My career was starting to pick up. Then we reached the FA Cup final. I was playing until the night before, when Wisey called me in and told me I was sub. He was going to start, play 50 minutes, and come off for me. I never got to play. He played 89 minutes, and brought on a young lad, Curtis Weston, for his debut instead. I have a lot of respect for Wisey as a manager and a player, but that hit me hard, really got me down. I'd obviously built up the fact I was playing.

'The club was soon transformed. The next pre-season was a shambles. The board was unsteady. There was no security. Players were coming and going. There was no money. I had so many managers. No one knew where they were. I played around 40 games that season. We got relegated, and in that situation, you're going to start picking up abuse. I was playing in a different position in every game. I was working hard, but was not talented enough to cope.'

Jackett, pitched into the lava stream, took soundings from former managers. He recognised Dunne as a victim of his versatility, but ran out of patience as he tried to strip back the layers of his personality. He told him he was surplus to requirements, and stepped back to observe. 'Everyone said Dunney had a lot of ability', he recalled. 'It wasn't his fault that he had been played in too many positions. He'd had his troubles, and almost needed to be left alone, to work through the issues.' Deployed as a right back, Dunne showed the Right Stuff:

'I was still young, a bit loud. Kenny and I didn't see eye-to-eye at first. I didn't think he knew who I was, and I don't think I knew who he was. We didn't gel as people, but he gave me a wake-up call. I was 25, and had always felt looked after. Suddenly, my career was in danger. It seemed my whole life was under threat. I knuckled down. He called me when I was on holiday in Florida. 'Come back, and have a go for me. Let's start from scratch.'

'I played 30 games last season. Being in the play-off final at Wembley was a big achievement for me. Things were starting to slowly turn around. The crowd gave me less abuse. The Den is a ruthless place. I have seen it break so many players. I knew it wasn't personal. Something in my body language was frustrating the fans. I had to correct that. I always knew I was good enough. It was just finding the bollocks to believe in myself. Once I found a position I could

work on, I knew my head wouldn't be filled with different scenarios. Your mind can go missing.

'Now I work, week to week, on what I'm doing. The hunger that maybe I didn't have at eighteen, without a wife and family, is there. I'm 27 now. I know what the club is all about. I know what the fans want. I know the lads are good enough. We respect each other. There's no one here who thinks he's better than he is. Sometimes it takes years to realise what makes a successful team. I'm learning all the time. We have had a rough time, and we want to achieve.'

That resolve would be tested at Colchester on Easter Monday. Football was reduced to its lowest common denominator at the Weston Homes Community Stadium, set in miserable isolation in a building site scarred by a moonscape of stone-encrusted mud heaps. It was yards from the A12 dual carriageway, but no access road had been built. Fans braved horrendous traffic jams on a two-mile diversion, where wardens lurked, ready to penalise those who parked on a grass verge. Sightseeing was restricted to a gypsy encampment on a roundabout. It consisted of six caravans and two wrecked cars, in which children and dogs played with customary vigour.

The away dressing room was similarly inviting. It had been halved in size in the summer, and painted black. The hum of pre-match drinkers carried through cracked plasterboard. All power points had been removed, and covered with a metallic casing. 'Fuck it', said Richard Shaw. 'If we ever have to come back here I'm bringing a screwdriver.' The players pooled their batteries, and cranked the communal iPod up to eleven. The sledgehammer sentiments of 'I Am Not a Whore', by American electro rappers LMFAO, filtered across the tunnel entrance to the home dressing room, where a sign read: 'You don't win on emotion. You win on execution.'

Colchester manager Aidy Boothroyd was big on slogan-eering. It played up to his image as a modernist, and played down the reality of his conservatism. The pitch had been narrowed and shortened to cater for a Route One approach. It was bare, compacted, and deadened the bounce of the ball. 'Everything in this place is dead', said Gary Alexander as he took his place on the bench next to me. 'Good players wouldn't want to play here, on such a small pitch. It's too congested.'

Colchester, aware of the dire consequences of defeat, launched their customary blitzkrieg. Danny Schofield headed David Prutton's twenty-yard drive off the line, Darren Ward made a saving tackle to deny Kevin Lisbie. Anthony Wordsworth and Ashley Vincent both missed when it seemed easier to score. Referee Andy D'Urso, who was to book seven players, turned down a penalty appeal after a Neil Harris shot appeared to hit John White's hand. Millwall's 3,000 travelling fans had regaled him with chants of 'D'Urso, D'Urso, you're a cunt' throughout the warm-up. He merely smiled, sardonically, at the welcome.

The bile settled, three minutes before half time, with the sort of goal that proved how far Steve Morison had come. He took David Forde's clearance on his chest, had the strength to shrug off and turn inside the expensive loanee Franck Queudrue. Changing feet as he entered the right-hand angle of the penalty area, he took the ball early, striking it with the outside of his right boot across goalkeeper Ben Williams, and into the far corner. Jackett shouting at him, that bleak November morning, seemed nothing more than a bad dream.

The manager's more immediate concern was over-hitting crosses and set-pieces. 'It's a postage stamp', he said, with ill-concealed contempt. Jackett recognised the significance of winning the first ball, and reminded Liam Trotter

that 'closing down, blocking and intercepting are more important than tackling in the modern game'. He did not bargain on an uncharacteristic fumble from Forde, which gave Lisbie the softest of equalisers, five minutes into the second half.

Paul Robinson chased the side-footed finish, to no avail. He saw a Millwall fan, behind the goal, bite the end off a twelve-inch hot dog and launch it, like a javelin, in disgust. Mesmerised by the incongruity of the moment, Robinson took the bun, complete with frankfurter and onions, between the eyes: 'It was comical. I was raging because we'd lost the goal, but I was laughing inside.' He maintained his game face, even if it was smeared with tomato sauce, as Millwall fans began to keep any balls that flew out of play. They threw six out of the back of the stand into the wilderness beyond, much to the disgust of the Colchester players. 'They were complaining to the ref, saying, "We're not going in there to get them back"', said Robinson. 'It's funny, but sometimes as a player, you get that feeling: "The fight will go out of these."' Sure enough, twelve minutes from time, Colchester succumbed to a self-inflicted wound. Substitute Shaun Batt, whose pace and unorthodox gait bewildered left back Marc Tierney, seized on an incisive Dunne throw, and volleyed it into the box. As it hit the head of Colchester substitute Danny Baath, Alexander screamed, 'It's in!' His striker's instinct had enabled him to read the flight of the ball quicker than anyone else.

I was about to go native.

Alexander and I were on our feet, in full eye contact. What we did was so wrong, it felt right. We paused, threw our arms around each other, and leaped up and down in unison like additive-crazed kids on a bouncy castle. I had finally lost my virginity, crossed that unspoken boundary between observer and participant. My professional

detachment, nurtured over 30 years watching sport at the highest level, had been fractured. I identified with these men, shared their values, felt their pain. God help me, I kidded myself I belonged.

They made a mockery of that dark, pretentious dressing room, when the most significant of wins had been confirmed. Jackett was effusive: 'Alright. You may say the ball was in the air, and the ref was a joke, but to get promoted you have to get through things like that. The last two games we've had two teams playing out of their skins against you. They've got nothing left. That's fucking fantastic, and I'm seeing it, week in, week out.'

The manager beamed at Batt – 'You gave that Tierney sea legs. He shat himself' – as Trotter banged on the iPod and threw some strange shapes to Dizzee Rascal. Joe Gallen, a dad rock refugee whose touchstones were U2 and Simple Minds, smiled and sagged back against the breeze-block wall. 'When you get promotion you see little signs, like that winning goal', he said. 'You feel things are going for you.' He hesitated as the door opened to reveal a Colchester steward. 'Anyone need the doctor?', he asked. 'Yeah, the ball', Harris replied, with perfect comic timing.

Life was being lived to the max. Harris, Essex Man, was in his element, on his patch. He was playing with a controlled rage, as if, deep down, he was proving something to himself. Morison was the new kid on the block; Harris was the elder statesman, asked to articulate the daily devotions that make up a winning mentality: 'It's a difficult thing to define. You've got to develop the intensity to be a winner, in everything you do. That means being the best, not just on Saturday afternoons, but in the five-a-sides on Monday morning, in the shooting practice after training. You know when it's time to relax, do something with the kids, but something makes you flick on Sky Sports News.

Who's doing what? You need to know. This is the business end of the season, when you are more conscious of everything that's going on around you. Football has to take over your life.'

The fans, needless to say, were revelling in their political incorrectness. An anonymous scallywag marked the next home game by erecting a sign on the travellers' mobile home compound beside South Bermondsey station. 'Gillingham F.C. Team Hotel' it read, in reference to The Pikeys, the Kent club's pet name down Millwall way. Sensitive souls appalled at such a social slur had the compensation of two suitably surreal cultural diversions, provided by the Royal Opera House and an urban art collective known as Dripping Paint.

The 'No One Likes Us' chant was a central theme of *Ingerland*, a short opera composed by Jocelyn Pook, a British pianist and viola player who might have been on more secure ground when she backed Massive Attack. The chorus line featured a group of Wags, agonising over cosmetic surgery, singing a paean of praise: 'Stevie, Stevie Gerrard, he's big and he's fucking hard.' A Royal Opera statement trumpeted: 'Football is a force that connects with primal human instincts of the oppositional, emotional and irrational. *Ingerland* brings all these elements together and presents a new perspective on the beautiful game.'

They speak of nothing else in Nunhead.

Dripping Paint, meanwhile, provided a piece of guerrilla art, a Neil Harris mural painted, in the style of Banksy, under the railway tunnel on Zampa Road, which leads on to the concourse at The Den. A tortured soul by the name of Wizywig, one third of the collective, explained: 'We saw it as an opportunity to do something positive for the club, to coincide with their recent results and push for automatic promotion. Because of the incognito nature of this work

it's not exactly something you want to be hanging around doing.'

Harris did his thing, heading in the final goal of a 4–0 win that presaged Gillingham's relegation. Tony Craig celebrated a two-year contract extension by adding to Batt's opening goal, while Danny Schofield marked his 30th birthday with his tenth and best goal of the season. He picked the ball up, just inside the opposing half, changing feet more than once during a mazy run capped by a delicately curled left-foot shot into the top corner. Defeats, endured by Swindon and Charlton, elevated Millwall into the automatic promotion position, a point ahead of third-placed Leeds. On cue, Jackett wheeled out hoary old clichés about taking one game at a time and concentrating on process, rather than outcomes.

The final home game of the season, against Swindon, had already sold out. Andy Ambler was working on two strategic plans, catering for promotion and ultimate disappointment. 'It's as if the club has skipped three generations, and is operating in the eighties', he said. 'The mentality is the same. Everyone, players, staff, management, directors and fans, are in it together. We're getting big gates not just because we're near the top. It's the way we're playing, the leadership. People respond to that. There is a lot of self-policing going on amongst the fans. We're getting a lot of feedback. We have some tasty supporters, believe me, but they do talk to you. Even those who know they do wrong basically love their club. We can't encourage vigilante action, but when they have a word, it helps. The hot dog man gave himself up.'

It was quiet out there, Carruthers. Too quiet.

Huish Park, Yeovil's neat, tree-lined ground, was a bucolic setting for a showdown the following Tuesday evening. Blossom drifted on a gentle breeze across the VIP car

park. A wedding marquee, erected on the other side of an all-weather training area, was open to the elements. The sun was losing its warmth, but illuminated the bay-windowed executive boxes that resembled a job lot from the Ideal Homes Exhibition. The Den, it ain't. Entertainment, of a sort, was provided by a trumpeter and a DJ with a fixation for the Dave Clark Five.

Harris was one of the first to strip, wandering into the shower area in black briefs for his normal pre-match massage from Chris Harvey. 'Do you know that conversation we had?' he said, as we swapped gossip. 'I just can't get it out of my mind. For me the best definition of a winning mentality is an absolute hatred of losing. That drives me, even during a game. I feel anger, disappointment. Afterwards, when I think through things, those feelings intensify. It's not a physical pain, but just an awful feeling.' Jay-Z was on the iPod, informing the troops he had 'Ninety-nine problems, but the bitch ain't one'.

John Berylson arrived an hour before kick-off. Jackett waited until Robinson returned from the referee's briefing before calling for silence. 'Last year we knocked on the door, and were denied entry', intoned the chairman. 'Five games left. Hunker down. Just go do it.' They didn't. There was no fluency. Ball retention was poor, as was pass selection. Jack Smith, recalled in place of the injured Dunne, was rusty, strangely muted and immobile. The game was run by Yeovil midfield player Gareth Williams. At half time Millwall trailed to an avoidable goal, a Darren Ward mistake allowing Williams to set up Dean Bowditch.

I was last to return to the dressing room, squeezing in before Adrian Wisson locked the door. His raised eyebrows were eloquent. Forde was railing at Ward: 'Have a look, man, for fuck's sake.' Harris suggested, 'We can't play that bad again', but Craig sensed danger: 'We fucked it up here

last year. Don't let it happen again.' Once Forde had delivered a second volley – 'We talk about second balls all the time. We've not won one all night' – Jackett moved to the centre of the room, a pencil and yellow sheet of paper in his right hand.

'We've had everything our way, haven't we?' he said, with that trademark stooped delivery. 'It's time to get your heads in the game. We need to start sliding balls down the sides, turning people. Jack, we need you tonight. Come on now. You can create, make the sort of play we need. Keep going. Keep your discipline. Keep defending. If it takes you 85, 90, 95, keep doing the right things. There has been fuck all in that half but that mistake. Don't lose your morale. This is where we find our spirit. We are the ones who will drive forward.'

Trotter, replaced at the interval by Scott Barron, was going nowhere. The door was thrown open and he was suddenly alone, the object of curious stares from the Yeovil scholars. He sat on a physiotherapist's bench, ice on his thigh, taking most of his weight on his hands. He had the pleading eyes of a puppy in a rescue centre. 'It's the hammy', he confirmed, in a desolate murmur. A scan, the following day, suggested he faced a minimum two weeks out.

The nature of Yeovil manager Terry Skivington's team talk was revealed by the running commentary he delivered to his players from the touchline. 'Oi, Oi', he screamed, as Millwall went back to basics with increasing desperation. 'Can we stand up to it? They're trying to nail us.' Harris, inarticulate with aggression, was replaced seven minutes into the second half by Jon Obika, who had played 22 times for Yeovil earlier in the season. Fate couldn't be that predictable, could it?

What do you think?

Only twenty seconds, of the four added minutes allowed, remained when Schofield fed Craig, who slipped as he

delivered a last-chance cross. Chris Hackett helped it on and Obika rose above goalkeeper Scott McCarthy, contracting his neck muscles and fashioning a backward header that looped into the net. The scorer chose dignity instead of delirium, refusing to celebrate out of respect to a small, warm club that had taken him to its heart. 'Crazy', he called it. Shaw was similarly incredulous: 'We do love a 94th-minute goal, don't we?'

'A good point from a poor performance', Jackett suggested. 'We lacked energy, sparkle. Was there anything in our preparations, travelling on the day? I'm looking for the reason why we were as flat as that. If there is anything, I trust you senior pros to tell me. It's easy when it's all going well. We can play a lot better but, fuck me, we've got to keep digging things out. Tonight was a lesson for us. It's all about Friday, and Huddersfield, now. We've got to have a hunger to press on. Bollocks. I think we'll go up Thursday. That might be better for us. Make sure you are fucking on it when we get there.'

I had seen enough of him to recognise the undercurrent of concern. He leaned on the bench once occupied by Trotter, and gnawed at a sandwich. In the shower area, Gallen was consoling Batt, who kept on his undershirt, ripped around the shoulder, as he sank into an inflatable ice bath. 'I felt really leggy', he complained. Like Hackett, he worried about the durability of his hamstring. These were young men reacquainted with their physical limitations. Jackett understood, identified Trotter as a symbol of the strain that assails contending teams.

'It's Liam's first full season of League football', he rationalised. 'To be honest, I had fancied him to be injured over the last couple of weeks. He was stretching himself too much.' A shrug was followed by a request for a summary of the night's results. Huddersfield had scored twice

in added time to win 4–3, at home to Walsall. Charlton beat Colchester by the only goal. Southampton, on a roll, had won 5–1 at Bristol Rovers. Leeds, 3–1 winners at Carlisle, were a point clear in second place. 'Fucking tight, eh? The lads are hanging together, just.'

The manager was in a thoughtful mood on the way home, which he reached just before 2.00am. Little more than twelve hours later, Frank Jackett, his father, tutor, and inspiration, was dead.

Chapter 20
Circle of Life

Death has no dominion in football. Life goes on, has its familiar cadences and challenges. There are teams to select, injuries to monitor, matches to win. Kenny Jackett had to deal with the minutiae of mortality, funeral arrangements and late-night family phone calls. He helped throw a protective cordon around his mother, a strong lady who had lost her soulmate. He tried to touch the void that separated his personal and professional lives. He thought of what his father would have wanted, as he drove to Toddington services on the M1, the day after Frank had passed away, to catch the team bus to Huddersfield.

It's in Jackett's nature to internalise issues, isolate problems. He shared his loss with Joe Gallen, but told no one else within the group. He needed no one's sympathy, denied himself emotional distractions. I had heard of Frank's death through my brother David and Tom Walley, Jackett's mentor. I caught Kenny gently by the elbow in the hotel car park, offered my condolences. He turned, said 'Thank you very much' with an earnest smile and an unwavering gaze, and kept walking. His response didn't surprise me. Jackett has an island mentality. He's not like some football managers who become emotional eunuchs because they fear everything they say will be used in evidence against them. He's honest, unafraid of candour, but reserved. He'd be the same if he was an assistant wages clerk at the Ministry of Work and Pensions.

'I won't lie to you and say it has been anything other than a tough time', he said later. 'There's no time to grieve, and suddenly the game is on you. Dad would have understood. He lived long enough for me to know what he would have said, and done, in any given situation. He would have been saying, "Do your job". Mum's struggling a bit at the moment, but she will come through. She talks about death in order. She said Dad lived a long and happy life. He was healthy for the vast majority of it. He had a good run, did very well. To lose people at other, younger ages, in different ways, can be truly catastrophic. It's a huge blow but it's the way of things. Dad's death is in order.'

Jackett was in a people business. He had to maintain focus, ignore the relative mundanity of the problems he was obliged to consider. Danny Schofield was one of several players running on fumes, worn down by the run-in. The game represented a poignant challenge for the winger, who had been a fan favourite at Huddersfield over a decade, after joining them from Brodsworth in the Northern Counties East League. He retained strong family ties in Yorkshire, but was becoming a cult figure among the urban foxes who form The Den's fan base. A quiet, uncomplicated character, he did his job effectively, without fuss.

Shaun Batt had physiological imbalances to address, and lacked aerobic fitness. Oblivious to the self-important rituals of live TV coverage going on around him, he washed his boots in the dressing room sink with a park footballer's relish. As he did so, Bobby Bacic knelt on the shower tiles to apply Kinesio tape, laterally, around Chris Hackett's groin and suspect hamstrings. The physiotherapist had seen the effectiveness of the tape in the NHS, where it was used to aid recovery from mastectomy operations. It relieves pain, supports muscle movement, stimulates bloodflow and removes

congestion in lymphatic fluid. Hackett had also convinced himself it worked. That helped.

The players were markedly quiet as they filed out to warm up, past a sign that crystallised their challenge. It highlighted one of Michael Jordan's many truisms: 'The hallmark of excellence, the test of greatness, is consistency.' Jackett sat quietly in the corner of the dressing room, reading the *War and Peace* of match programmes, while Joe Gallen oversaw preparations. I sensed a wistfulness, sorrow soothed by small talk. 'Programmes at Wembley these days cost a tenner', Jackett said with unreconstructed amazement. 'They say there's no money about, but how much do people spend at Wembley? What's a burger? Six quid? Whatever happened to taking sandwiches to the match?'

Frank did that with him, as a child. They pored over team sheets, form guides. They saw something noble in statistics, something admirable in the professionalism of the players they had come to analyse. The manager's reverie ended when David Forde returned early. Adrian Wisson habitually produced his notebook, which outlined who would take Huddersfield's penalties, and where they would probably be aimed. The goalkeeper was half-listening. He winced from a stabbing pain from his left heel, his standing foot. 'I've had it for a while', he confessed, while imploring Bacic to make the painkillers 'as strong as you like'.

A big man, a big personality, had reached ground zero. 'Is there anything else you can do?' he pleaded. Bacic had a one-word answer: 'No.'

Huddersfield's strength was on the flanks. Jackett understood the strategic importance of Jack Smith's ability to readjust to a regular place at right back. Richard Shaw's concerns about his mental attitude in the reserves – 'I see him saying to himself, "I ain't playing with no kids"' – led to the manager taking Smith to one side. 'Get angry', he told

him. 'So you've not been in the team. Do something about it. That's football. That's life. Fight back. Don't stay there, feeling sorry for yourself.'

Marc Laird, facing his first start of the year as Liam Trotter's replacement, reached for the smelling salts as Gallen reminded the team: 'There's plenty of space to play.' The Scot sensed he was playing for a contract extension. The Galpharm Stadium, set against a wooded hillside, was modern, airy, but lacked atmosphere. As so often happens in this age of plastic fans, the club distributed flags, and vuvuzelas to create a wall of noise that lacked the mortar of passion. Millwall started poorly, losing Batt to an ominously predictable injury within four minutes, and fell away.

The nature of the goal, by which they trailed at half time, grated. It was a set-piece move identified in pre-match video analysis by Gallen, an outswinging Danny Drinkwater corner driven at Peter Clarke, accelerating into space at the far post. Darren Ward, Clarke's marker, was distracted by Forde's decision to come for the ball. The goalkeeper was caught under it, allowing the home captain to score with a firm header. 'Sorry, lads', he said quietly, when they returned to the dressing room. Ward was exasperated: 'Fuck's sake, this is doing my head in. There are three games after this. Do you want to go up?'

Jackett's eyes flickered around the room. He didn't like what he saw. Too many were studying the floor, covered in a film of mud, moisture, and discarded bandages. 'Let's see your eyes', he snapped. 'It takes fucking guts when things go against you. I want more. There's no talking. Don't want to see the shutters going up. Don't want to hear this "It's a big game" bollocks. There's fuck all to be frightened of. Give it everything. We can talk about how long and how hard a season is, but this is about us sticking together. Get in the game. Listen, teams are afraid of you. You're relentless.

Whatever happens, I don't want to see your shoulders stooped. Don't ever turn your back when you're in my fucking team. We graft, we go all the way. Remember, after all the hype, we have conceded from a set-piece. A fucking set-piece.'

Millwall rallied, but succumbed to only their second defeat in twenty matches. Jon Obika, Batt's substitute, headed against the crossbar, and the relief with which Huddersfield celebrated at the final whistle was revealing. Lee Clark hailed it as the most significant result of his managerial career. Jackett, acting out of character, waited at the mouth of the tunnel to confront referee James Linington, who had enraged him by abandoning the multi-ball system when they were chasing the game.

'Son, that was one of the worst performances I have ever seen.'

'Kenny, don't be silly.'

'It's my opinion.'

'It's a silly opinion.'

'I've been in this game 30 years and I know what I'm talking about.'

The playground point-scoring, conducted on the walk down a narrow corridor, was interrupted by a scuffle between Forde and a Sky functionary, hustling Huddersfield players to the interview room. 'Don't get ideas beyond your station', yelled the goalkeeper, as he was ushered into a dressing room that seethed with frustration. 'Not enough bollocks in this room', announced Neil Harris. 'You need bollocks to play for Millwall.'

'It's easy when you come in here after a good win', said Jackett. 'Keep your spirit, keep your morale. If things need to be said, say them. But we're a tight group. No backbiting. You battered them in the second half, but there's no question there was not enough from all of us in the first. We

looked tentative, a bit nervous. I know a few of you haven't trained, but we have got to have enough confidence and guts to go for teams like that. Understand this. They are absolutely fucking delighted to scrape a 1–0. Lads, we can get nine out of nine, can't we? That's what we have to focus on. We've lost a bit of rhythm, that's all. I'll watch the DVD later and see a drawn game. Think about how you want to be for this club. If something goes wrong, don't withdraw. Take pride in being fucking horrible. We have got to move on quickly.'

Jackett knew it was not that simple. He sensed injuries coming, saw physical frailty and mental tiredness in his players. He consoled Tony Craig, who had sustained what appeared to be a season-ending ankle injury in a block tackle. Across the room, in the shower area, Paul Robinson's face was creased with concern as he was examined by Bacic. Three red weals, scored diagonally across his back, were not the issue. He had damaged an intercostal muscle, and convulsed when the physiotherapist found the seat of the problem. The pain literally took his breath away.

The following day Jackett, who did not get home until the early hours, watched Leyton Orient, Millwall's next opponents, beat Stockport 2–0. Results elsewhere went for him. Leeds and Charlton both lost. Swindon could only draw. Millwall remained third, a point behind Leeds. Hackett couldn't have cared less. He was in the labour ward with his partner Zabeena. Complications meant she was denied pain relief, but Amelia, their first child, was delivered safely on Sunday. Hackett cut the umbilical cord and, like any new father, was consumed by his insignificance. 'You look at your partner in a different light after something like that', he said. 'There's such respect for what she went through.'

The sense of wonder survived his return for training, when he admitted he had barely slept for 72 hours: 'You

know what it's like. I keep peering into the cot, checking she's still breathing.' Jackett knew that Hackett would have an important role to play against Orient, who played four central midfield players and conceded space on the flanks. He worked with him in training, urging him to take an extra fraction of a second to consider his options on the ball. Hackett set up several chances from set-pieces, but as he flagged, he was substituted by Gary Alexander.

Anxiety dissipated when Robinson gave Millwall a 70th-minute lead, a low shot after Scott Barron's deflected cross had fallen at his feet. The game was safe ten minutes later, when Barron, put through by a sublime Alexander pass, was brought down by Adam Chambers. Harris instinctively grabbed the ball, but tossed it to Steve Morison, whose successful penalty was his 20th goal of the season. The sloppy concession of a Ben Chorley goal, deep into added time, meant Millwall had the same goal difference, but one point less than Leeds. There were only two scheduled stops left on the emotional rollercoaster. A visit to Prenton Park would be followed by a last-day showdown against Swindon at The Den.

'It's very intense, but you've got to realise these are the good times', Jackett rationalised. 'It's horrible to be in the position of someone like MK Dons, who are safe, but have been redundant for the last three months of the season. Colchester might be thinking they're now in the same position. We have done well to keep our season alive. You have to enjoy it, give yourself a pat on back, and remember the basics, your gameplan in and out of possession. A promotion race is full-on, but I've been through plenty and find I can switch off from it. There's enough to do at home, when I walk through the front door.'

He was not entirely convincing. Successful managers don't do indifference. He pored over his training diaries,

played a succession of DVDs on the PC in his study. He had huge respect for Les Parry, the physiotherapist who succeeded John Barnes as Tranmere manager. 'How the fuck has he kept that lot out of the bottom four?' he asked his coaches, who were similarly baffled, and impressed. Jackett saw them lose at Brentford, where he also saw enough to recall Lewis Grabban from a productive loan spell.

Grabban had come to symbolise one of the defining challenges of management, keeping players happy when they are out of the team. They lose focus, try too hard, or not at all. Some tinker with the component parts of their game, entangle themselves in a thicket of confusion. A quietly effective, short-passing, get-and-give midfield player might suddenly try a succession of Hollywood cross-field passes in a doomed effort to impress. Central defenders forget their trade, which is to kick it and head it, and behave as if they are Beckenbauer incarnate, with predictably calamitous consequences.

'There's a crossover between confidence and attitude', explained Jackett. 'You can look at a footballer and think he has a poor attitude, but put yourself in his shoes. You're 21. You think you're not getting the opportunities you deserve. You're lacking in confidence. It's a grey area in management. You see a player who, at one club, is not trying. He goes to another club, and looks a different player. It's hard to discern, sometimes. Lewis has had a positive month, building up his confidence. He played in every game, didn't lose, and scored a couple of goals. He'll be looking for his next opportunity.'

Perspective is hard to find in a promotion race, which induces a collective nervous breakdown. But it came in the form of Frank Jackett's funeral on 27 April. He was borne into West Herts Crematorium on the northern edge of Watford by six grandsons, to the strains of 'What

a Wonderful World' by Louis Armstrong. I took my father, who wanted to pay his last respects. Millwall were represented by John Berylson, who had made a 24-hour flying visit from Boston, and Andy Ambler. It was standing-room only on the second tier of one of those spare, white-walled chapels that seem to soak away the emotion.

Alan Jackett recalled a proud man, who told him never to think he was inferior to anyone. Kenny spoke of 'the straightest man I ever knew', with whom he shared pilgrimages to the great golf courses of the United Kingdom. Both followed their father's instruction, to be a good listener. In a little under half an hour, after the congregation had sung 'Bread of Heaven' in homage to Frank's Welsh heritage, we filed out to the accompaniment of Frank Sinatra singing 'My Way'.

We all had our private thoughts of mortality. Mine were triggered once again, in the most unexpected of circumstances. On the morning of the Tranmere match, I logged on to the House of Fun, one of three Millwall fan forums, to try to gauge the mood. There, among the ritual pessimism and desperate hope, I was confronted by the seismic reality of what it means to lose a father. Tom Marshall, a young fan, had posted the following, entitled 'A Fallen Lion', at 11.32pm, the previous night. It's worth reproducing in its entirety.

'Today my Dad passed away. Totally out of the blue. Only 42 years old and was mad about Millwall. Absolutely gutted he hasn't got to see the season out at least and gutted that I've lost the man I looked up to as a kid and made sure I didn't go down the wrong paths when growing up. He wasn't the best Dad in the world, but he tried as hard as he could for me, my mum and brother and loved us with all the love he could give, but he was still the best Dad to me.

'Just wish I could have got to say that goodbye to him, walked to Millwall that one last time with him, shout MIIIIIIIII that one last time with him or even have that one last beer with him. My Dad was having a severe heart attack this morning, I had to perform CPR on him and I was told that if I hadn't done what I done, then he would have died before the paramedics arrived. At least I know that the one last thing I got to do with my old man was save his life, even if it was for another hour, it's something I'll take with me forever that I returned the favour of 19 years of my life he devoted to me by saving him for that little bit longer. Also, I hope he has a beer waiting for me when I next get to see him in the next world! He owes me one!

'Although his death is out of the blue, it was still contributed by years of alcohol & drug abuse. Here's a poem that he related to during his difficult time.

I am your Disease.

To all who come in contact with me, I wish you death and I wish you suffering.

Allow me to introduce myself; I am the disease of addiction, Alcoholism, Drugs and Eating Disorders. Cunning, Baffling and Powerful! That's me. I have killed millions and I am pleased. I love to catch you with the element of surprise. I love pretending I am your friend and lover. I have given you comfort, have I not? Wasn't I there when you were lonely? When you wanted to die, didn't you call me? I was there. I love to make you hurt, I love to make you cry. And better yet, I love it when I make you so numb that you can neither hurt nor cry. You feel nothing at all.

This for me is true glory. I will give you instant gratification and all I ask of you is long suffering. I've been there for you always. When things were going right in

your life, you invited me. You said you didn't deserve these good things and I was the only one who agreed with you. Together, we were able to destroy all the good things in your life.

People don't take me seriously. They take Strokes seriously, Heart Attacks seriously, even Diabetes they take seriously. Fools that you are, you don't know that without my help, these things would not be made possible.

I am such a hated disease and yet I do not come uninvited. You choose to have me, so many have chosen me over reality and peace.

More than you hate me, I hate all of you who have a 12-step program. Your programs, your meetings, your Higher Power; all weaken me and I cannot function in the manner I am accustomed to.

Now must I lie quietly. You don't see me, but I am here, growing bigger and stronger than ever. When you only exist, I can live. When you live, I can only exist. But I am here. And until we meet again, if we meet again, I wish you death and suffering.

Sincerely,
Your Disease of Addiction

'Rest in Peace Dad. I hope Millwall can get promoted for you and I'll make sure that I make you proud.'

I suspect I was not the only one who cried into his cornflakes that morning. Pete Garston, the fans' representative on the board, posted, under his pen-name Gordon Hill: 'RIP. There but for the grace of God, go I.' It had a haunting quality. The simple eloquence of loss remained with me when I walked into the visitors' dressing room at Prenton Park. The rituals were familiar, reassuring. Bacic and Chris

Harvey worked in the shower area. Players flicked through the programme before changing, slowly. Wisson handed the coaches their tea in polystyrene cups. As I sat next to Gallen in the corner, he passed me the scouts' report. My eye was drawn to the line: 'They are all with the manager, but lack of goals might cost them.'

Tranmere knew they would probably have to win both their remaining games to stay up. It was not an occasion for niceties, and the pitch, which looked like a potato patch, was rutted and well grassed. I sat with Jackett in the dug-out as he watched his opponents prepare. There was a brief moment of epiphany when Bas Savage jogged towards us to recover a ball. He was the former Millwall player who sought Wisson's counsel when the Cold Blow Lane End took against him. I saw his corn-rowed hair, dyed electric blue, and realised his qualities as a footballer had only a peripheral role in his rejection. Fur coat, no knickers. Not Real Wall.

Neither were Millwall, in a first half that reached an infuriating climax. They ignored the basics, at their peril. Andy Frampton, starting for the first time since the FA Cup tie at Derby, was lucky to escape embarrassment when he lost his man at the first corner. Forde insisted on maintaining an argument with Ward, even as another corner was being taken. When Ian Thomas-Moore artfully tripped himself up, under challenge from Robinson two minutes into added time, referee Neil Swarbrick awarded a penalty. Thomas-Moore, son of former manager Ronnie, feigned innocence, and calmly waited for Forde to commit himself before he claimed his undeserved reward.

'A dive, yes?' Jackett asked Robinson, who nodded his head ruefully. Anger was counter-productive, for the moment at least. The manager took his coat off, and began to illustrate his tactical strategy on a whiteboard. He moved

the red counters into wide areas to illustrate the need for the delivery of quality crosses into the corridor between the goalkeeper and his defenders. There were the usual entreaties, but the aggression proved illusory.

Millwall lacked leadership, lost their shape. Grabban, a 52nd-minute substitute for the ineffective Barron, flickered briefly. There was no way back when, mid-way through the second half, Morison lost a 50–50 ball and Jimmy Abdou allowed Andy Robinson to run off him. His 30-yard drive flew past Forde who, strangely, jumped without extending his arms. News that Leeds were losing at Charlton, and the denial of a valid late penalty appeal, added to the gnawing sense that a huge opportunity had been squandered.

A solemn silence settled quickly on the dressing room after the game. Celebratory yelps from across the corridor filtered through a locked door. Jackett politely asked two drug-test officers, who had come for Smith and Hackett, to wait beside the urinals while he addressed his players. He leaned over a skip and, with a dramatic flourish, ripped an A1 sheet of paper, onto which he had transcribed the Tranmere team, from the wall. His tone was caustic, contemptuous, as he screwed it into a ball.

'See this? It's a relegation team. I can't believe they beat my team. There's not one of us worthy of the shirt. They couldn't run. They had no legs. There's no fucking excuses for anyone, and I include myself in that. I tell you what, we haven't turned up in the last three away games. We've had our chances in this League. When I think of the money we've spent this past couple of days, it disappoints me. When I think of the work other people did, to allow you to train at Everton yesterday, it disappoints me. After all that graft, you've been poor. So poor.

'I tell you what. I feel embarrassed. We were crap today. We played into their hands. We gave them an easy ride.

That fucking second goal – we gave him too much time and space. Our delivery from wide free kicks and corners – poor, time and time again. If you ever think in this game that it's just going to happen for you, you're wrong. It will kick you up the arse. There's been too many pats on the back. Do you sense it? The others are coming for you.

'I ain't fucking having it. Where were our runs, our shape? Where were our angles? We had forwards staring back at people. The relationship, between back and front, just wasn't there. It fucking wasn't there. I will take responsibility for our pattern. We will get it better for next week. I will get it better. I will ask myself why some people turn up at The Den, and not away from home. 2,000 people travelled here to see you today. Think of what that meant to them. I felt terrible for them. What did you give them? You should have taken responsibility. I'm thinking fuck off. It ain't good enough.'

He sat down in the corner, and began making notes on the back of a copy of the official team sheet. Gallen scanned my BlackBerry, which carried the day's results, and winced. Millwall would be one of five teams with a chance of automatic promotion on the final day. I escaped the oppressive silence, and walked down the stairs to the pitch with Ward, who wanted to warm down. 'This is doing my head in', he said. 'It will be going round and round in my head all weekend. It will kill me. I'm moody in training because I go in there to work. That's what you learn from the top guys – mental strength and the determination to work, work, work.'

I couldn't get the image of Tom Marshall, and his stricken father, out of my mind. They were complete strangers, but I was enraged on their behalf. I learned later that Tom had bought a ticket for Prenton Park as a surprise present for his Dad. It was an eerie, alien experience. Even Gallen, a bubbly character, was depressed. Like Jackett, he didn't

expect Leeds to squander their third chance to go up, a home game against Bristol Rovers. 'Three more weeks', he said, as if the play-offs were a jail sentence. He spoke privately to senior players, who understood the implications of their capitulation. 'They know they need to be better. They said it was a one-off. Good: it has to be.'

The response justified the element of calculation in the manager's outburst. He had set the agenda, created the mood. By the time the players reported for duty on Monday morning, he had worked through a series of key messages with his staff. Two pattern of play sessions, on Tuesday and Thursday, were designed to enhance the cohesion of the front two, who were too static to be effective. Passing needed to be sharper, more accurate. The easy option of playing back-to-front had to be resisted. Ward and Robinson would be given extra heading practice, to prepare for the expected barrage.

'You see human faults in a pressure situation like this', Jackett explained. 'When you have people working for you, in any business, you have to decide what you want out of them. Most managers like it, prefer it, if there are a few rucks around the club. You see timid people and you wonder whether, underneath it all, they really give a fuck. The best people, the strongest characters, transmit a certain confidence. Apart from that it's pretty simple. Be clear, in your own mind, why you didn't win, and know what you need to put it right.'

Gallen expanded on the theme: 'Players become the people they really are when they go out on the pitch. I used to think I could change them, make them mentally stronger. That's bollocks. They are who they are. They reflect where they have come from. David Forde has been David Forde for 30 years. Am I going to change his character in two weeks? It's not going to happen. All I can do is be ready for them

when they come into work. I was devastated on Sunday, but now I'm renewed.'

He was in Tigger mode, bounding around the training pitch with infectious enthusiasm as he supervised a set-piece session and shooting practice. 'Let's score as many goals as possible', he announced. 'Enjoy it. Scruffy goals are the best goals. Don't dwell on a miss. Expect the keeper to make a mistake. Be bright, boys. Everyone reacts. Energy. Last week was last week. This week is this week.' It wasn't what he said, but how he said it that was important.

Shaw, given the sensitive task of shepherding the waifs and strays, was in more reflective mood. His reserve team had gone through their season without a win, and he despaired of the sustained disaffection of some of the younger pros. 'I've learned a lot about myself', he said, as he stretched like a cat in the warmth of a late spring afternoon. 'It will stand me in good stead. How can people not get themselves up for a game of football? Take today. What a great day to get the boots on. I've been on suicide watch recently. If I had my way, I would take some of them off after ten minutes. I know that's not what the gaffer wants, because it impacts on their fitness, but it's what they deserve.'

No one really wanted to think about events conspiring to leave Swindon celebrating a win, and promotion to the Championship, at The Den. As Gallen said: 'That's the nightmare scenario. If they go up, and their fans get on the pitch, there will be a riot. They are who they are at this club. They'll see that as them being disrespected, on their manor. They will not have it.'

The defiant screech of tribal reaffirmation that greeted Swindon's third-minute goal by Danny Ward set the tone for a manic, multi-dimensional afternoon. Morison's equaliser, an emphatic penalty following a lunge by Jonathan Douglas on Batt, was greeted with a growl of appreciation. This was

an interactive experience, a cross between the video-game mayhem of *Call of Duty* and the childish extremes of snakes and ladders. Charlton went up the ladder on their way to a comfortable win at Oldham. Huddersfield slithered down the snake, subsiding to defeat after taking a second-minute lead at Exeter. An electric shock of expectation passed through the crowd when news came through that Leeds had been reduced to ten men at Elland Road. Jackett, who had instructed Wisson to keep him abreast of developments, clung to the basics of his trade like a shipwreck survivor clings to driftwood.

The essence of his pre-match team talk – 'We have to be diligent in the nasty side of the game, the stuff you don't see on Sky Sports' – carried through to his half-time address. He had detected an undercurrent of unease when Grabban failed to commit himself to a physical challenge. 'As well as you have done, Lewis, you have to put your head in there', he said. 'This is Millwall. They expect it, even if you get a kicking.' Grabban was uncomprehending. He was pursued into the toilets by Tony Burns: 'You know what he was saying there, don't you? It wouldn't hurt to ding their guy in that situation. So you get booked. So what? Rap him, if you get the chance.'

Jackett reminded his players to 'concentrate on what you do, not what's going on elsewhere', but it was impossible. The Den resembled a mosh pit. Strangers bounced off each other in unfettered joy when Bristol Rovers took a 48th-minute lead at Leeds. They fell, headlong, down rows of seats when Morison's run and cross led to Gordon Greer's 62nd-minute own goal. It was a distinctive initiation for guitarist Boz Boorer, a friend of Gallen who was visiting Millwall for the first time. Boorer, Morrissey's musical director, looked around at the tumble dryer of humanity and exclaimed: 'Man, what an awesome vibe …'

Millwall were in the automatic promotion place for four minutes, all it took for Leeds to score twice. A superb dipping volley by Morison coincided with a false rumour that Bristol Rovers had equalised. Hope was throttled slowly, agonisingly. A late Billy Paynter goal was irrelevant, and unused squad players, clustered around a television in the staff dining room, saw Leeds see out four minutes of added time.

The cruelty of their fate confirmed, Jackett's team threw shirts into a heap in the centre of the dressing room. Before they went out to endure the empty ritual of a lap of honour, the manager called them to attention. He was self-contained, several steps ahead of them: 'Lads, 85 points and third place is something to be proud of. Our season is still in front of us. Get over this, physically and mentally, and come back to work on Monday, ready to win the play-offs.'

Family Guys

The build-up began with a bit of a domestic. Alan Dunne, afforded overdue respect by his Player of the Season award, returned to training and collapsed under a clumsy challenge from Gary Alexander. He lay face down, apparently inert, before springing to his feet with a war cry of 'Cunt!' He slapped Alexander in the face, and was slapped in return. The friends began flailing at each other, without making a fist, as the traditional crowd scene ensued. It had the entertainment value of watching two secretaries fighting over a spotty youth at kicking-out time, following a night on the Bacardi Breezers.

Neil Harris dived into the scrum and led Alexander away towards the corner flag. Dunne was consoled by a gaggle of team-mates. Richard Shaw, on the touchline, chuckled and came over all nostalgic: 'I used to get the first punch in, and leg it. That worked until I had a spat with Iain Dowie at Palace. He said, "Right, me and you, in the car park, after training". I was shitting myself, but had to front up. We ended up going down the pub and getting legless.'

Kenny Jackett stood, right foot on a ball, and watched impassively from the centre circle. He had a pattern of play session to complete, and didn't want to waste time with inquests. It was obvious Dunne had hurt more than his pride. He limped away to consult with physiotherapist Bobby Bacic. His signature season was over. He had rolled his damaged foot, which was quickly encased in an airboot.

The crutches, so recently discarded, were retrieved from the boot of his Porsche Cayenne. 'I was pushing it anyway', he said ruefully.

Worse was to come. Two minutes after Dunne's departure, Chris Hackett pulled up sharply. He tried to struggle through another sequence of play, but cupped his head in his hands and followed the full back's path towards the treatment room. As he did so, he faltered and glanced longingly over his shoulder, like a lover saying a protracted farewell at an airport departure channel. Bacic was soon trotting over to Jackett to confirm the inevitable. Hackett had pulled a groin muscle. He had, at best, an outside chance of playing at Wembley if Millwall reached the play-off final.

13 May was not proving particularly lucky. Forty-eight hours remained until the first leg of their play-off semi-final at Huddersfield. Deeply ingrained instincts kicked in, and, like all football men, they made light of adversity. 'I've got my boots', shouted Shaw. Tony Burns ran maniacally down the touchline, burbling, 'No players, and we're still gonna win'. Jason Price, who returned from Cumbria to complete the formalities of seeing out his contract – 'Professional, ain't I?' – was suddenly a candidate for the bench.

'I'm not one to bleat about injuries', said Jackett. 'Dealing with them is a part of the game I enjoy. It's about challenging yourself, deciding what you can do to make a difference. Don't make a fuss, just do it. It's the same with the play-offs. People talk about the pressure, but I don't feel any different now than how I felt pre-season. If I was drained, tired, I'd blame myself. It would mean I'd got my time management wrong. The simple fact is, it's all about what we do over 180 minutes.'

There were minor irritations – Liam Trotter and Shaun Batt were temporarily living in a hotel because the lease of their rented houses had ended with the League season, on

8 May – but life went on. Jackett reviewed a list of targets for the following season with chief scout Jamie Johnson, with special emphasis on players who would offer depth in wide positions. They were impressed by the potential of Tottenham winger Andros Townsend, and had to balance the pace and power of Arsenal's Jay Emmanuel-Thomas, on the right side of a 4-3-3, against his laid-back nature.

Ikenna Ofoche and Hassan Janneh, who had been released six weeks earlier, called Scott Fitzgerald, asking for permission to use the gym. He refused. 'I know it sounds brutal, but they've got to learn to stand on their own two feet', he said. 'This is the first day that their situation has hit home. This club has been their life, and it's not there any more. I'll do all I can to help them, but I also have to tell them, "Sorry, you don't work here any more".'

And it was work. Jackett toyed with playing Jimmy Abdou in front of the back four in a 4-1-2-3 system, but opted for 4-4-2, with Marc Laird filling in for Hackett on the right. Danny Schofield, replaced on the left by Scott Barron, was denied another reunion by a calf injury, which Bacic put down to his 'tippy-toed' running style. Jackett also made contingency plans for the absence of Steve Morison, who felt pain in his gluteus maximus muscle – backside to you and me – when he volleyed the ball. Those plans didn't include Lewis Grabban, who had not made enough of his opportunities.

The essence of a big-game player is discipline. He detaches himself from the importance of the situation, ensures that excellence recurs as part of a process. Millwall had failed five times previously in the play-offs, over twenty years. Rather than be intimidated by such a record, they heeded the wisdom of Brazil captain Lucio: 'Use the past as a trampoline.' Barron, in particular, was rising to the occasion. The Ipswich Academy graduate, technically adept but

a little lightweight, had been on the fringes of the team. Now, with everything on the line, he excelled.

Barron had valid claims for a 12th-minute penalty at Huddersfield turned down, when Peter Clarke blocked his goal-bound shot with his arm. Then, when he was tripped by Clarke early in the second half, he went into 'my Italian waiter routine', spreading his arms imploringly, to no avail. Conspiracy theorists seized on the identity of the referee, who also booked Harris for punching in a Barron cross. It was Darren Deadman, the official sanctioned by the Football League for his orgasmic yelp of self-congratulation when he played advantage to Harris' benefit against Carlisle, back in August.

Coincidence? Of course.

Jackett knew the pointlessness of paranoia. He had been amused by Huddersfield's gamesmanship in only watering the half they were attacking, to aid speed of distribution on the counter-attack. He was buoyed by the discipline of his defenders in the goalless draw, and knew The Den would be a uniquely forbidding place in the return leg. The tribe trusted him. Their emotion was extreme, but deflected by the heat-shield of the manager's personality. They responded to someone being true to himself. They would do their bit by over-acting, in the manner of the ghoulish extras from Michael Jackson's 'Thriller' video.

In the sanctuary of his office, two hours before the second leg, Jackett tempered the temptation to gamble on the fitness of returning players. He was convinced by Schofield's strength of character when the winger insisted he would be OK to play on a single day's training. Barron's emergence, and Schofield's comfort on either flank, gave him the option of easing Batt back into the group after his hamstring injury. 'Shaun's standing on the edge of a cliff', said Bacic, who was working his 23rd straight day. 'I'm telling

him to jump, make that leap of faith.' Jackett nodded, his mind made up: 'He will be relieved to be a sub. Sometimes, when you have those sorts of injuries, they are worse in your own mind.'

With that, Jackett walked out into the changing area to give his final team talk at The Den for the season. He was five minutes early, but his players were waiting. They had the air of students, determined to make the most of a final revision session on the eve of an important exam. They instinctively understood the manager's line of thought that their role was to enlist the crowd as twelfth man. Millions of words are wasted on that link between footballer and fan. Most clubs use it blithely as a marketing tool, to build brand loyalty. But in this context, used privately and deliberately, it mattered.

'Our approach is the same as Saturday', said Jackett. 'All the things we imposed on them, we do again. They are a counter-attacking side. If you give them space and time they'll build confidence. Deny them that, get after them, and we will bring the crowd into play. I'm not underestimating us on the ball, lads. We have stepped on, in possession, as a team. Our passing, the development of the ball, breeds confidence in you, and the supporters. Our performance, our body language, how we respond to each other, will bring them into play. I'm telling you, lads. That will be a massive thing.'

He was not wrong. The banshee wail, when Huddersfield went out to warm up, was a taste of things to come. To the home players, such bile was breast milk. They fed off it, filtered it. The sense of intimacy, before they went out to perform, was close to suffocating. It found its voice in Darren Ward: 'Round each other', he intoned. 'Doing your job, winning your tackles, wanting that ball, showing some bollocks.' Joe Gallen caught the mood. 'There's a lot of

experience in this room', he said, before pointing at the door in the direction of the visitors' changing room. 'There are young players in there. Sweep through them.'

Shaw sensed that the match was won in the tunnel. The players had to wait for Sky, whose indulgence led to them having to apologise for Paul Robinson's profanities. It gave Huddersfield's players time to consider their fate. Some blinked a little too quickly for comfort. Others couldn't resist the temptation to half-turn and investigate the fog-horn at the end of the line. It was David Forde, master of ceremonies. The goalkeeper boomed, basso profundo: 'C'mon Millwall. They're ours.'

Millwall took the lead mid-way through the half. Tony Craig, who had overcome ankle problems through sheer willpower, hooked a high ball towards Harris, who fell under Robbie Williams' challenge. Referee Anthony Bates played advantage, allowing Schofield to advance to the byeline. Goalkeeper Alex Smithies could only parry his hard, low cross into the path of Morison, who swept in his 23rd goal of the season. Barron bounded after him, and rode piggyback during the striker's final strides towards the touchline.

Jackett understood the dynamics of the situation. He needed to maintain his team's intensity – 'Keep running and fucking running' – but prevent them from over-heating. As a result, his half-time address was more collegiate than normal. He generated discussion, sought the views of the players on a number of issues. It was agreed that Forde should speed up his distribution, with the proviso that it didn't place unreasonable demands on Trotter and Abdou, who had to be in a position to be tight enough to win second balls.

His players had, literally, paused for breath. Craig closed his eyes, turned to the wall. Ward sat, ramrod-straight, and stared into the middle distance. Batt picked his toenails.

Schofield deliberately peeled off his socks and shin pads, dried his feet, and put on a new pair of boots. They were not the garish green pair he had been given by the Nike rep: 'I'd never have the bottle to wear them here.' He was on the chain gang, not the catwalk.

Barron hit the woodwork, mid-way through the second half, and triggered a tsunami of noise. It started in the upper tiers, flowed through the lower sections of the three stands that contained home supporters, and convulsed the entire ground for several minutes. It was the sound of decades of defiance, which came from the belly of the beast. The only time I had heard something similar was in a Glasgow derby, when Celtic won the Scottish League title at Rangers' expense. Even referee Bates admitted: 'I have never heard anything like that in years.'

Up in the commentary box, Dion Dublin noticed how reluctant the Huddersfield wide players were to get close to the touchline. As they melted, Millwall gathered momentum. The TV cameras captured Huddersfield manager Clark exclaiming: 'I hate this fucking place.' Victory, and a return to Wembley, was secured by Robinson's 82nd-minute header from Barron's right-wing corner. Any steward inclined to stop the inevitable pitch invasion at the final whistle deserved a VC. Ward had the shirt stripped from his back; Morison, whose bandaged head received a battering from well-wishers, danced with all the grace of Pinocchio.

The survivors of the throng returned to the dressing room, one by one. The first request for Wembley tickets, texted to Dunne, was received within two minutes. 'What a place to come to work', yelled Forde, exultant after keeping successive clean sheets against the Division's top scorers. 'What a place to play your football.' There was a lightness of being, an intoxication of the spirit. Forde jokingly demanded Armani suits for Wembley, instead of the previ-

ous year's ensemble, £90 off-the-peg outfits from Top Man. He was to get neither.

Millwall would turn up for work against Swindon Town on 29 May in specially embroidered tracksuits, the equivalent of a labourer's hard hat and donkey jacket. Their dress sense was a statement of intent. 'Don't go into holiday mode', warned the manager. 'We'll keep everything as normal as possible up to, and including, Wembley. We keep working. We keep playing. The stakes are big. We have the opportunity we have been talking about for so long, for too long.'

Privately, Jackett was consumed by pride. 'That is the best atmosphere I have generated, as a manager, since I've been here', he admitted. Clark, his opposite number, was suffering death by a thousand cuts in the corridor, where he endured a series of increasingly truculent interviews. It was only when he was in Jackett's office, among football people, that he could allow the tension to dissipate. His fate had been sealed, his demons had been released.

Before he joined the respective coaching staffs, who were sharing a beer in the corner, Clark toured the room with quiet dignity. He shook everyone by the hand, looked them in the eye, and wished them well at Wembley. It was an impressive gesture of respect. Clark's temperament had been an issue since September, when defeat at The Den was visibly traumatic. But now, in his lowest moment, his reputation soared. He thanked Andy Ambler, who had organised a couple of crates of Becks for the Huddersfield team bus, and prepared for the purgatory of his summer holiday.

In the home dressing room, memories of Wembley 2009 lingered like anti-perspirant spray. Hackett, who had been an uneasy spectator, veering between feigned indifference and manic involvement, captured the mood: 'I never again want to feel what I felt last year, lying there on the pitch

after we had lost. It was the worst thing. At least we know now we have a job of work to do. We won't be tourists.'

Individuals came to terms with the challenge in their own way. Forde was in a reflective mood: 'I'm very deep about my game. I go into everything in minute detail, and that's something Burnsy is working on with me. It's a lonely place, being a goalkeeper. If you make a mistake you've got to do the next thing right. I reckon our familiarity with Wembley will give us a slight advantage. It says a lot for this group, and the staff, that we've been able to refocus after the disappointment of last year. There's this drive about us. Ask anyone in this Division who they don't want to play, and they don't say Norwich or Leeds. They say Millwall.'

Robinson drew on his sense of deprivation: 'I felt I missed out on everything last year. There's this huge sense of emptiness when you're a loser at Wembley. All that build-up, all that talk of what you can achieve, and then nothing. It's weird. All you're left with is questions. Why? How? It takes time to come to terms with it. Fortunately, the moment it happened, the manager spoke really well. He'll get us to use that anger, to drive us on.'

Jackett's existence was even more schizophrenic than usual. He oversaw photo-calls, conducted interviews, became an ambassador, when all he wanted was to immerse himself in the mechanics of his trade: 'I'm preparing, in my own mind, for any eventuality. I'm going through details of set-pieces, looking at my options from the bench, thinking about what technical changes I can make during the game. I'm deciding how I'm going to be with the players. I want them to think about nothing else but what they are going to do when they cross those white lines.'

He took great personal delight in Ian Holloway's triumph in reaching the Premier League through the play-offs with Blackpool, but turned even that to professional advantage:

''Olly said he concentrated on three or four things, pretty much what he had been saying to the players all season. He created a sense of normality, ignored the peripheral stuff. All said and done, a play-off final is a game of football. Plan accordingly.'

He was true to his word. The final would be the 1,670th match of the Football League season. A match like no other, treated as if it was business as usual. Jackett went through the formalities of the press day, 48 hours before the game, but asked for the cameras to be switched off before he did his final tactical session, on a training pitch freshened by early morning rain. He had spotted some weaknesses in the Swindon defence at set-pieces, and ordered two youth players to stand precisely five yards apart, seven yards away from the goal. Four players, two from each flank, aimed a succession of corners into the space between them.

Halfway through the drills, Jack Smith limped off with a tight hamstring, which he had first felt two days earlier. Jackett was unamused. After shooting practice, he called his squad together. 'There are too many groins and fucking hamstrings at this club', he said. 'It means you are not working hard enough on your preparation. I can't do anything about this week, or Saturday, but if I'm doing my job, I'm making sure you are doing your job.'

Millwall were, to use Forde's phrase, 'playing in the biggest playground in the world'. Their willingness to see themselves through the looking glass of others' lives was revealed when a nervous eleven-year-old boy was ushered into the away dressing room at Wembley. George Mizen, mascot for the day, wore his murdered brother's name, Jimmy, on the back of his shirt, along with a number nine in homage to his hero Neil Harris. His presence was an affecting act of affinity with a special family. George's mother, Margaret, missed the match because she was climbing Scafell to raise funds

for Jimmy's Foundation. There was a catch in the soft voice of his father Barry when he admitted: 'Without Millwall, the family would have gone under.'

'Hiya Georgie', said Harris, who had been applying black shoe polish to his boots in an ante-room that contained two physiotherapists' benches and a fridge full of isotonic drinks. He ruffled his hair, and with a jaunty 'Come with me', took him into the inner sanctum and introduced him to the players, who were changing in individual dark walnut compartments. Robinson knew what his theme would be, as captain in the pre-match huddle: 'We're playing for the people who hate their jobs, who'd love our lives. Let's give them something special.'

There were small concessions to the magnitude of the match. Gallen had prepared thirteen set-piece charts instead of the usual seven. He consciously slowed down the warm-up, and remembered to bring a whistle. The previous year, he had been unable to make himself heard above the hubbub of the crowd. In the coaches' room, however, Jackett applied cold, hard logic to a familiar dilemma. Smith was vacillating about his fitness, so he took the decision for him, and left him out of the biggest game of his career. Barron would play at right back, and be expected to counter the dangerous Danny Ward.

Outside, in the rain, 40,000 Millwall fans were gathering. They were invisible, inaudible. No one can hear you scream, if you're playing at the Venue of Legends. Pre-match imprecations that sound convincing in less exalted surroundings – 'Relentless, boys ... It's all about us ... winners, we're winners' – seem strangely hollow. The intensity of Jackett's final address, three minutes before the players were summoned to the tunnel, changed the mood. He leaned against a bench in the middle of the dressing room. In the corner, boxing from Las Vegas was showing, mute,

on TV. He spoke of solidarity, in terms a squaddie would understand:

'You never want to feel you are alone on a football pitch. Support each other. That's what a team is all about. We are united. We don't go quiet on each other. If we need to bollock each other, we bollock each other. We respond. We're not dead to each other. Never, ever. Run for your mate. Support him, encourage him. He will do it for you. I guarantee that. We are here to win. That is all that matters. We're not here for the occasion, for the crowd. Bollocks to that. We are all men. We have put our work in. We're fucking together. They can't live with us.'

There were now 90 seconds to go. Time enough for the final rituals. Robinson turned left out of the inner dressing room and put his head under the cold tap. Water was still dripping down his face as he paused, turned, and screamed at the players shuffling into single file behind him: 'We go to work, boys. It's our time. We make it our time.' With that the outer dressing room door, black and heavy, opened. They walked into a halo of TV arc lights, and the hum of 73,000 expectant fans.

The Swindon players, who had proved their durability by outlasting Charlton in the other semi-final, looked nervous. Only one, Jon Paul McGovern, laughed when Harris announced, a little too reasonably to be convincing, 'We're Millwall, we're fucking horrible'. Sure enough, Danny Wilson, their manager, was soon on the touchline, screaming at his team to 'wake up'. The chocolate box clichés of their specially recorded song, a dirge entitled 'Achieve the Dream', could have been dipped in cyanide.

Kevin Amankwaah had particular reason to regret what he wished for. Booed relentlessly by Millwall fans, following his ugly spat with Harris at the County Ground in October, he lumbered through a living nightmare. His headed own

goal, disallowed because Trotter was fractionally offside when Batt delivered a telling cross from the right, had the fourth official scuttling to check a Sky monitor, to see if the linesman's decision was correct.

Six minutes before half time, Amankwaah inexplicably dipped under Schofield's left-wing corner, driven at the area Jackett had identified in that final tactical session. The ball fell at the feet of Robinson, who remained composed and flicked the ball in off the end of his right boot. A boyhood fantasy, enacted with his brother in the back garden, had become flesh. Millwall led, but quickly had to deal with the loss of Craig, who went down on the far side of the pitch. Andy Frampton exhaled, silently ripped off his sweatshirt, and went out to remind himself he still had a career.

'Framps, you OK?' asked Jackett, who gave him the option of missing the half-time team talk, to warm up properly. Frampton, taut and stern, stayed put. 'We were ahead this time last year', warned the manager. 'We've done fuck all yet. I know it's easy for me to stand here and say it, but it's time to be brave. You have the personality to make things happen. If we can turn everything into a fight, we are going to win that fight. Is anybody struggling? I need to know.'

Craig was lying on a bench outside, being tended to by Imtiaz Ahmad. His face, red and blotchy where he had wept surreptitiously, was crumpled like week-old bed linen. He had broken two metatarsal bones, and could deal with the pain. The sudden sense of impotence was harder to endure. We had spoken beforehand, of his determination to seize the day. 'Last year went by so fast I can't remember a thing about it', he said. 'I want to enjoy Wembley, see my family and friends do the same thing.' No further words were necessary, or appropriate. I silently threw a consoling arm around his shoulder, and, suppressing a sense of guilt, rushed back to the bench.

Craig made his way there, on crutches, just in time to share the final's defining moment. Robinson saw his football life flash before his eyes when his misjudged headed clearance sent Charlie Austin clear. He turned to chase, to see Forde advancing, with a bellow of rage, to narrow the angle. Faces around me, on the bench, were frozen in horror. Respiratory systems were shutting down. Austin, recruited from non-League football in October, had built a burgeoning reputation on converting such chances. Yet, as he shaped to shoot, the ball bobbled off the patchwork quilt of yet another relaid pitch. To universal astonishment, he shinned his shot wide.

It was Millwall's time.

What's it like to win at Wembley? You look upwards, from the centre of a scarred pitch, at a mass of humanity, writhing ecstatically. You narrow your focus, see small boys weeping, along with their Dads. You finally understand why Millwall fans couldn't follow a sanitised club. Their football is not a middle-class diversion, where spectators graze in concession stands, and leave early to get a seat on the tube. It's an act of faith, undertaken by their forefathers. They honour the fallen, like Tom Marshall's father, and Alan Baker. The game is in their DNA, a genetic inheritance. They savour life's small successes. There's a link with the players, who climb 107 steps up to the Royal Box, football's Mount Olympus, and pass an angular piece of silverware down the line.

Real Wall, meet Wonderwall.

The players are crying too. Robinson's dark-ringed eyes are streaming. His face is gaunt, yet radiant. You're given his man of the match award for safe-keeping. Forde squeezes the life out of you, and talks emotionally about the debt he owes Burns, who has the smile of a man who has the secret of eternal youth. Harris, who understands the gift of life, laughs at the incongruity of being a middle-class kid who

has become a working-class hero. Trotter is struck by the status symbol of a small red carpet, the privilege of big players in big games. Frampton, freed from collective responsibility, finally unburdens himself. He shares the anxiety he has felt at being pushed to the margins. His nemesis Craig, who must cancel his holiday to undergo surgery, is waving his crutches and moon dancing in an airboot.

In the dressing room, they celebrate with plastic bottles of lager and cans of Tetley's Bitter. Gallen sneaks next door, to the warm-up area, for a sandwich and some chips. Adrian Wisson has died and gone to heaven. Players play up to the cameras, daub strawberry recovery drink over Harris' head. They guffaw like naughty schoolboys at the Sky fixer's astonishment, when John Berylson lights up the sort of cigar that keeps Fidel Castro in power. The chairman's having an out-of-body experience that would cost north of $1 billion in the NFL. Health and safety? Smoke-free stadia? Forget it. This is Millwall we're talking about, a proper football club.

The first person you meet at the promotion party is Hackett, pushing Amelia across the hotel lobby in a mobile crib. 'Beautiful, isn't she?' he says. Robinson and Dunne are cradling their infant daughters. Cameron Harris is marshalling the older offspring, who use balloons as footballs in an impromptu game on the dance floor. In the Premier League, this would be an occasion for self-glorification, conspicuous consumption. This has the feel of a wedding reception, without the obligatory brawl. Barron has come of age as a professional footballer. He is attentive to his parents, but sneaks off for the occasional Sambuca slammer. Morison, whose emergence has impressed Wales manager John Toshack, is playfully derided as an opportunist for revealing that his late grandmother, Martha, was born in Tredegar. He's put up with worse, in four and a half years waiting to launch a secondary career in the Football League.

Gallen promises to dine out on that dire night against Yeovil, when he told disbelieving directors that Millwall would be promoted from the play-offs. Board members affect amnesia. Pete Garston, who cancelled a chemotherapy session rather than miss the West Ham match, is buoyant after the worst year of his life. Trevor Keyse necks beer from the bottle and resurrects the legend of that Thames barge named *Promotion*. Constantine Gonticas, the financier, reflects on the discovery of something money can't buy. Demos Kouvaris is on the BlackBerry, claiming bragging rights in Boston.

Ambler, the chief executive, has deals to do. Tomorrow. Ward exudes quiet dignity, and tours the room with his brother Elliott. He will soon sign a three-year contract extension. Batt and Trotter, who eventually go out clubbing with Barron, will make their loan moves permanent. They belong. Ali Fuseini, who knows he's about to be released, gets his mates to sign a Millwall flag for old times' sake. You begin to think of the ghosts in the machine, victims of the season, the system. They have an ethereal presence.

Danny Spiller's YouTube advertisement earns a contract at Gillingham. Danny Senda reinvents himself at Torquay United. Jordan Anderson seeks yet another chance, after being released by Charlton. Simon Walton, released after 33 appearances for Crewe Alexandra, suffers a serious knee injury after being picked up by Sheffield United. George Friend leaves Wolves for Doncaster. James Henry remains on the radar, and will be signed from Reading in July. Kiernan Hughes-Mason is lucky to have a second chance. Jason Price and Adam Bolder will extend their careers at Carlisle United and Burton Albion respectively.

The free bar shuts at 3.00am. The Guvnors – Frampton, Forde, Robinson, Craig, Alexander and Dunne, a new candidate – are still in the saddle, but swaying slightly. They've

morphed into the History Boys. Harris, the Legend, is in magnanimous mood. He reveals that he approached a distraught Amankwaah at the final whistle. He foreswore vengeance, offered his hand, which was accepted. Alexander still has an issue to address. He had been stripped, and was ready to go on as substitute for four full minutes, but never made it over the white line. 'Eh, gaffer', he shouts across the bar, 'I'm still waiting …'

Jackett throws back his head, laughs, and waves. 'There ain't many, in or around that training ground, who are wrong 'uns', he says. He senses the group's hunger, trusts their character, but will not shy away from the hard call. Change in football is constant, inevitable. Alexander, an impeccable professional and a Millwall fan, will be sold to Brentford three days before the start of the following season.

Sam Jackett hints at the cost of her husband's job, the dark nights that define the loneliness of the modern football manager. But such realities, such forbidding memories, do not belong here, in the basement of the Royal Garden Hotel in Kensington. You remember the delight on Jackett's face when he lifted that trophy, repeatedly, to a roar of appreciation from the massed ranks of Millwall fans. You understand why it meant so much to him when he saw Sam, his sons David and Ryan, and his Mum, in the Royal Box. You know, also, he sensed the spirit of Frank, his father, friend, and guide. He did his job.

The family is complete.

Losing My Religion

The knife left its mark. Alan Baker's right breast is disfig-
ured, numb to the touch. Occasionally, when he sleeps in
an awkward position, he is woken by a sharp pain across his
chest. He finds himself unconsciously protecting the scar
tissue when he plays with his grandchildren. On this day,
as on many others in the two years since he was stabbed as
he approached Upton Park, his life passed before his eyes.
The sight of so many West Ham shirts stimulated his senses,
triggered his imagination. He could taste the blood, feel
the pain, and, perversely, the pride.

A thunderstorm passed, rolling in the direction of the
Rotherhithe Tunnel. It was the perfect weather in which
to end a textbook security operation, and suited the fleet-
ing darkness of Baker's mood. Millwall's goalless draw with
West Ham satisfied tribal loyalties, without diluting enmities.
Baker walked through rivers of rainwater that coursed across
the car park at The Den, and drew me into a damp embrace.
'So many different emotions', he said, gruffly, quietly. 'Today
was another step closer to closure, but it doesn't go away.'

Baker is just another unsolved case number on the
Metropolitan Police database, a victim of attempted mur-
der, denied justice. His assailant, protected by the chaotic
nature of the gang that attacked his family, still walks free.
It was natural to scan the away end, on the afternoon of
17 September 2011, and wonder whether faceless, nameless
men shared a secret. 'I live through what happened every

single day', said Baker. 'Revenge? I thought about it. I could so easily have gone that way. I asked myself, "Is it worth it?" I looked at my grandkids, and thought to myself, "Just enjoy life". I know how lucky I am, still to be here. I look at football in a different light, but the old bonds are unbreakable. The club – players, staff, everyone associated with Millwall – have eased me through the bad times. They understand. We stick together.'

The match ball, a gift from Tom Pratt, its sponsor, has pride of place on Baker's breakfast table. It wasn't much of a match, to be honest. But the fact that it took place, on equal terms, was testament to Millwall's progress. Kenny Jackett's reputation had soared. His squad over-achieved on their return to the Championship, finishing ninth after extending their attempt to reach the play-offs to the penultimate match of the season. The House of Fun celebrated by hiring a light aircraft to fly over Wigan's DW Stadium as West Ham's relegation from the Premier League was confirmed. The banner it trailed – 'Avram Grant – Millwall Legend' – entered folklore as an epitaph to the ineffectual Israeli who was quickly replaced as West Ham manager by Sam Allardyce.

The match programme contained a heartfelt tribute to Frank Whipple, who had passed away, aged 103. He would have enjoyed the rivalry, visceral and ritualistic. One Millwall fan cancelled his vasectomy, scheduled for 7.00am at a clinic in Blackheath, because doctors refused to guarantee his release in time for the lunchtime kick-off. Ken Chapman had contacted the Football League as early as 15 March, to ask that they consider his contingency plan that any home game against West Ham should finish in daylight, and not be staged in midweek or on a Bank Holiday. There was one potential breach of the peace, inadvertently created by referee Lee Mason.

He failed to warn David Forde that the match had kicked off. The goalkeeper was behind his goal, fussing over his water bottle, when Henri Lansbury shot from just outside the centre circle at an unguarded net. Mercifully, it rolled wide of the right-hand post. 'If that had gone in, there would have been a riot', Forde reflected later, wide-eyed. 'They'd have fucking killed me, and then killed the ref.' As he spoke, he peeled off his black jersey, and swept a film of sweat onto the floor. Alan Dunne, who sat silently beneath the next peg, nodded slowly, knowingly. The scene was comfortingly familiar, but the dynamics of the dressing room had changed in the year I had been away.

I had missed the war cries, drowning out the death-rattle of studs on a tiled floor. Forde led the way, booming: 'Fire in the heart. Cool in the head.' Dunne backed him up: 'Let's see the fear in their eyes, boys.' Paul Robinson was less theatrical, more menacing: 'Our ground, our fucking ground. This is ours. This is us. How much do they want it?' But the group had evolved, absorbed different personalities. It was quieter, less emotionally driven. Hameur Bouazza, a French-Algerian winger recruited from Arles-Avignon, prowled around, head down, murmuring 'We can do this' to himself. Tamika Mkandawire, a revelation in his first season, was reserved, assured yet understated. John Marquis, the man-child doing a man's job, barely blinked. Endearingly, he wiped his wet hands on a towel before we clasped palms in the pre-match bonding session.

Jackett was characteristically concise in communicating salient points from the seven closely-typed pages of his scouting report. But his emphasis on collective confidence hinted at underlying issues: 'This is not just about stopping them. Remind yourself: I am a good player, good enough to impose my personality on you, and this game. Don't get too

disappointed. Support each other. Don't get pissy with your mates. Keep your morale.'

I thought of absent friends.

Gary Alexander, the first of the Guvnors discarded by Jackett, had a ticket for the game. 'This club is so difficult to walk away from', he explained wistfully. He was recovering from having his knee drained, and decided, reluctantly, to cancel plans to watch the first half. There was no way he could traverse London in time for a 2.15pm rallying call in the home dressing room at Griffin Park. Alexander had fitted in well at Brentford, but in best Real Wall tradition, had blagged a Millwall kit from Adrian Wisson, to wear during personal appearances. He coached at Millwall's Centre of Excellence, where his eldest son George played for the Under 11s. Even at that level, the DNA was easily definable: 'The kids have that Wall spirit. They run through people. Teams crumble against us.' Danny, his four-year-old son, sang 'No One Likes Us' as his party piece.

Neil Harris, the embodiment of that culture, made his comeback from a groin injury that afternoon, playing the final 36 minutes of Southend's 2–0 win over Plymouth. He was at his boyhood club, in a different world. He trained at the Boots & Laces ground, where Paul Sturrock, his manager, tended an allotment and prepared the players' lunch from freshly-sourced vegetables. The security of a three-year contract, at 34, did not entirely compensate for the gnawing frustrations of his final season at Millwall.

Harris started only eight League games, and 'realised, early on, that I was going to be a bit-part player'. The loss of status imposed subtle strains, and brought out the darker side of his character. During one training session that spring, he had thrown an elbow at Connor McLaren, a second-year scholar who was nipping at his heels. Instead of flinching, the kid flew at him, and had to be ushered away.

It was an act of disrespect, readily excused, that had inescapable significance. The tipping point, for Harris, came at Coventry on 16 April, when he was sent off for stamping on Aron Gunnarsson within seconds of coming on as a half-time substitute. Harris sat, alone, in the dressing room, and stared into the deepest recesses of his soul.

'I had no problem with Connor, you know. He wouldn't back down, and it was left until later. He apologised to me quietly, in the gym. There are fine lines. You need that fiery attitude, and Connor stood up for himself. He's well liked by everyone, and he's got his pro contract. Good luck to him. I never fell out with the manager, but I never let him off the hook. I wanted him to see the hunger in my eyes. He knew what was coming when he opened his office door and found me there. "Why aren't you giving me a chance? I know I can play in this team." The sending off was a big sign the frustration had got to me.

'The guy blocked me off. I didn't control myself. I didn't say anything, but thought, '"You're going to get it", and stepped on him. At my age I should have known better. I like to think I'm a nice guy, a good pro, but I've always had that edge. It's part of being a winner. It's not a violent streak, in the sense that I want to beat people up, but certain things are like a red rag. It was all my fault, and I realised I had reached a bit of a crossroads.

'My wife told me it was murder for her, and the kids. She'd come home from the school run, and didn't know what mood she'd find me in. I wasn't nice to live with. There's nothing emptier than a footballer on Friday who knows he's not going to play on Saturday. Football is a short-term game, and I want to play as long as possible, until I'm 36 or 37. Millwall is a huge part of my life. I miss my mates in that dressing room, more than I thought I would. But I've gone back to my roots. I've gone from being a play-

off winner, a Championship player, to League Two. It just shows you how quickly life can change in football.'

Harris could have stayed at The Den to see out the final year of his contract. Jackett stressed his belief in him, as an impact substitute. It took Harris a month to take the plunge, after Southend had made an official approach in May, and he used Andy Ambler as a sounding board: 'Neil just wanted someone to listen and give an opinion. I found it nice that he was comfortable with me. As chief executive you have to keep your distance. You can't be too pally with the player because of the nature of the job. Neil was trying to weigh everything up, what was best, not just for him but his family.'

Jackett understands the implications of Harris' iconic status – if his departure had been messy, the chaps would not have been pleased – but his respect goes beyond professional expedience: 'I admire him, as a player and a person. You see so many lethargic people, players with real ability, who don't want to put themselves out. They drive me crazy. Neil has that burning desire, deep within, that carries him onwards, and upwards. It can spill over into frustration, but I don't mind that. I like people who love the game, and live their life around it. Sometimes, that is to the detriment of your family, but that's the way it is. It took Neil a while to get his head around leaving Millwall. It must have been a massive thing for him. He has a unique position at this club, and he is someone on whom I knew I could rely. He was in the budget. I told him no one would think any less of him for leaving. He has closed nothing down. Millwall will be an option for him, in the future.'

While Harris was reacquainting himself with Roots Hall, Andy Frampton was captaining Gillingham to a 6–1 win at Hereford. He had endured a cheerless, grimly ironic year, in which he ultimately failed to save Swindon Town,

Millwall's play-off final opponents, from relegation. There was an ominous symmetry to his fitness problems. He hurt his left ankle in the first half of his loan debut for Leyton Orient, and injured his right ankle in the first half of his Swindon debut, when he collided with the goalkeeper, stumbled, and got his foot stuck in the turf.

'To be honest, my ankle was never quite right when I was at Swindon. The defeats hurt, believe me, but as a loan player I was caught between two stools. I'd come from a club with great camaraderie and togetherness, and I was seeing a team fall apart around me. They were good lads, good players who should never have been in that position. No matter what we did, we couldn't get a win. It was a real shame, especially for the boys who'd been at Wembley.'

Times were sombre. The recession was beginning to bite, and a lot of players in their early thirties were being forced into premature retirement. Scott Fitzgerald's homily – 'Good characters will find work in the game' – was more relevant than ever. Frampton was protected by his reputation for making the most of himself, and those around him. Gillingham manager Andy Hessenthaler, who made his first approach to sign him in the summer of 2010, identified him as the tough, principled leader he required to get them out of League Two.

Jackett was unsurprised: 'Framps is a very intelligent, articulate man, who has a lot to offer football. He is going to end up with many options. A lot depends on which way he wants his life to go. He's well capable of becoming a successful manager or coach, but it's a fickle world in which you could be working at the other end of the country from your family. It earns you a good living, but do you want to miss your children growing up?'

Frampton relished the release of watching his son Dominic play for Barming Under 8s, in tournaments

around Maidstone. The bloodlines were obvious: 'He might score a great goal, but he comes off and says, "Did you see that tackle, Dad?" He absolutely loves it. I love to see him enjoy it. Pros play with pressure, and the kids help me to put things into perspective. I'm taking my badges, but want to play as long as I can. Being captain at Gillingham is an honour, because it indicates what people see in me. They do their research. They know about your character. If you don't do the right things they come back and bite you.

'It's very tough when your contract is up. You've got to retain your self-belief. In football there's very little middle ground between the mega-rich and the ones who are really struggling financially. That PFA list of unattached players is getting longer every year. It's a reality check we've all got to come to terms with. You can't say, "If I'm not getting x amount I won't bother". I see a lot of good-calibre players, younger than me, who can't find clubs. The way the game is going is worrying. Clubs are looking for youth and energy, especially lower down the Leagues. It's a cheaper way to go.'

Danny Spiller, who had consolidated his career alongside Frampton at Gillingham, understood the wisdom of his new captain's words.

I had underestimated him, on that bleak, brutal day at Bromley, when he left Millwall. I made the mistake of pigeon-holing him as a victim, rather than the everyday hero the game breeds in the lower Divisions. 'I've been a pro for fourteen years, and I can take the rough with the smooth', he explained. 'I like to think I'm an honest pro, not only to myself, but others.' His determination in the face of adversity identified him as a true football man, and it was no surprise to learn that he, too, harboured management ambitions. He faced another three months out, after sustaining an ankle injury at Southend on 13 September, but had set himself to return, fitter and stronger.

Simon Walton, who needed nine months to recover from his knee injury, had also shown greater reserves of resilience than I suspected. He was captain at Plymouth, being paid only occasionally as the club teetered on the edge of oblivion at the bottom of League Two. At 24, he was the elder statesman, an admirable leader of a young team, chasing the dream in a nightmare scenario. In such a context, his unsuccessful trial at Millwall was a minor irritation.

Other alumni of Millwall's school of hard knocks were surviving and, in some cases, thriving. Danny Schofield and Lewis Grabban were reunited at Rotherham. Marc Laird joined Leyton Orient. Ashley Grimes' fifteen goals in 27 games were insufficient to keep Lincoln City in the Football League, but earned him a free transfer to Rochdale, where he flourished under former Manchester City youth coach Steve Ayre.

Jason Price qualified as a plumber, was surprisingly released after a month's contract on 'embarrassing' money at Barnet, but made the most of a subsequent three-month deal at Morecambe, his tenth club. To everyone's delight, Danny Senda was given a twelve-month contract at Underhill, following his release by Torquay and Bristol Rovers. He was consumed by the privilege of his profession, working assiduously in the gym and relishing each game as if it were his last. Fittingly, for someone whose Twitter time-line was punctuated by quotations from the Dalai Lama, he had found inner peace.

Shaun Batt, who had not kicked a ball in anger since Wembley, craved such serenity. He suffered a catastrophic knee injury in a pre-season friendly at AFC Wimbledon on 16 July 2010. A newly signed three-year contract offered a degree of security, but the blow to a young player who had chased the dream of a professional career around such non-

League outposts as Arlesey Town, Cheshunt, Ilford, Leyton and East Thurrock United, was profound.

Bobby Bacic rushed from Millwall's photo-shoot to the operating theatre, where Batt underwent two separate procedures. His anterior cruciate ligament was reconstructed. Lateral knee ligaments were reattached, as was part of his hamstring. There was no nerve damage, but Bacic knew Batt's rehabilitation would be painful and prolonged. The player's anger was raw, corrosive. As the months stretched into an imaginary infinity, he underwent further surgery to remove scar tissue. Batt was a naturally impatient patient.

'It's weird. The boys probably think I coped quite well. They see me with a smile on my face, ready for a laugh and a joke. But it's a front I put on. I'm not like that away from the training ground. There have been some very, very down days. The seriousness of the injury shocked me. I didn't handle it too well. It was a case of, "Why me? Why now? What did I do wrong? What did I do to deserve this?" It took time for me to come to terms with it, to tell myself, "It's done, it's happened". I could wallow in self-pity, and let it affect my life, or fight back.

'There's been a lot of stress in my relationship with Bobby, but he has been there for me, one hundred per cent. I needed him so badly. I had to grow up a bit, take better care of myself away from the club. There were moments I felt like giving up. There was nothing left. I could do no more, physically or mentally. I learned a lot about myself. I'm tougher, mentally, than I thought. I've avoided bitterness and jealousy, but there have been times when I watched the lads train, and dreamed of just putting my boots on and getting out there with them.

'When I do eventually play again, it will be like Christmas morning. It will be one of the happiest moments of my life. It's all about setting myself small goals, while I'm working

towards the big one. My motivation at the minute is not the first team, or scoring my first goal. It's little things, like being able to play in the park with my daughter, being able to run around with her, without worrying about doing myself damage. I just want to be normal again.'

Fate toyed with him as the new season dawned. He trained with the first-team squad before succumbing to a series of calf injuries, as his body over-compensated. Unforgivably, just before the West Ham game, one alleged fan accused him, on Twitter, of being indolent. His reply was a strangled scream: '14 months. 3 ops. 1 manipulation. 3 injections. 2 sessions a day, 6 days a week, treatment and gym. 2 trips to Lilleshall. Yet he says I'm lazy.' He was inundated with supportive messages. The most significant, and heartfelt, came from Senda: 'It's a long dark road but I'm buzzing for you. Keep the faith, mate. Whoever said that will never understand what it takes to get back.'

Batt grew up slowly. Marquis grew up fast. He was unrecognisable from the youth who unwittingly played for his future at Basingstoke. Richard Shaw described him as 'nineteen, going on 27'. Of the young forward's year group, only Chris Hegarty, given a second season by Glasgow Rangers, retained a realistic shot at redemption. Kiernan Hughes-Mason was on the bench for Tooting and Mitcham during a 3–0 defeat in the first qualifying round of the FA Cup, on the day Marquis threw himself at West Ham. He quickly moved on to Kettering Town. Striker Aiden O Brien, the latest Fitzgerald protégé, made his debut at Wolves in the Carling Cup on 20 September. He will take a season or so to live down his schoolboy error: wearing a scarlet gilet and sparkly purple headphones to training. Dunne stole them, and posed for photographs.

Survivors tend not to be shrinking violets, or shirkers. Marquis had texted Wisson within twenty minutes of the

announcement of the departure of Harris. He wanted the icon's number nine shirt. Jackett gave it to him, because 'asking straight out, like that, showed some bollocks. John believes he's a single-digit footballer. He's a man in the group. No one in that dressing room underestimates him.'

The senior pros, quietly canvassed by Robinson, were impressed by his work ethic. He stayed on after training every day to work with Shaw, who shared the secret fears of a defender as he chipped 100 balls at him, to hone his technique. Joe Gallen worked with him on his shooting, and provided a striker's insight into avoiding the blind alleys of the penalty area. During games his heart rate – above 200 beats per minute – was comparable to that of a long-distance Olympic swimmer.

Marquis' father, also John, died when he was five. His mother Jane subjugated herself to her son's promise, arranging her work schedule around his youth football commitments. His elder sister, Alex, was dragged along to school playing fields and leisure centres set in concrete canyons. Just as there's something refreshingly old-fashioned about his buccaneering style, Marquis is an authentic working-class boy with an unfashionable set of values. He feels the loss of his father deeply, and gestures to the heavens after every goal.

'I know Dad's looking down on me. He's brought me luck. I look up to my parents. They brought me into this world. They taught me the rights and wrongs of life. You have to grow up fast in football. Maybe losing my Dad made me more independent than most. I look at players of my age at Premier League clubs. They've obviously got bags of ability, but if they have to drop down, they'll struggle with the reality check. They've never cleaned boots, swept the dressing rooms, like we have. Young players in the lower Leagues appreciate things more. Ask them what they consider their

greatest achievement, and they will usually say it's proving people wrong. At Millwall you start at the bottom, and work your way up the hierarchy.'

Steve Morison, the player Marquis initially understudied, was living the dream, scoring goals for Wales and for Norwich City in the Premier League. His decision to submit a transfer request to trigger a £2.8 million move was viewed by many fans, on a deeply personal level, as a betrayal. He had signed an improved £7,000 a week contract in January. As so often in the game, it was an irrelevance. Jackett understood, and was not entirely unsympathetic to the unrealised ambition of the late developer he had rescued from the Conference.

'On a personal level you put yourself in his position, and understand his attitude. A player might only get one shot at playing in the Premier League. But as the manager of Millwall I wanted him to stay, and build things around him. It boils down to how far you are prepared to go to look after yourself. Football has a revolving door. The person who is most vulnerable is sat in my chair. Managers are moved on more quickly than players.

'I sensed I was losing Steve in the last month or two of the season. Part of that was down to the speculation, but it wasn't that straightforward. Steve did fantastically well to push his body to the limit, and beyond. He played when he had no right to play. People forget that players have lives too. Steve had his first child and didn't sleep for a month when they took him home. His world stood on its head. The strain told on him, but, to be fair, he never coasted. To be truthful, it was a transfer that had to happen. We had to try and wring every last penny out of the deal.'

No one within the dressing room begrudged Morison his good fortune. He could have left with more dignity, scrabbling to backtrack after suggesting he had 'been hung

out to dry' by his former club, but he was now a member of a protected species. Premier League clubs employ individuals like Joe Ferrari to bubblewrap players. As Norwich's head of media, he was indifferent to my request to interview a player I had got to know well. It would have been relatively simple to source Steve's new contact details, but I chose not to, because the episode highlights the absurdity of the system.

On the ball, City? I'll leave it to you to decide.

The nature of the challenge was changing. Millwall's wage bill had inflated from £5m in the first season back in the Championship, to almost £7m. It was still one of the smallest in the Division, and left them vulnerable to asset-strippers. It doesn't take much to prise a team apart. Clubs connive. Agents whisper. Players moan. Envy enters the equation. Ambition mutates into avarice. Aspects of character, previously hidden or addressed, become an issue. Before a manager knows it, he's fighting fires with a water pistol.

Jackett acknowledged: 'If we sell any more, too cheaply, we might be perceived as a soft touch.' He rejected a series of 'derisory' bids from Ipswich Town for James Henry, who appeared to lack the maturity to cope. Liam Trotter's form faded as the number of Premier League scouts monitoring his progress multiplied. The interest was understandable, as was Millwall's response, an improved three-year contract. Trotter had developed, under Jackett's tutelage, into an intelligent, technically adept modern midfield player. He was diligent, well-built, but almost too aware of his body. He felt every twinge, and was unsettled by a series of hamstring problems.

Forde, another conspicuous success story, also attracted admirers. He had fulfilled his childhood fantasy by representing the Republic of Ireland. Giovanni Trapattoni was

impressed by his strength of character, as much as the twenty clean sheets he kept in his first Championship season. Forde, at 31 the oldest player to make his Republic debut since the Second World War, barely touched the ball during an eighteen-minute cameo appearance in a 5–0 thrashing of Northern Ireland on 24 May. His first start, a 2–0 win over Italy on a rain-sodden pitch in Liège on 7 June, had an ethereal quality.

'It's something they can never take from me. It was strange. I was nowhere near as nervous as I imagined I was going to be. You just settle into the rhythm of the game. It's only afterwards that you realise what it means, not only to those closest to you, but to those who judge you from a distance. You are judged by entirely different standards. Your life is in transition. As a footballer you are used to change, but it can creep up on you.'

Jackett gave him time to rest, because his season finished a month later than the rest of his squad, but was perturbed by the persistence of Forde's achilles injury. It was not enough to prevent him playing, but his international commitments disrupted the continuity of his work with Tony Burns. Though third choice, behind Aston Villa's Shay Given and Sunderland's Keiren Westwood, Forde was in a world where the pecking order of wealth and status was even more pronounced. His volatility – 'You know me, I'll have a barney' – could not be ignored.

Forde's run of 141 consecutive League appearances ended on 20 August, when he was dropped for the 1–0 defeat at Southampton. The sub-plot was a dressing-room confrontation with the manager, triggered by the loss of a two-goal lead in the previous match, at home to Peterborough. Henry lit the fuse by questioning whether the goalkeeper should have been beaten from distance. Forde's scream – 'Are you fucking sure?' – signalled a crimson tide of anger.

Unusually, Jackett was drawn into the maelstrom, and stood toe-to-toe with him. I was next door, in the manager's office with Jamie Johnson, making small talk with Peterborough manager Darren Ferguson. Jackett hid his emotions well, when he appeared with apologies for his lateness, but I saw the shutters were up. He couldn't wait to get into his car, and attack the M11 and M25.

The row blew over long before Jackett turned down a £700,000 bid from Reading for Robinson, who opened negotiations for an improved contract rather than agitate for a move. The captain was playing without the aid of anti-inflammatory tablets for the first time in three years, after an operation to cure persistent tendinitis. He was a loyalist, but also a realist: 'Football is a process of continual evolution. If I look at the players who were in that bar, on the night we won at Wembley, a lot aren't around. If someone leaves, someone else steps up. We've lost some strong characters, and it's important to let the new lads know what it takes at this club. They'll find out soon enough, of course.'

My journey ended where it all began, at Vicarage Road. Watford came from behind to beat Millwall 2–1 on 27 September. It was a gruesome match, between teams stripped of belief. Liam Feeney's deflected goal, Millwall's first in six matches, was not enough to prevent them sliding into the relegation zone. A long hard winter stretched ahead. An increasingly vocal 'Jackett out' minority firebombed the message boards. Sam, his wife, was a guest of Graham Taylor in the chairman's suite. She wore a wan smile and sketched a circle in the air with her index finger. It signified the circle of life, for a football family.

It was the night the game officially went mad. In Munich, Carlos Tevez allegedly refused to play for Manchester City in the Champions League. What better time to lose my religion? 'My' team, Watford, had eked out a vital win, yet I was

desolate. I had no affinity with the club that nurtured my love for the game. I instinctively disliked the new owner, who had changed his name from Laurence Bazini to Bassini when he was made bankrupt in 2007. I despaired of happy-clappy fans, who only raised their voices when their team were allowed back into the game.

Forgive me, father, for I have sinned.

I wanted Watford to lose. I involuntarily clenched my fists when Feeney scored. I urged John Berylson to 'take a deep breath'. He reassured me that his faith in Jackett was undiminished. I swapped texts with Harris, who was in the stands. I cared. I had made my choice, and was as comfortable as a philanderer trapped in a room with his wife and mistress. I realised I had fallen for Millwall, warts and all. They represented the freedom I knew as a child, when I travelled to Watford's away matches in a neighbour's side-car. I sensed a struggle ahead, but was sanguine about the prospect of failure.

The Family was lumbered with an adopted son.

Author's Note

When I returned Paul Robinson's man of the match award to him as he sat beneath his peg in the Wembley dressing room, he rose and drew me into an embrace. 'What a final chapter', he exclaimed, not knowing that, a year later, I'd be back on his case for the epilogue. By broadening the context of his most fulfilling moment as a pro, Robbo made me realise the limitations of my trade. Journalism is a dispassionate business, in which a writer is routinely denied the time to truly know his subject. I was given that time by the Millwall players, the coaching staff, and the teams behind the team. I thank them for that rare opportunity.

When I first approached Kenny Jackett with the idea for this book, he was characteristically decisive. 'Let's do it', he said, after a brief pause for thought. 'It will be good for the club.' Millwall FC doesn't deserve its one-dimensional reputation, which is being countered by some good people. They know who they are. I thank them for small acts of kindness, and large dollops of patience.

Some didn't make the final edit, but I remain in their debt. Thanks to Lorraine, for tea and sympathy at the training ground, and to Yvonne Haines and Jess Newman, the heartbeat of the club. Thanks to Deano Standing and his press team, Lucy Pepper and Andrea Warth. Ray James and Jeff Burnidge are also helping re-shape perceptions. The three main external sites – MISA, Millwall Online, and House of Fun – and the fanzines *NOLU* and *The Lion Roars*,

are required reading. Lions Live Radio is also well worth a listen.

I was humbled by the response to the original, self-published edition. Recognition, in the form of nomination as Football Book of the Year in the British Sports Book Awards, was hugely encouraging. I was struck, also, by the emotional intensity of the feedback from supporters, who viewed the book as a reaffirmation of faith. I am indebted to Ian Marshall and Simon Flynn, of Icon, for their vision and support in bringing *Family* to a wider audience. The professionalism of their colleagues Duncan Heath, Andrew Furlow, Henry Lord and Madeleine Beresford is appreciated.

Thanks also to Paul Moreton, for his support, and Geoff Fisher, of CPI, for his initial guidance. I value the wisdom of Dr Ben Wilson, and his father Marco. Tom Keeley is a terrific designer, no matter what he tells you. Alex Skelton, and his team at webdna, have overcome my ignorance, and produced www.michaelcalvin.com. I thank Fergus McKenna, of Mirrorpix, for permission to reproduce Kent Gavin's brilliant cover shot. Brian Tonks and David Walker were with me every step of the way.

I've not been the easiest to live with during the gestation process, so thanks most of all to my family. I owe my Mum and Dad everything. I've been insulated from the real world by my wife Lynn. Our children – Nicholas, Aaron, William and Lydia – are a constant source of pride. My life in sport has taught me one thing, which I have tried to pass on. Follow your dream. Work hard enough and, invariably, it will come true.

Michael Calvin
October 2011